Snapshot Stories

Snapshot Stories

Visuality, Photography, and the Social History of Ireland, 1922–2000

ERIKA HANNA

UNIVERSITY PRESS

Great Clarendon Street, Oxford, OX2 6DP,
United Kingdom

Oxford University Press is a department of the University of Oxford. It furthers the University's objective of excellence in research, scholarship, and education by publishing worldwide. Oxford is a registered trade mark of Oxford University Press in the UK and in certain other countries

First Edition published in 2020

Impression: 1

Published in the United States of America by Oxford University Press
198 Madison Avenue, New York, NY 10016, United States of America

British Library Cataloguing in Publication Data
Data available

Library of Congress Control Number: 2019945444

ISBN 978-0-19-882303-2

DOI: 10.1093/oso/9780198823032.001.0001

Printed and bound by
CPI Group (UK) Ltd, Croydon, CR0 4YY

Acknowledgements

This book was only possible because I was so lucky that many people were so generous in talking to me about their lives in photography, and sharing personal archives with me. A very special thanks to Derek Speirs, Joanne O'Brien, and Frankie Quinn for sharing so many reflections on how and why they became photographers, and what photography means and has meant in Ireland. Thanks also to Alan Lund, Eamon Melaugh, Helena O'Donnell, Mick Rafferty, and Jackie Redpath for sharing their reflections on how they have used photography in campaigning and politics. Thanks to Tanya Kiang for sharing her immense knowledge of Irish photography. Anyone who has ever worked with images knows what a frustrating, time-consuming, but ultimately rewarding experience it is. This book is the product of the time and labours of many people, who care about photography, and who have given up their time to collect and archive photographs, and make them accessible. My thanks are due to all of those who have gone far beyond the call of duty in helping me access and study images. This includes James Harte at the National Library of Ireland, Nora Thornton and Elizabeth Kirwan at the National Photographic Archive, the staff at Galway County Archive, Waterford County Archive, Special Collections at UCC and NUIG, the Irish Architectural Archive, the National Archive of Ireland, and the Public Record Office of Northern Ireland. Vivienne Pollock is sadly missed. She went far beyond the usual duties of archivist by giving me a lift to and from the Ulster Folk and Transport Museum archive when I was on crutches.

This book has benefited from the inspiration and patience of many scholars. Thanks to Roy Foster, Simon Gunn, and Elizabeth Edwards for asking big questions, querying crucial details, and being indispensable with their support. Thanks to Matt Houlbrook for his unique blend of insights on bikes and the paradoxes of cultural history. Charlotte Greenhalgh read and commented on the whole manuscript with her characteristic sensitivity and insight, and was encouraging and critical at just the right moments. It is an exciting time to be an Irish historian, and I value my cohort of scholars very much for smashing disciplinary boundaries with such good humour—thanks especially to Caoimhe nic Dháibhéid, Ultán Gillen, Carole Holohan, Matt Kelly, and Colin Reid. This book was written during the time when

I was what is now known euphemistically as an 'early-career researcher', and as such it has found a home in many locations. Thanks to all the colleagues who made the process so enjoyable, including Victoria Bates, Robert Bickers, Tim Cole, Julio Decker, Amy Edwards, Su Lin Lewis, Will Pooley, Richard Sheldon, James Thompson, and Beth Williamson. At Bristol, I have been part of a department which values creativity in all its forms, and lucky enough to work with a group of people who have taught me to play with language and weigh words carefully. My third-year special topic 'Documentary, Society, and Conflict in Modern Ireland' has been the testing ground for many of the issues in this book; my students have been enthusiastic and inspiring, and many of their insights are now in the text. It has also been an exciting and energizing time to be an academic and a historian as a feminist, and I am very grateful to all the women who have been part of these conversations, in particular the women who make me swim and write every January: Lucy Donkin, Marianna Dudley, Margery Masterson, Josie McLellan, and Kat Peddie.

This book has also been enabled by money which has allowed me to travel, to write, and to cope with the expense of working with photographs. This project began with a Leverhulme Early Career Fellowship at the Centre for Urban History, University of Leicester. Funding also came from the Carnegie Trust, and the Universities of Bristol and Edinburgh. I am indebted to all of them. Many people have been incredibly generous in sharing their photographs with me and allowing me to publish them here. Every effort has been made to contact the copyright owners of the images, but in some cases this has proved impossible or provenance has been unclear. Please do contact me if you are the photographer or copyright owner of an image and have not corresponded with me already.

Finally, thanks again to my friends, Lu Hiam and Ellie Austin, for putting up with this again and daily being an inspiration about how women can change the world when we put our minds to it. Thanks to Rob Priest for pithy insights and truth bombs. Thanks to my family, David, Rebekah, Adam, Josh, Izzy, Logan, and Ivy, and especially to Rosalind for forensically reading the manuscript and spotting my errors, grammatical and historical. Finally, thanks to Max and Will Harding for keeping me going and putting up with me. In particular, thanks to Will for all the laughter and adventures, and for all the things which begin as this book ends.

Contents

List of Figures

List of Abbreviations

CIÉ	Córas Iompair Éireann
DCC	Dublin Camera Club
FDG	Fatima Development Group
IAA	Irish Architectural Archive
IALS	Institute for Advance Legal Studies
IC	Inner City [magazine]
IFSC	International Financial Services Centre
IRA	Irish Republican Army
NAI	National Archives of Ireland
NCCCAP	North City Centre Community Action Project
NIVAL	National Visual Arts Library Archive
NLI	National Library of Ireland
PCL	Polytechnic of Central London
PSI	Photographic Society of Ireland
PSNI	Police Service of Northern Ireland
RTÉ	Raidió Teilifís Éireann
RUC	Royal Ulster Constabulary
UCD	University College Dublin

Shut your eyes and see.

—James Joyce, *Ulysses* (1922)

Introduction

Visuality, Photography, and the Social History of Ireland, 1922–2000

This is a book about what it meant to see in Ireland during the twentieth century. The starting point for this exploration into visuality and history is an anonymous photograph album, tucked away and ignored, today known by a string of letters and numbers in an archive. Inside its browning pages, in small photographs, are glimpses of lives, loves, and emotional bonds which once had meaning for a family, but which now have seemingly passed almost entirely out of historical view: three brothers on bicycles on a day out, a family group picnicking on a blustery headland, empty sepia landscapes reached by new motor-cars (Figure 0.1).[1] Incidental and ephemeral in themselves, these images serve to prompt questions. Here in these photographs are a wealth of stories, relating to how ordinary citizens saw their world; how they made sense of the social and cultural contexts they inhabited, what they valued, and whom they loved. There are stories too in the things which are hidden and missing: photographs ripped out, images cropped, and faces without names. Through scribbled notes and duplicated photographs, we get a sense of how they communicated an image of their life to their extended family, to siblings and cousins living across the globe, and passed on these curated mnemonic tokens through generations. Their lives, connections, and ties of affection spilled out across Ireland, the Irish world, and the twentieth century, cutting across the chronologies and geographies that we as historians take for granted. I wonder how these people, in their now-strange clothes, became detached from a family narrative, how it became an 'unknown' photograph album, and how it ended up in an archive. Indeed, the photographs are increasingly fading, bluish, and the disappearance of this family is becoming ever more literal. In the pages of this photograph album lies a story of intimacy and distance, family stories and family secrets,

[1] NLI Alb424d Family Holidays Ireland Album 4 (1929).

Snapshot Stories: Visuality, Photography, and the Social History of Ireland, 1922–2000. Erika Hanna, Oxford University Press (2020).
DOI: 10.1093/oso/9780198823032.001.0001

Figure 0.1 The Glenmacnass valley and river Co. Wicklow from the waterfall (1929). Image Courtesy of the National Library of Ireland.

which is repeated in millions of iterations across Ireland during the twentieth century. Despite (or maybe because of) the commonplace nature of the images in its pages, the stories it contains seem strangely absent from history books, and as such poses fundamental questions for the way which we write the social history of modern Ireland.

Visibility has a history, and visibility in Ireland has its own distinctive past.[2] Over the course of the twentieth century, issues of visibility have been at the centre of a series of crises regarding the nature of society in modern Ireland. Individuals and families presented themselves as respectable, communities marketed themselves as tidy and industrious, while the states north and south were shown at home and abroad as prosperous, pious, and distinctively modern. Visibility costed money and was a social and economic privilege. In all these cases, how the individual, the community, and the state appeared, and how they disseminated these images, were of central importance to the regulation and self-perception of Irish society. These images were slowly interrogated by an increasingly active civil society which revealed new—different—images of Ireland: of poverty, abuse, and marginalized groups.

Languages of visibility have also been fundamental to the way that Irish people have explained and understood society. Metaphors of shadows, darkness, and invisibility are commonplace in the words we choose to make sense of Irish life. The original 'hidden Ireland' was the beleaguered Gaelic culture which survived in eighteenth-century Munster; however, since this turn of phrase was coined, the notion of 'hidden' aspects of Irish culture has been repeatedly used in a variety of divergent contexts.[3] Seamus Deane's memoir of his childhood in Derry and the family secrets which were whispered behind closed doors was entitled *Reading in the Dark*.[4] In the

[2] Sydney Walker, 'Artmaking in an Age of Visual Culture: Vision and Visuality', *Visual Arts Research* 30/2 (2004), 23–37; Martin Jay, 'Scopic Regimes of Modernity', in Foster, Hal (ed.), *Vision and Visuality* (San Francisco, 1988), 3; Liz Conor, *The Spectacular Modern Woman: Feminine Visibility in the 1920s* (Bloomington, IA, 2004), 6; Janet Wolff, 'The Invisible Flaneuse: Women and the Literature of Modernity', *Theory, Culture, Society* 2/3 (1985), 37–46; Phillip Ayoub, *When States Come Out: Europe's Sexual Minorities and the Politics of Visibility* (Cambridge, 2016), 22; see also Mary Gray, *Out in the Country: Youth, Media, and Queer Visibility in Rural America* (New York, 2009); Rosemary Hennessy, 'Queer Visibility in Commodity Culture', *Cultural Critique* 29 (1994–5), 31–76; James Scott, *Seeing Like a State: How Certain Schemes to Improve the Human Condition Have Failed* (New Haven, 1999); Chris Otter, *The Victorian Eye: A Political History of Light and Vision in Britain 1800–1910* (Chicago, 2009).

[3] Daniel Corkery, *The Hidden Ireland: A Study of Gaelic Munster in the Eighteenth Century* (Dublin, 1924); Robert James Scally, *The End of Hidden Ireland: Rebellion, Famine, and Emigration* (Oxford, 1996).

[4] Seamus Deane, *Reading in the Dark* (London, 1996).

later twentieth century, narratives of 'invisibility' were often used to describe those who remained in poverty as Ireland modernized. For example, in 1990, Colm Tóibín described Cumberland market, to the east of O'Connell Street, as 'the Dublin you don't see any more, the Dublin that doesn't appear on television... This, in the thin Baltic light, is the hidden Ireland.'[5] Similarly, the Irish community in Britain were frequently described as 'hidden' during the twentieth century, demoralized by poverty, racism, and distance from home; Mary Hickman and Bronwen Walter, for example, described the community as 'invisible' in their 1997 report on discrimination in London.[6] Since the 1990s, the repeated scandals which have surrounded the Catholic church have also been written through discourses of visibility; for example, Carole Holohan's report into abuses by priests for Amnesty International was entitled *In Plain Sight*, while public debate often rested on questions of how we 'turned a blind eye' for so long.[7]

Historians of Ireland also use metaphors of visibility to talk about the past. During the Decade of Centenaries, historians have also been using the language of visibility to discuss those excluded from the historical canon and their recuperation, most notably with reference to the 'invisible women' of the Irish revolution.[8] Indeed, the threads of visibility—of revealing, unearthing, exposing—run through social historical research. Women were 'hidden from history', waiting to be uncovered by feminist historians, queer men 'become visible' through activism and scholarship, while social historians have 'uncovered' working-class experience.[9] In Joan Scott's canonical essay 'The Evidence of Experience', she made the link between vision, historical knowledge, and modernity, describing how 'the visible is privileged; writing is then put at its service. Seeing is the origin of knowing.'[10] Histories that document 'hidden' worlds 'show the impact of silence and repression

[5] Colm Tóibín, 'Introduction', in O'Shea, Tony, *Dubliners* (Dublin, 1990), 16.

[6] Mary Hickman and Bronwen Walter, *Discrimination and the Irish Community in Britain: A Report of Research Undertaken for the Commission for Racial Equality* (London, 1997), 7.

[7] Carole Holohan, *In Plain Sight: Responding to the Ferns, Ryan, Murphy and Cloyne Reports* (Dublin, 2011).

[8] Mary Cullen, 'Invisible Women and their Contribution to Historical Studies', *Stair: The Journal of the Irish History Teachers' Association* (1982), reprinted in Mary Cullen (ed.), *Telling it Our Way: Essays in Gender History* (Dublin, 2013), 49–64; Maeve Casserly and Ciaran O'Neill, 'Public History, Invisibility, and Women in the Republic of Ireland', *The Public Historian* 39/2 (2017), 10–30.

[9] Sheila Rowbotham, *Hidden from History: 300 Years of Women's Oppression and the Fight Against it* (London, 1977); Leela Dube, Eleanor Leacock, and Shirley Ardener (eds.), *Visibility and Power: Essays on Women in Society and Development* (Oxford, 1986); Maria Luddy, 'Writing the History of Irish Women', *Gender and History* 8/3 (1996), 467–70.

[10] Joan Scott, 'The Evidence of Experience', *Critical Inquiry* 17/4 (1991), 776.

on the lives of those affected by it and bring to light the history of their suppression and exploitation'. But Scott goes on to push at the logics which structure these narratives; as she shows, the project of making experience visible 'precludes critical examination of the workings of the ideological system itself'.[11] Celebratory stories of people or issues becoming 'visible' have often implicitly presupposed the gaze of a historical establishment. But the range of memory work going on outside these groups is often held to be 'invisible', only celebrated as 'visible' when it is co-opted and validated by the mainstream historical institutions. Therefore, discussions of 'disappeared', 'invisible', and 'hidden' histories require critical reflections on the position, values, and assumptions of the historical profession. Indeed, as Scott avers, our job as historians is not just to excavate the past, but to understand why some pasts are unseen, and to comprehend the processes whereby people, events, and systems are rendered 'invisible' as part of our past.

While the language of visibility is pervasive, it is less frequent for historians to ask questions about what it means to see in the present and in the past. Indeed, through tracing how people understood and debated ideas of visuality in their own lives, we can understand ways of seeing Ireland as a 'contested terrain' where a variety of social and cultural anxieties played out.[12] Indeed, repeated platitudes that Ireland is not a 'visual' culture tell us less about the island's rich visual history and more about anxieties about the cultural status of visuality in Irish life. These sorts of statements serve only to naturalize—and hence obscure—the operation of power and capital that the visual embodies.

In this book, photography is used as a way in to explore the history of visuality in Ireland. Photographs—the residue of light on paper—have been imbued with a wide variety of profoundly felt cultural resonances, from keepsake, to craft object, to evidential document. Since the invention of photography, its status has been exhaustively debated; in particular, the photograph's seemingly unique relationship to reality has formed an essential part of its cultural significance.[13] The way in which the camera mechanically transmits shadows onto a negative without the interference of human hand—that is, the photograph's indexical status—has since the invention of the technology given the camera a unique status as conduit of visual fact

[11] Joan Scott, 'The Evidence of Experience', 778.
[12] Jay, 'Scopic Regimes of Modernity', 4.
[13] Susan Sontag, *On Photography* (Harmondsworth, 1979).

and truth.[14] As such, since the nineteenth century, the camera has been put to a range of uses in science, discipline, and surveillance. Even if people did not refer to it by its name, it is the quality of indexicality that has given photography its status and emotional power—the power to connect people with their own childhood memories, with long-dead ancestors, or with geographically dispersed relatives. While this veneer of veracity has been repeatedly deconstructed,the emotional and social resonance of the image persists. Indeed, many of photography's genres are still premised on the notion of indexicality; for example, photographic heritage projects are based on the camera's ability to record and taxonomize, while the profession of photojournalism is based on continued popular understanding of photography's ability to document and expose. As John Roberts has shown, 'claims to "knowledge" and "truth" still haunt the social functions of photography today.'[15] Moreover, cultural understandings of visibility map on to the qualities of the camera. Roberts goes on to note that 'notions such as "making visible", the "memory of the working class", "historical consciousness" and "counter-knowledge" are part of a shared commitment to what are perceived as the "truth telling" powers of photography'.[16] Photographs form only a small part of broader ways of seeing, but nonetheless they provide a useful exemplar for exploring a broad range of issues surrounding the cultural politics of sight. Indeed, through photography we can chart the material as well as the ocular qualities that comprise visuality; we can trace how photographs were reproduced, where they were disseminated, how they circulated, and how those who looked at them interacted with them to provide a textured understanding of how Irish people saw and were seen. Often stories of 'hidden' Irish histories and 'invisible' people are presented in the passive voice. Using photography allows us de-naturalize these processes, to reinsert actors into these sentences, and to think harder about processes and practices of revealing and concealing in Irish life.

Photography has played a fundamental role in shaping these ways of seeing. After the introduction of the Kodak Box Brownie in 1900, young people increasingly compiled photograph albums to curate and narrate their lives.

[14] Mary Ann Doane, 'Indexicality and the concept of medium specificity', in Kelsey, Robin and Stimson, Blake (eds.), *The Meaning of Photography* (Williamstown, MA, 2008), 4. Douglas R. Nickel, '"Impressed by Nature's Hand": Photography and Authorship', in Howells, Richard and Matson, Robert (eds.), *Using Visual Evidence* (London, 2008), 44.

[15] John Roberts, *The Art of Interruption: Realism, Photography, and the Everyday* (Manchester, 1998), 1.

[16] Roberts, *The Art of Interruption*, 3.

Young men and women began to take their own family photographs of days out at the beach, parties, and family groups, which they then stuck into photograph albums, with days and people carefully labelled: a way of seeing family life shaped by the global aesthetic conventions of Kodak marketing campaigns. Echoing Tolstoy's truism that 'All happy families are alike; each unhappy family is unhappy in its own way', families were presented as happy and alike, while the unhappiness which made each family unique was omitted from vision. James F. used his photograph album to explore his own development as a young man, using the conventions of Kodak photography to explore intimacy and his sexuality. The difficulties and complexities of distance and emigration were excluded from William C.'s photograph albums, with the images instead pulling the family together across great distances. Complex personal histories were also occluded from the image-frame. Dorothy Stokes had a long-term relationship with another woman, but this is entirely absent from the albums she made throughout her life. Within these conventions, photograph albums rendered family life increasingly similar and respectable. Studio portraitists also played an important role in creating images of family moments for much of the twentieth century. A close examination of the collections and papers of studio portraitists across provincial Ireland shows how photographer and sitter worked together to emphasize certain qualities and downplay others, and create idealized images of individuals and family groups to send to their extended families across the Irish world. Families presented themselves in their Sunday best, while photographers used backdrops, props, and lighting to create an image of family that conformed to aesthetic and social standards. Moreover, studio portraitists adapted their prints to erase wrinkles, worn hands, and blemishes, removing markers of poverty and aging, and enabling their subjects to conform to visual markers of respectability. This formation of norms around 'ways of seeing' Ireland was also a part of the practices of photographic societies. Clubs such as the Photographic Society of Ireland (PSI), Cork Camera Club, and Belfast Camera Club ran classes in photographic practice, teaching their members how to understand and value qualities of the Irish landscape through the visual conventions of pictorialism and the picturesque.[17] In replicating a formal pictorial style, these club photographers erased both indicators of poverty and modernity in their depictions of a

[17] Pierre Bourdieu, *Photography: A Middlebrow Art* (Stanford, 1990), 7.

rural pastoral, which created an image of a timeless Irish landscape that mapped onto a broader nationalist discourses.

From the 1970s, photography was used more often to document and reveal injustice, and the consistent ways in which Ireland had been represented to this point began to break down. This process was shaped by international shifts within photographic theory, enabled by new forms of photographic activism and new types of publishing and journalism. Photography became a central part of revealing 'the invisible' stories of Ireland, while the rhetoric of 'revealing' also characterized much photographic practice in this period. Influenced by developments in Britain and America, the community photography movement spread across Ireland from the early 1970s, emphasizing access to creativity and the democratization of cultural value as fundamental photographic values. This movement had a particular traction in Northern Ireland, where darkrooms and exhibition spaces such as Derry Camerawork, Shankill Darkrooms, and Belfast Exposed were set up to provide space for these new photographic practices. In Dublin, the North Centre City Community Action Project also ran courses in photography. Activists taught photography to young people, women, and the unemployed in inner-city areas, enabling them to produce their own—more representative—photographs of their neighbourhoods as a way of building self-confidence, community spirit, and empowering individuals and groups. Professional photography also took on a more interrogative tone from the 1970s. Indeed, photographic culture was profoundly shaped by the impact of a pack of international war photographers, such as Gilles Peress, Don McCullin, and Clive Limpkin, who descended on Northern Ireland in this period, depicting the conflict as a series of 'flashpoints' at street corners. Ireland also had its own first generation of celebrity photojournalists, such as Colman Doyle and Fergus Bourke, who captured the drama of high politics and violence on the streets for the news media.[18] This activity was accompanied by image makers, such as Frankie Quinn, Brendan Murphy, and Bill Kirk, who attempted to resist this portrayal and present a more authentic image of the conflict and other aspects of life in the province.[19] Working in a similar idiom, Derek Speirs photographed a range of issues including the poverty faced by Travellers and the poor physical conditions of psychiatric hospitals, Brendan Walsh photographed inner city communities, Joanne O'Brien captured women's experiences of

[18] John Quinn and Colman Doyle, *All Changed: Fifty Years of Photographing Ireland* (Dublin, 2004); Brendan Murphy, *Eyewitness: Four Decades of Northern Irish Life* (Dublin, 2003).

[19] Colin Graham, *Northern Ireland: 30 Years of Photography* (Belfast, 2013).

emigration, while Clodagh Boyd documented the activities of the women's and LGBT movements. These photographers were part of a febrile political climate which was increasingly pushing at the boundaries of political discourse in Irish life during the 1980s. However, in line with broader social and cultural change in this period, this is not an entirely celebratory or progressive narrative. Like any other genre, these photographs were only ever small glimpses of the world, and excluded far more than they showed. Moreover, visibility could border on voyeurism; individuals in difficulty could become exemplars of 'social problems'; and people had the complexities of their lives understood through media paradigms. Ways of imaging Ireland rose and fell: while increasingly from the 1970s, photographers were developing ways of imagining a new urban Ireland using tropes from the documentary movement, so—with a few exceptions—the realities of rural life and middle-class culture during a period of change were progressively ignored in the press. Each photographic genre mediated a different relationship between individual and community, and public and private. These genres each have their own history, which were often in conflict with each other in the way they depicted place and people; however, across all these different types of image-making, the early 1970s was a crucial turning point in the introduction of new modes of representation. Indeed, an examination of these divergent photographic practices in tandem demonstrates how the history of Irish modernity is inextricable from the history of visuality, and hence from the history of the camera.

This social history of visuality builds on an exciting field of Irish photographic history. The pioneering figure in the field is Edward Chandler, whose book *Photography in Ireland* traced the emergence of photography as a commercial practice during the nineteenth century.[20] More recently, Justin Carville has examined the dynamics of power and colonialism written through the practices of a range of photographers working in the nineteenth and twentieth centuries, from the ethnographic work of J. M. Synge to the street photography of J. J. Clarke.[21] Gail Baylis has explored themes of

[20] Edward Chandler, *Photography in Ireland: The Nineteenth Century* (Dublin, 2001); Edward Chandler and Peter Walsh, *Through the Brass Lidded Eye: Photography in Ireland 1839–1900* (Dublin, 1989).

[21] Justin Carville, 'Mr. Lawrence's Great Photographic Bazaar: Photography, History and the Imperial Streetscape', *Early Popular Visual Culture* 5/3 (2007), 263–83; Justin Carville, '"My Wallet of Photographs": Photography, Ethnography and Visual Culture in J.M. Synge's Aran Islands', *Irish Journal of Anthropology* 10/1 (2007), 5–11; Justin Carville, 'Visualizing the Rising: Photography, Memory and the Visual Economy of the 1916 Easter Rebellion', in Perreault, Jeanne, Warley, Linda, and Kadar, Marlene (eds.), *Photographs – Histories – Meanings* (New York, 2010).

absence and presence in photography of the Irish landscape, in particular with reference to the work of Robert French, and the creation, use and circulation of such visual icons of Irishness as the colleen and the 'gap girl'.[22] The contours of Irish photographic modernism in the early years of the new states has been excavated by Orla Fitzpatrick, who has researched both aesthetic practices and the commercial circulation of photographs and photo books.[23] Colin Graham has also examined in great detail the work on contemporary photographers in Northern Ireland, many of whom have gained international recognition for their considered responses to violence and post-conflict society.[24] This survey, while foregrounding the dynamism and variety of contemporary photographic research, is also suggestive of the large amount of work still to be done on Irish photographic culture. Moreover, it indicates the disparate nature of the field of 'history of photography', which is characterized by the heterogeneity of its research questions, methods, and approaches.

The history of photography in Ireland has principally been read through the dynamic of the colonial gaze. In a well-known article from 1986, Luke Gibbons describes J. M. Synge's journey to the Aran Islands with a camera. The resulting photographs 'captivated the native islanders' who 'scrutinized the pictures until every person in them had been identified'. He went on:

> Irish people in general have often felt like the Aran Islanders when confronted with images of themselves. The absence of a visual tradition in Ireland, equal in stature to its powerful literary counterpart, has meant that the dominant images of Ireland have, for the most part, emanated from outside the country, or have been produced at home with an eye to the foreign (or tourist) market.[25]

[22] Gail Baylis, 'Gender in the Frame: Photography and the Performance of the Nation Narrative in Early Twentieth-Century Ireland', *Irish Studies Review* 22/2 (2014), 184–206; Gail Baylis, 'Exchanging Looks: Gap Girls and Colleens in Early Irish Tourist Photography', *Early Popular Visual Culture* 10/4 (2012), 325–43; Gail Baylis, and Sarah Edge, 'The Great Famine: Absence, Memory and Photography', *Cultural Studies* 24/6 (2010), 778–800; Gail Baylis, 'Metropolitan Surveillance and Rural Opacity: Secret Photography in Late-Nineteenth-Century Ireland', *History of Photography* 33/1 (2009), 26–38.

[23] Orla Fitzpatrick, 'Modernity and Irish Photographic Publications, 1922 to 1949' (PhD thesis, University of Ulster, 2016).

[24] Colin Graham, *Northern Ireland: 30 Years of Photography* (Belfast, 2013).

[25] Luke Gibbons, 'Alien Eye: Ireland and Photography', *Creative Camera*, (December 1986), 10; for a more recent discussion of this position, see Justin Carville, 'Refracted Visions: Street Photography, Humanism, and the loss of innocence', in Maher, Eamon and O'Brien, Eugene, *Tracing the Cultural Legacy of Irish Catholicism from Galway to Cloyne and Beyond* (Manchester, 2017), 70–88.

In this reading, Irish photography has played a key role in both the symbolism and constitution of colonial and neo-colonial relations. However, in the thirty years since Gibbons wrote, the field of visual culture has been transformed. No scholar today could argue that Ireland lacked a 'visual tradition', in light of the wealth of recent work on Irish visual and material cultures.[26] However, Gibbons's reading of the interaction between colony and metropole has played a decisive role in the formulation of studies of Irish visual culture.[27] Indeed, the critical mass of scholars have situated the impact of colonialism as crucial to understanding Irish visual culture, and have pursued themes of colonialism through a diverse array of visual sources, from the newssheet ephemera, to lantern slides, to sober paintings displayed in solemn institutions. This has led to long running debates regarding the nature of these images drawing in scholars including Roy Foster, Fintan Cullen, and Perry Curtis.[28] However, in pursuing this project, photography and photographers that do not fit within this paradigm have often been passed over and the complexity and diversity of Irish visual production has often been overlooked. Throughout *Snapshot Stories* I reveal a visual landscape where the optics of Ireland are more partial, contingent, and mobilized to tell a range of stories. The social history of Irish photographic practice has been largely unexplored; this study excavates the practices of a myriad of previously unstudied photographers, and in particular contributes to unexamined histories of how women used image-making to make sense of their lives. In so doing, this book reveals a lively visual culture which existed beyond the realms of galleries, interpreting and exploring the visual production of a wide spectrum of Irish people through a range of new and productive theoretical lenses. Moreover, while the effects of colonialism are

[26] For example: Paul Caffrey, 'Irish Material Culture: The Shape of the Field', *Circa* (2003); Claudia Kinmonth, *Irish Country Furniture 1700–1950* (London and New Haven, 1993); Claudia Kinmonth, 'Survival: Irish Material Culture and Material Economy', *Folk Life* 38/1 (2000), 32–41; Lisa Godson and Joanna Brück (eds.), *Making 1916: Visual and Material Culture of the Easter Rising* (Liverpool, 2016).

[27] Following Gibbons, Justin Carville has proposed a nuancing of this positioning, arguing instead the utility of the concept of 'visual culture' in substitution of Gibbon's 'visual tradition'. Justin Carville, 'Visible Others: Photography and Romantic Ethnography in Ireland', in McGarrity, Maria and Culleton, Clare (eds.), *Irish Modernism and the Global Primitive* (Palgrave, 2009), 97–9.

[28] See, for example: L. Perry Curtis, *The Depiction of Eviction in Ireland, 1845–1910* (Dublin, 2011); Perry Curtis, *Apes and Angels: The Irishman in Victorian Caricature* (Smithsonian, 1997); Michael de Nie, *The Eternal Paddy: Irish Identity and the British Press, 1798–1882* (Madison WN, 2004); Roy Foster, 'Paddy and Mr Punch', in *Paddy and Mr Punch* (London, 1993), 171–94; Fintan Cullen, 'Marketing National Sentiment: Lantern Slides of Eviction in Late Nineteenth-Century Ireland', *History Workshop Journal* 54/1 (2002), 162–79.

unavoidable in Irish culture, this book foregrounds a different—if allied—story which focuses on issues of power, truth, and authority.

Even as historians of photography conduct research and adopt new theoretical insights, there remains a disjuncture between the critical and considered approach of work on Irish photography from scholars working in art history and cultural studies, and the plethora of publications produced every year for the mass market. Glossy coffee table books, compendiums of local memories, and collections of national idiosyncrasies use photography either to propagate an image of Ireland as rural pastoral or to reproduce older photographs of the country as a way of accessing a simpler Ireland prior to social and economic modernization. The interventions of photographic historians have also had little impact on how those working in history departments use photographs within their publications. To date, the photographic material employed by historians can be limited, and used in limited ways. Social, political, and economic historians often use no photographs whatsoever, and when they do use photographs, they use them for merely illustrative purposes—in order to reinforce a narrative already made through textual sources and statistics.[29] In so doing, they draw upon notions of photographic realism in order to reinforce or add authenticity to a narrative garnered elsewhere, or to draw the reader into an affective relationship with a historical subject, based on an often unarticulated idea of an emotional connection between viewer and viewed, transcending historical time, through a photographic image.

The history of Ireland since partition was dominated for a long time by political narratives focused on party infighting and state formation. However, social history is currently having something of a revival. An active cohort of social historians made use of institutional archives to excavate the interlinked power of church and state in post-partition Ireland; this material could, however, through its focus on an institutional gaze, at times seem almost empty of textured experiences of individuals. More recently, historians such as Carole Holohan, Lindsey Earner-Byrne, and Caitriona Clear have done important work in considering how these forces shaped the lives of individuals, using sources such as letters and diaries to make sense of subjective experiences of social and cultural change.[30] *Snapshot Stories* is

[29] Peter Burke, *Eyewitnessing: The Uses of Images as Historical Evidence* (Cornell, 2002), 10.

[30] Diarmuid Ferriter, *The Transformation of Ireland, 1900–2000* (London, 2007); Rosemary Cullen Owens, *A Social History of Women in Ireland, 1870–1970* (Dublin, 2005); Tom Garvin, *Preventing the Future: Why Was Ireland So Poor for So Long* (Dublin, 2004); Caitriona Clear, *Women of the House: Women's Household Work in Ireland 1921–61: Experiences, Memories, Discourses* (Dublin, 2000).

informed by this new work in social history; but while historians working in this field have overwhelmingly focused on written sources to apprehend this story, this book draws these themes into conversation with approaches from visual studies.[31] An apprehension of the complex interplay of the image's visuality, materiality, and mobility, drawing on work from art history, anthropology, and sociology, provides the historian with new conceptual tools for rereading Irish social history.[32] This turn to the visual adds the perspective of those outside formal structures of power to this story, and reveals a more complex interplay of agency and resistance than has hitherto been apprehended. It shows how people used photography—portrait, landscape, and documentary—in a whole host of complex ways in order to mediate, interpret, and interrogate their understanding of state and nation, and their place within it. Furthermore, photographic sources provide a crucial forum for making sense of new themes: how power functioned across society, how ideas of exposure and concealment were mediated, and notions of the visible operated, both north and south of the border. Indeed, an examination of this story shows how photographers were an essential part of an expanding public sphere, and how their images played a crucial role in creating and shaping the Irish crises of legitimacy in the latter part of the twentieth century.

There are a huge number of photographs scattered in archives across Ireland. The most important collections are housed in the Public Record Office of Northern Ireland (PRONI), the Ulster Folk and Transport Museum, and the National Library of Ireland (NLI). The collections of these institutions by photographers such as William Lawrence, Robert Welch, and Elinor Wiltshire have increasingly come to define an image of the Irish past. Smaller collections are also housed in universities, county archives, and specialist archives. The country tends to be better served in terms of coverage of the nineteenth and early twentieth centuries. As temporal distances narrow the density of photographic archives diminish, creating a strange sense of the distance of the near present. Some collections are in better

[31] Matt Houlbrook, *Prince of Tricksters: The Incredible True Story of Netley Lucas, Gentleman Crook* (Chicago, 2016); James Hinton, *Nine Wartime Lives: Mass Observation and the Making of the Modern Self* (Oxford, 2010); Claire Langhamer, *The English in Love: The Intimate Story of an Emotional Revolution* (Oxford, 2013); Michael Roper, *The Secret Battle: Emotional Survival in the Great War* (Manchester, 2009).

[32] Elizabeth Edwards and Janice Hart (ed.), *Photographs Objects, Histories: On the Materiality of Images* (London, 2004); Penny Tinkler, *Using Photographs in Social and Historical Research* (London, 2013); Gillian Rose, *Visual Methodologies* (London, 2013); Pierre Bourdieu, *Photography: A Middlebrow Art* (Stanford, 1990); Geoffrey Batchen, *Each Wild Idea: Writing, Photography, History* (Cambridge MA, 2001).

condition than others, and some are better archived. Indeed, it is often the case that the textual and photographic elements of a collection are separated for cataloguing and preservation, meaning that images are separated from their archival context. However, the biggest challenge—and opportunity—facing scholars of the visual is digitization. Digitization of photography—as with other historical data—has resulted in a simultaneous opening up and a narrowing of the field as scholars are repeatedly drawn to the huge numbers of photographs available online, just as many more gather dust in county archives across the country. Online photographs are also bereft of the large amount of information that can be garnered from their materiality and their context, and even quite simple data such as what is written on the reverse, their size, or the order in which they were inserted into an album.

Today these documents are often in boxes in attics, scattered in junk shops, interleaved in long-forgotten books and personal papers. These photographic archives are often full of absences or silences—blurred faces stare out unnamed from images, rips and tears are testament to long forgotten family feuds, while creases and thumb prints imply photographic afterlives which can only be guessed at. As historians, we often find ourselves waging a war of attrition against our sources, and the historical actors under our scrutiny, in our attempts to reconstruct the meaning of their lives, or to fit their archive into a broader historical narrative. However, this can be a distorting process which renders the contours of subjectivity flattened under the historian's need to uncover and catalogue. But sometimes it is more useful not to uncover these stories, to leave these stories as they appear in the photographs: unfinished. Instead, thinking with these unfinished histories pose useful questions about how the archive functions, how historical subjects kept secrets and destroyed traces, and how the past can slip out of view. As Elizabeth Edwards has indicated, following Frank Ankersmit, the melancholia of old photographs is 'not merely a melancholia for a lost past in the face of modernity, but a melancholia for a future unaware of its past, poised in the tensions of historical desire between discovery and recovery, loss and love'.[33] It is worth taking these emotions, gaps, and silences seriously. In this context, these hurdles can provide us with a way of uncovering a textured and nuanced understanding of the nature of social history and its boundaries and enable us to use photography to pose fundamental questions about the nature of the historical past.

[33] Edwards, 'Photography and the Material Performance of the Past', *History and Theory* 48/4 (2009), 150.

As this discussion demonstrates, visual sources pose a series of questions about the nature of historical practice. As well as being a social history *of* photography, *Snapshot Stories* is also a social history told *through* photography, which uses archival scholarship as an opportunity to examine the possibilities and challenges provided by photographs for rewriting the narrative of post-partition Ireland. Produced in enormous quantities by individuals and families across Ireland, photographs signal the potential to write a history of Ireland from the outside in, exploring the experiences, perceptions, and aspirations of those on the margins of power. Many of these photographs, recording personal perspectives and quotidian moments, display events and phenomena which are simply absent from any other type of archival record. Moreover, detail in the background, events caught by chance on the periphery of the frame, and photographs taken by accident all intimate a plethora of stories absent from contemporary narratives. John Berger has argued that photographs represent an 'opposition to history' by which ordinary people affirm the subjective experiences that modernity, science, and industrial capitalism have done so much to crush: 'And so, hundreds of millions of photographs, fragile images, often carried next to the heart or placed by the side of the bed, are used to refer to that which historical time has no right to destroy.'[34] These photographs, while seemingly commonplace, destabilize overarching themes through which we understand the Irish states after partition and, through the recovery of these incidental moments, provide profound challenges relating to the way Irish history has been researched, practised, and understood.

Today these photographic stories are changing again, as Ireland has evolved through waves of both prosperity and austerity, and the nature of visibility shifts with the revolutionary potential of social media. But visuality in the twentieth century had its own distinct tenor, fashioned in photomagazines, portrait studios, and family albums. Ireland is often stated as not a 'visual' society, but this book aims to show the opposite: that the politics of visibility has always been crucial, heightened, and constantly contested in Irish life. As the twentieth century recedes into the realm of historical time, intimate memories pass beyond out of our grasp, but patterns reveal themselves which were not visible up close.

[34] Susie Linfield, *The Cruel Radiance: Photography and Political Violence* (Chicago, 2010), 6.

1

Beaches and Sunlight

Photograph Albums and Youthful Memories, *c.*1922–50

Happening upon a photograph album in an archive or a junk shop produces a strange paradox of experiences, of belonging and knowing, yet anonymity and distance. We have seen all the photographs before: friends hastily assemble on blankets for a picnic on a rare sunny day, sisters smile begrudgingly on their first day of school, hands rest proudly on bonnets of new cars, and families huddle together, grimacing at cameras on sandblasted days at the beach. Nearly recognizable faces stare out at ours in colour and in black and white, while images, holidays, and days out which were once almost ours provide us with nostalgia for events we cannot quite remember. Leafing through these pages, we see the patterned rhythmic similarity and familiarity of other lives to ours. We see the concertinaed chronologies folded into the album's pages, as *cartes-des-visites* give way to dewy and sentimental studio portraits, and then to small snapshots. We get a sense of nostalgic recall of 'endless summer days' of youth through the thematic arrangement of the album's pages. Here too, however, we are also simultaneously forced to confront the album's inscrutability. Uncaptioned images of blurred faces seemingly provide us with no way of finding a path backwards through time to discover the identity of these people, or to link their lives to broader historical narratives. The album frustrates as it beguiles.

From the advent of the Kodak Box Brownie in 1900, the photograph was a relatively affordable way of recording life events for Ireland's more prosperous young people. During the 1920s and 1930s, camera ownership was advertised and sold in the Irish press as part of modern self-fashioning and taking photographs was a key part of the leisurely free time of affluent and single twenty- and thirty- somethings. Youth and the shifting character of the life-cycle have been increasingly studied by historians of Ireland in recent years; indeed, the increasing distinction between life phases was a feature of an Ireland in modernity, with shifts in the financial and personal

Snapshot Stories: Visuality, Photography, and the Social History of Ireland, 1922–2000. Erika Hanna, Oxford University Press (2020). © Erika Hanna.
DOI: 10.1093/oso/9780198823032.001.0001

independence of young people being differentially experienced in urban and rural areas.[1] In the early part of the twentieth century, this phase of life was structured by the new spaces of the city and the town: the cinema, the dancehall, and the coffee bar which provided new opportunities for experimentation and the construction of an identity beyond the remit of the family. Indeed, the photograph album can be understood as another of these spaces, and thus provides an important source for accessing these histories. The album served as a visual record of lives between childhood and marriage, recording family events, parties, and days out. Moreover, these albums allowed young people to narrate a sense of belonging to family while also establishing distance from its structures through charged forays into individuality, desire, and independence.[2] These personal stories were refigured and reframed in line with advertising, combining local particularities with themes inspired by Kodak marketing. The fictive and the real intertwined and became indistinguishable as events and scenes were constructed to be photographed and photographs were chosen for albums based on their similarity to photographic ideals. As such, these albums contain a wealth of detail about how identity was imagined, belonging was narrated, and the boundaries between public and private were negotiated.

However, these photograph albums are scattered. As part of the individuality of youth, they were often discarded and forgotten once the owner got married and started their own family. They frequently reside in damp boxes in garages and attics, looked at infrequently, as those pictured within them recede from memory. Filled with unnamed figures on unknown holidays, these albums rapidly lose their emotive power, becoming only curiosities evoking how strange our great-grandparents looked and how foreign their lives seem. However, at moments when these lineages rupture, such as personal tragedy, family crisis, or emigration, these objects instead become homeless, sometimes finding their way into junk shops, eBay, car-boot sales, or the bin.[3] Sometimes, they find their way into archives. Since the close of the twentieth century, the photograph album, in its traditional paper format, is now rarely made and, consequentially, there has been a more

[1] Carole Holohan, *Reframing Irish Youth in the 1960s* (Liverpool, 2018); Catherine Cox and Susannah Riordan (eds.), *Adolescence in Modern Irish History* (London, 2015).

[2] Penny Tinkler, '"Picture Me As a Young Woman": Researching Girls' Photo Collections from the 1950s and 1960', *Photography and Culture* 3/3 (2010), 262.

[3] Jacollette collects and displays a wide variety of found Irish photography: http://www.jacolette.com.

self-conscious effort to collect, archive, and digitize these ephemeral documents. Currently the *Photograph Album of Ireland* project run by the Gallery of Photography is touring the country, collecting, archiving, and displaying snapshot photography.[4]

The National Library of Ireland (NLI) has over 400 photograph albums, largely dating from the nineteenth century.[5] For example, it holds the album of Alfred Ternan, who charted the development of his family life alongside the growth of the young state. He was a housing architect with Dublin Corporation, while his father had been a prominent city doctor, and at one time resident medial officer at the Royal Hospital for Incurables, and this civic perspective is visible in the way that he framed his family's life. Interspersed with family photographs are images that tie together the familial and the national story. He documented the key civic moments of the first decade of independence, including the funeral of Kevin O'Higgins, reconstruction of the Four Courts, a visit of William Cosgrave to Ardnacrusha, the Eucharistic Congress, mixed with scenes of picnics and trips to the beach.[6] James Bone, a farmer from Irishtown, Co. Mayo, began his album with a photograph of a Land League demonstration and an image of his parents, and filled the rest of its pages with bought and self-taken images of religious processions, local landmarks, and political ephemera, alongside photographs of his extended family posed in various domestic gardens.[7] Vincent Byrne's album begins with a crucial milestone—his class photograph on finishing school, and the photograph of the altar in his neighbourhood church. From these markers, this is a story of his foray into adulthood: a photograph of himself and another young man in trench coats, hair slicked back, one meeting the photographer's gaze, taken by Arthur Fields on O'Connell Bridge. From there the tone changed again, with Byrne's move to Australia, now depicting the outdoorsy emigrant culture and new scenery: young men posed on rocks or against huge and exotic trees, a different configuration of masculinity and landscape to that which he had left in Ireland.[8]

[4] Erika Hanna, 'Life's a Beach: The Photo Album of Ireland', *Source* 80 (Autumn 2014), 54–5; Karen Downey and Pauline Hadaway, *Portraits from a 50's Archive* (Belfast, 2005).

[5] For example, Galway County Archive (GCA) GP8 Minihan family collection, NLI Alb. 162 Ternan family collection; PRONI D4122/B Arthur Campbell albums; and a wide variety of photographs online at Waterford County Museum: http://www.dungarvanmuseum.org/exhibit/web/BasicImageSearch.

[6] NLI Alb162 Ternan Photograph Album.

[7] NLI Alb428 Mayo Photograph Album.

[8] NLI Vincent Byrne vtls 531,462.

These albums are a demotic form of life curation that open up new possibilities for historians beyond traditional objects of study such as diaries and letters. They provide a huge wealth of resources for considering the lives of young people, and a view of social and cultural change from the perspective of those outside authority. Indeed, as the twentieth century recedes from view, and the album increasingly becomes a historic form, it is essential that social historians develop a method and a vocabulary in order to use these documents. However, to do so requires developing appropriate methodologies and research questions to make full use of the information they may contain. When gathered around old photograph albums, the often-repeated questions circle around establishing the names of people in the images, and the dates and locations at which the photographs were taken. However, albums in archives often lack this sort of biographical information, or any discernible way of finding out, and can therefore leave the researcher with few clues with which to begin research. Moreover, approaches to these photographs from art history also present a further, different, set of issues. The academic study of photography has, in the words of Geoffrey Batchen, been 'anxiously, insecurely, focused on originality, innovation, and individualism' in terms of its methods and research agendas.[9] However, these albums cut against these tendencies, displayed by the rotating cast of characters within the images which demonstrate that the camera has been passed between many hands, and that most of the photographers had a total lack of interest in marking either photographs or albums as their own creation. Further, as Batchen goes on to warn, a consideration of these albums in terms of their artistic merit can only provide us with the response that these are 'boring photographs' and reveals the biases implicit in much of the methodological apparatus surrounding the history of photography.[10] Approaching these photograph albums forces us to work harder with our sources, to look again, and to examine the resources we do have present for making sense of these artefacts. Indeed, the insurmountable empirical barriers which many of these albums seemingly present provide us with an opportunity to both foreground and question research methods implicit to historical study, and consider how we can use new approaches to make the most of our sources.

[9] Geoffrey Batchen, 'Snapshots: Art History and the Ethnographic Turn', *Photographies* 1/2 (2008), 123.

[10] Batchen 'Snapshots', 121.

Historians of Ireland have to date tended not to research with photograph albums, however, a wide variety of scholars—in particular from cultural studies—have theorized their meaning and use, exploring notions of nostalgia and memory, examining albums as objects of affect across time and distance, and using them to study power and the gaze within the family.[11] Scholars have also discussed the dialogic relationship between photographic convention and concealment. In this literature, Kodak marketing has come to epitomize certain forms of photographic practice which has placed the leisure time of the middle-class family at the centre of snapshot photography.[12] This adherence to a small set of visual clichés has been argued to have played a fundamental role in the consolidation of the nuclear family during the twentieth century, but in so doing perpetuated snapshot photography's role as a mode of concealment, which demanded adherence to unrealizable societal norms and intentional forgetting.[13] In particular, Jo Spence and Patricia Holland's diagnosis of the photograph album has had a lasting impact on the shape of the field. In *Family Snaps*, they explore the suffocating replication of convention within the photograph album, and argue that 'the fascination of such pictures is precisely this embrace of the conventions. Pictures which match up to expectations give enormous pleasure, partly because their familiar structure is able to contain the tension between the longed-for ideal and the ambivalence of lived experience.'[14] In Annette Kuhn's *Family Secrets*, the family album took on a dual significance, displaying her mother's need to force her to play certain roles both in the home and in photographs, and to hide certain painful memories not only from public view, but also from personal recall. Later, as an adult, scholar, and feminist, the album took on a new meaning, providing her with the materials to work through her memories and explore the affective agency of nostalgia and loss.[15]

This chapter builds on this literature and considers its themes in the context of Ireland after partition. Here the focus is on how young people curated

[11] The literature is extensive; see for example, Gillian Rose, *Doing Family Photography: The Domestic, the Public, and the Politics of Sentiment* (London, 2010); Richard Chalfen, *Snapshot Versions of Life* (Wisconsin, 1987); Marianne Hirsch, *The Familial Gaze* (Dartmouth, 1999); Marianna Hirsch, *Family Frames: Photography, Narrative, and Postmemory* (Cambridge MA, 1997).

[12] Nancy May West, *Kodak and the Lens of Nostalgia* (Virginia, 2000).

[13] Lynn Berger, 'Snapshots, or: Visual Culture's Clichés', *Photographies* 4/2 (2011), 175–90.

[14] Patricia Holland, 'Introduction: History, Memory, and the Family Album', in Jo Spence and Patricia Holland (eds.) *Family Snaps: The Meanings of Domestic Photography* (London, 1991), 4.

[15] Annette Kuhn, *Family Secrets: Acts of Memory and Imagination* (London, 1995).

and narrated stories of their lives, explored their relationship to family, community, and nation, and used their albums to tell stories and hide secrets. This chapter was written through surveying the hundreds of photographs albums that are now in PRONI, the NLI, and the National Archives of Ireland (NAI). The focus is on a detailed study of three suggestive examples of three young people who were compiling albums in the twenty years after independence, which, for various reasons, have ended up in archives: Dorothy Stokes, a piano teacher who recorded her sociable life in Dublin in albums; James F., a Fermanagh solicitor who made albums depicting his leisure time; and William C., who worked his way across Africa and Canada, and who used his album to record his relationship with his family in Ireland.[16] Throughout this chapter, I consider the photographs these people placed in their albums, the stories these photographs told, and—inversely—what information resided beyond the albums' borders. Stokes, F., and C. all found different ways of curating information about themselves and their social circles in their albums, and all dealt with issues of family, politics, and sexuality in differing—partial—ways. However, our ability to extract these narratives has a short half-life, and is based both on close readings of photographs and on the assessment of the album as a whole against other archival material assembled on the people pictured within them. Moreover, to attempt to trace the boundaries of the visible in this fashion also requires the development of a sophisticated way of making sense of what *cannot* be found out from photograph albums. Here I attempt to think with the lacunae and absences which these photograph albums present, in contrast with the historian's usual instinct to work around these empiric deficits and to paper over absences in their writing. Paying attention to stories of presence and absence rereads the photograph album in an alternate light. Rather than trying to uncover a whole, genuine, or unified historical subject hidden within layers of photographic convention, instead I attempt to consider the fine grain of stories they wanted left behind, and recover a sense of their agency in their attempts to create an image, or hide details about their lives, for their contemporaries, posterity, or the historian's gaze.

Each photograph album is examined with a differing photographic methodology. With particular regard to the albums of Dorothy Stokes, I focus on the semiotics of her images. In particular, I explore how she situated her

[16] Some names have been changed.

photography within the repetition of content and form of snapshot photography, a phenomenon which Geoffrey Batchen has described as 'the visual economy of same but different'.[17] Stokes's images replicated two contemporary styles: snapshot and ethnographic photography. Tropes were not only disrupted and manipulated but photographic conventions were also unself-consciously and serendipitously re-figured.[18] I explore how, for Stokes, assimilating and subverting genre became a way for her to make a range of comments on her identity and social world—sometimes consciously, sometimes less so, and both represent and constitute an oppositional private life which resisted state and religious discourses of womanhood. Secondly, with regard to F.'s album, the practices and pleasures of taking photographs, and the spaces of sociability the presence of the camera opened up for young people are given priority. This builds on work by Josie McLellan, who has reconstructed from snatched glimpses in photographs a life-world of a group of East German queer men; here she finds experiences, emotions, and excitement which have tended to be omitted from historical work on sexuality under communism and shows how the camera played an important role in creating moments of fun and group cohesion.[19] With reference to F.'s album, I explore how these 'quotidian moments' were given a new significance and potency by the presence of a camera.[20] Finally, the chapter turns to the album of William C., and an examination of the narratives embedded in histories of photographs when they are considered as objects. A careful exploration of when photographs were produced, when they were pasted into an album, and how they have moved between individuals can provide a complex story. In reading C.'s photograph album, I compare the stories which are produced by the materiality of the images against narratives embedded in content of the photographs and examine what the assonances and dissonances between these two divergent methods can mean.

It soon becomes apparent how the objects and images examined in this chapter do not always fit with current historiographical paradigms for making sense of photograph albums. It is notable how context-specific and ahistorical many of the approaches and assumptions made about snapshot

[17] Batchen, 'Snapshots', 125.

[18] Elizabeth Edwards, *The Camera as Historian: Amateur Photographers and Historical Imagination, 1885–1918* (Durham NC, 2012), 28–9.

[19] Josie McLellan, 'From Private Photography to Mass Circulation: The Queering of East German Visual Culture, 1968–1989', *Contemporary European History* 48/3 (2015), 405–23.

[20] Maiken Umbach, 'Selfhood, Place, and Ideology in German Photo Albums, 1933–45', *Central European History* 48/3 (2015), 336.

photography are. In Ireland, where conventions around sexuality and relations between genders were constrained, photography provided new avenues for action, performance, and sociability. These photographs were anything but conventional—indeed, they opened up new possibilities for the person holding the camera and the subject in the viewfinder to move beyond the ordinary into the fantasy world of the image frame. In this schema, the use of 'convention' provided both photographer and subject with another device for creating or representing themselves, as such 'convention' does not dull the analytic utility of the snapshot but rather is another mode of representation worth exploring. Exploring how they adopted, assimilated, and subverted convention can provide us with a whole host of information regarding their self-fashioning within contemporary axes of class, power, and consumption in Ireland.[21] However, Kodak did not simply provide a conduit for a more liberal, Americanized mode of self-presentation; indeed, while it opened up some themes, others—of loss, disappointment, political or financial instability, and homosexuality—were strictly beyond the realm of the image. Recognition of these photographic affordances poses a whole new set of questions regarding how Irish people conceived of, and made accommodations with, national discourses and social and religious norms, and reorientates a social history which has largely been written through civil society and institutions towards the politics of the everyday. Although photographs are often discussed in terms of their conservatism, these albums suggest that historians need to look harder, look for longer, inspect in detail every single photograph in the album rather than just those which already conform to our assumptions of what snapshot photography should look like. Here in these quiet details stories run against the grain, waiting to be seen.

Dorothy Stokes and the Unique Oscillations of Convention

Four young women look towards a camera as if they are laughing (Figure 1.1). They seem happy, unposed, and informal; clothed in swimming caps and bathing dresses, standing beside outdoor swimming baths, they also look very cold.[22] The caption tells us the names of the four smiling bathers—'Eleanor

[21] Edwards, *The Camera as Historian*, 1–30.

[22] National Library of Ireland (NLI) Dorothy Stokes Collection (DS) Alb. 215 (1925) (where known, dates are included in brackets after the reference number).

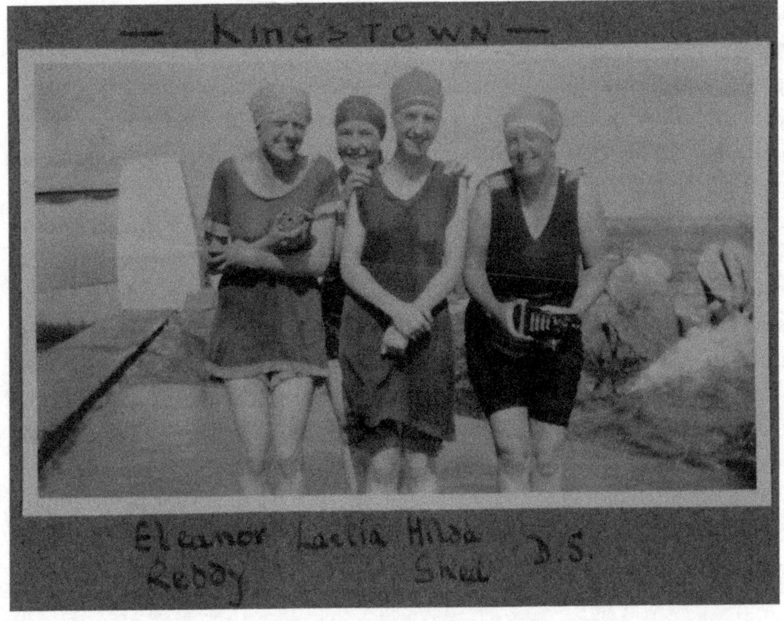

Figure 1.1 Kingstown (1925). Image Courtesy of the National Library of Ireland.

Reddy, Laelia, Hilda Shea, D. S.'—and records that the photograph was taken in Kingstown in 1925.[23] The photograph strikingly attests to the popularity of photography for young women in this period: two of the women hold their own cameras, while the existence of the photograph indicates a third camera which took the shot. In order to make sense of this image, it is worth noting that it does not stand on its own; it is one of fifty others in an album and that this album is one of twenty-nine, all containing similarly appealing and yet unrevealing images of days out at the beach amongst other celebratory occasions.

The D.S. on the right of the photograph was Dorothy Stokes, the owner of the album. She was born in 1898 in South Africa to Irish parents from the well-known Stokes medical family, but as a child her parents sent her back to Ireland to live with a governess in Glendalough.[24] Ten years later, she appeared on the 1911 census as living with her mother in Sandymount, a coastal Dublin suburb.[25] Stokes was a member of the Church of Ireland, a group which historians have often characterized as existing in a state of 'internal political exile'; however, she took a very active role in Irish civil society and national culture through her career in music.[26] In her youth she attended the Royal Academy of Music, and during the 1920s and 1930s she had a successful career as a pianist, combining playing musical accompaniments for theatre, playing in the orchestra at the Gresham Hotel and performing on Radio Éireann. She was also on the organizing committee of Feis Ceoil (a festival of Irish and classical music) and the Culwick Society (a choral society). In later life, she spent most of her time teaching the piano: she taught private lessons in her studio in Fitzwilliam Place, and taught music at Alexandra College, eventually becoming Professor of both Theory and Piano at the Royal Academy of Music, retaining a connection with that organization until her death in 1982.[27]

Stokes's other love was photography. Her first album, made in 1925, contained a diverse array of images; it opened with images of Dalkey Lodge, the Scalp, Ann's Gift Fethard, and the Rock of Cashel, followed by photographs of dogs, a display by Cossacks at Landsdowne Road and days at the beach at

[23] 'Kingstown' had been renamed Dun Laoghaire in 1921; this label probably refers to how those in the photograph referred to the town.

[24] Census 1901, http://www.census.nationalarchives.ie (accessed 20 February 2015).

[25] Census 1911, http://www.census.nationalarchives.ie (accessed 20 February 2015).

[26] R. B. McDowell, *Crisis and Decline: The Fate of Southern Unionists* (Dublin, 1997), vii.

[27] Album of Alexandra College Dublin photographs NLI DS Alb. 228; *Irish Times*, 24 June 1925, 8.

Greystones and Dun Laoghaire.[28] In the following thirty years, the way that she arranged her pictures into her albums remained markedly consistent: four small photographs on a grey or black background, all carefully captioned with the place the photograph was taken written above the image and people identified below. Stokes conformed with many of the trends regarding the growth of popular photography in Ireland during the twentieth century. She complied with the common themes and subjects of amateur photography as designated by the marketing of Kodak cameras, using her camera primarily to record her leisure time with her close friends in Dublin. This included parties, days out at the beaches near the city, and walks in the Dublin Mountains.[29] She also dedicated much album space to recording her holidays in Ireland and Europe, chronicling her travels to Connemara and Achill, Northern Ireland, the Lake District, and Scotland, and driving holidays through Europe to Switzerland, Austria, and Italy. Conversely, certain themes were rarely represented: images of work, or depictions of the streets of Dublin, almost never featured. These similarities continued with regard to her equipment and training; like most of her contemporaries who owned a camera, she never joined a club, took lessons, or learned how to develop her own photographs.

Despite these points of convergence, Stokes departed from the standard themes of twentieth-century snapshot photography in significant ways. She used her albums to document an urban—even bohemian—Irish life after independence, which stood in contrast to the modes of amateur photography and entrenched images of Ireland. Stokes remained unmarried; instead of a focus on family life and children, the albums display the sociable and full life of a single woman, comfortable at the centre of a large and unconventional circle of friends of musicians and actors. A central part of this active, urban life was her group of intimate female friends, with whom she holidayed and socialized. Indeed, the camera became an important part of designating and marking their experiences: Stokes took photographs of the group when they reached the Hell Fire Club, when they kissed the Blarney Stone, and when they walked the Cliffs of Moher. When Stokes, along with friends Nancie and Lily climbed to the top of Nelson's Pillar, they took each other's photographs in poses evocative of fashion photography as they perched on the railings.[30] Many of the photographs she took were of days out at the beach, where the assembled group changed into swimming

[28] NLI DS Alb. 215.

[29] West, *Kodak and the Lens of Nostalgia*, 36–73.

[30] NLI DS Alb. 222.

costumes and swam and lay on the sand. A photograph of a woman in a swimsuit, caught mid-leap, on Keel strand was entitled 'Nancie disporting!' (Figure 1.2).[31] A photograph of Maisie, taken at Shankill, just south of Dublin, shows her standing confidently posing in front of the camera, her wet swimsuit revealing the contours of her body.[32] These women also showed no compunction about being captured smoking, despite the fact that smoking in public was often criticized as being symptomatic of the declining morality of 'modern' women; rather they enjoyed posing with their cigarettes as a symbolic display of their contravention of the rules of social propriety.[33] However, Stokes did not solely portray this group of women as glamorous and sexualized. She also took—and appeared in—photographs where they discarded all conventions of feminine presentation or propriety; for example, shivering on the beach and climbing walls (Figure 1.3).[34] When the group stripped off down to their bloomers in order to have an impromptu paddle, they laughed as they took each other's photographs.[35] A well-composed photograph of a woman sitting on a rock on the beach, smiling towards the camera, and with her feet dangling in a pool, was disrupted by the caption 'Skerries: Nora corn curing!'.[36] The intimacy of the group of friends was reflected in how they arranged themselves to have their photograph taken: at the Blarney stone they stood bundled together with their arms around each other, and this informality was echoed by the off-centre framing and high-angle of the photograph.

While her friends often performed for the camera, Stokes herself was self-conscious in front of the lens she was more used to being behind. Indeed, she often guided the unseen observer who might leaf through the album in the way they would receive the photographs, perhaps aiming to pre-empt and so deflect negative reception of her appearance, by first appending a derogatory comment of her own. This was particularly the case when Stokes donned a bathing suit or went swimming. She captioned a photograph of herself on a rock by the sea, taken on holiday in Glengarriff in 1929, 'Self, not looking as fat as expected'.[37] A photograph of her by the seaside at Baily was captioned 'Some water nymph', while she entitled a photograph of her swimming at Roundstone 'Some mermaid'.[38] It is striking

[31] NLI DS Alb. 218 (1933). [32] NLI DS Alb. 242.

[33] Louise Ryan, 'Negotiating Modernity and Tradition: Newspaper Debates on the "Modern Girl" in the Irish Free State', *Journal of Gender Studies* 7/2 (1998), 187.

[34] NLI DS Alb. 218a (1933). [35] NLI DS Alb. 220. [36] NLI DS Alb. 214 (1927–8).

[37] NLI DS Alb. 224 (1929). [38] NLI DS Alb. 242; NLI DS Alb. 217 (1942).

Figure 1.2 'Nancie disporting!' (1933). Image Courtesy of the National Library of Ireland.

Figure 1.3 'Two Nymphs' (1933). Image Courtesy of the National Library of Ireland.

that she chose to include these photographs while simultaneously disparaging their subject. Indeed, it was not only her appearance, but also her status as a single woman without a family which caused her unease in front of the lens. A photograph she included in her album played on this disjuncture; it showed her, sitting in her car, holding her dog Barney, and was jokingly entitled 'Stokes Family!'.[39] The tension between her enjoyment of photography with the role that camera culture played in constructing the nuclear family meant that her hobby could lead her towards some discomfort in the way that she viewed herself. To Stokes, the camera, and having her photograph taken, could function as painful reminders of the role of an unseen societal gaze in constructing femininity and her failure to conform to these perceived ideals.

Stokes seems to have suffered less from her unease under the photographic gaze when she was photographed beside her car. Indeed, her albums contained forty-nine photographs of her various vehicles, and she included herself in many of these pictures. On a driving holiday to Norway in 1950, the first photograph in the album pictured her standing on the front seat of her car with the roof down, and a cigarette clenched between her teeth.[40] More often, however, she placed herself beside the car, with a hand proprietarily laid on the bonnet, and, on several occasions, she provided the caption 'Owner and Owned'.[41] This pride in her vehicle is hardly surprising: the cars she owned were some of her most expensive possessions and still a relative luxury and rarity, especially for a woman in 1930s Ireland. As Sean O'Connell has observed, during the interwar period the car 'was accorded an important symbolic role in growing female emancipation'.[42] Her car gave her the ability to travel widely and independently; it was technology which, alongside her camera, constituted and represented her sense of herself as affluent, mobile and, above all, modern. In the Irish context, the motor car also had further significance with regard to Stokes's sexual and social independence. During the 1920s and 1930s, it was the subject of a moral panic regarding the respectability of women; as Maria Luddy has shown, the Catholic hierarchy frequently asserted its belief that the mobility and privacy of the car as providing new territory for sexual impropriety.[43] Significantly, the car

[39] NLI DS Alb. 242. [40] NLI Alb. 236 (1950). [41] NLI DS Alb. 242.

[42] Sean O'Connell, *The Car in British Society: Class, Gender, and Motoring 1896–1939* (Manchester, 1998), 50.

[43] Maria Luddy, 'Sex and the Single Girl in 1920s and 1930s Ireland', *The Irish Review* 35 (2007), 82–3; Diarmuid Ferriter, *Occasion of Sin: Sex and Society in Modern Ireland* (London, 2009), 185.

also had an impact on how Stokes was able to portray herself. It served as the focus of the photograph, and, pushing the photographer back in order to get the whole vehicle into view, she was able to remove herself from the close scrutiny of the lens and depose herself to the edge of the image.

Most summers, Stokes and her companions travelled by car around the West of Ireland. For example, in 1929, she went to Glengariff in Co. Cork, while in 1930, she went on holiday to Kilpeacon Rectory, Co. Limerick and visited the Cliffs of Moher, the Shannon and Ennis.[44] In 1942 and 1943, she holidayed at Letterdyfe House, Roundstone, Co. Galway (Figure 1.4).[45] When she returned from holidaying in these locations, she compiled albums as souvenirs, which she filled with photographs of empty roads, ruined cottages, and towering mountains. Unlike the oppositional representations and social practices seemingly underlying her photographs of friends, her images of the Irish landscape largely adhered to notions of the nation and the visual spectacle of the west which preceded her, representing the Irish countryside as sublime and picturesque. The images she recorded in these locations drew on the combined genres of the tourist gaze and the visual tradition of depictions of the Irish nation, enabled by the mobility provided by her car. In so doing, she drew on a visual tradition which went back to the Romantic Movement, and which had been taken up by the Gaelic Revival, the 'West of Ireland' imagery of Synge and Yeats, the scale and composition of Paul Henry, and even the nation as visualized by Éamon de Valera.[46] For example, her album of photographs of her holiday in Roundstone included views of the Twelve Pins cloaked in mist, empty white beaches and stone covered fields on Inishere, all bereft of people, animals, or any discernible signs of modernity.[47] Following customary portrayals of the Irish landscape, her photographs aestheticized or occluded obvious markers of poverty: these images of empty roads or rundown villages were by no means critical reflections on the iniquities of British colonialism, the failings of independence, or the ravages of depopulation, but rather soft and romantic views of a rural scene from which, driving through, she was distanced. Commerce and visible signals of British or American culture were also excised, as was the presence of Stokes and her companions having been there taking their snapshots. Indeed, she did not only follow the visual framing of artists before her, but

[44] NLI DS Alb. 216 (1929/30). [45] NLI DS Alb. 217 (1942).

[46] Patrick Duffy, 'Writing Ireland: Literature and Art in the Representation of Irish Place', in Brian Graham (ed.), *In Search of Ireland: A Cultural Geography* (London, 1997), 64–83.

[47] NLI DS Alb. 217 (1942).

Figure 1.4 Holiday in Galway (1942). Image Courtesy of the National Library of Ireland.

she also followed them to the same locations: for example following in the footsteps of William McEvoy, who painted *Glengariff from the Kenmare Road, Evening*, in 1862.[48]

Alongside her landscape photography, Stokes also photographed people and social customs while travelling in the West. Carville has noted that, during the nineteenth century, 'peasant types such as the "Irish Fisherman", the "Spinning Woman" and the "Colleen" were as much a tourist attraction for photographers as the picturesque landscape'.[49] Stokes also slipped into these recognizable visual vocabularies. In Glengariff, she took 'Two turf gatherers on the Sneem-Kenmare Rd' and a photograph of an old woman in a black shawl weaving, entitled, 'Mrs O'Sullivan spinning/weaving for Home-Spuns on the road from Kenmare-Killarney' (Figure 1.5).[50] Similarly, in 1942, she photographed Pat Carroll, shoeless, leading a donkey laden with peat.[51] She also took photographs of other recognizable 'types' of Irish rural life, such as gnarled old men with fishing boats, and women working around a hearth.[52] The straight lines and centred composition of her ethnographic photographs of the communities of the western seaboard stand in contrast to the informal framing which she used for photographing her friends. This formality connoted dignity and respect, and also the influence of the composition of previous generations of ethnographic photographers such as J. M. Synge. However, unlike the photographers of the Gaelic Revival, she was not always deferential or unable to mock the tourist spectacle in which she partook. On the same holiday where she photographed Mrs O'Sullivan, she took a photograph of a bearded man in a hat and long raincoat playing the violin by the roadside, which she captioned: 'Dan Darley, aged 34, who danced to the tune of Pop Goes the Weasal [sic], he knew no Irish airs at all!! A fake Irishman.'[53] In this irreverent caption, Stokes revealed a keen sensitivity to the location of authentic national identity and its boundaries, the complex reality behind the serious, yet contrived, images of Gaelic communities, and perhaps also a sense of her own wayward position in this schema.

Like her albums, Stokes's letters were also exercises in self-fashioning; however, in these two forms of self-presentation she created very different narratives of herself and her relationships. In comparing her photograph

[48] Vera Kreilkamp, 'Visualising History', in Mary McAuliffe, Katherine O'Donnell, and Leeann Lane (eds.), *Palgrave Advances in Irish History* (Basingstoke, 2009), 258.

[49] Carville, *Photography and Ireland*, 99.

[50] NLI DS Alb. 224 (1929).

[51] NLI DS Alb. 217 (1942).

[52] NLI DS Alb. 220.

[53] NLI DS Alb. 224 (1929).

Figure 1.5 Mrs O'Sullivan (1929). Image Courtesy of the National Library of Ireland.

albums with her letters, we can consider the photographs that were never taken, and themes which she left out of her albums. During the 1930s, Stokes was involved in a tortuous relationship with another musician, Harold Johnson. His letters to her provide a microscopic view of a slow collapse of a relationship: Johnson's protracted withdrawal of affections, excuses, followed by guilty and painful apologies.[54] Juxtaposed against the passion and complexity of these letters, Stokes's photo albums created a much more stable picture. In her albums from the mid-1930s, Johnson certainly features more often than any other person, and photographs of him sunbathing on the beach at Howth perhaps can be read to betray a certain sexual longing. A photograph of Johnson lounging on the sofa in Stokes's flat with a pipe and newspaper also alludes to a certain degree of intimacy, although the fact that she chose to photograph this commonplace domestic moment might also be an indication of how rare these moments were.[55] But these visual signals would not have taken on this meaning for the historian in the archive without the accompanying letters.[56] A decade later she was engaged to Michael, who wrote long, thoughtful letters every day from Inishere of his attempts to learn Irish, to understand Ireland, to learn to be creative in an Irish register, and of the life they would build together after the war.[57] But that relationship too ended. Perhaps because their relationship took place during the Emergency, when film was expensive and difficult to get hold of, there are simply no photographs of Michael at all in Stokes's extensive collections. Finally, in 1956, she embarked on a passionate and emotionally intense relationship with a widow, named Cynthia Garrett, with whom she would spend the rest of her life. At this time, Garrett was living with her deceased husband's sister, and their correspondence that summer speaks of the excitement of the new relationship but also the necessity of secrecy: furtive and frustrating conversations on the telephone in the hallway, Stokes's undisguised pleasure in getting her small flat ready for Cynthia's snatched visits, airing the rooms, and changing the sheets on the bed.[58] However, having made twenty-three albums between 1925 and 1953, the latter date marks a twenty-year hiatus in albums. The absence of albums from this period appears to be linked to Stokes's relationship with Garrett—either the photographs she took were never made into albums, the albums were never deposited in the archive, or Stokes stopped taking photographs. All three

[54] Uncatalogued letters, Stokes Collection, NLI.
[55] NLI DS Alb. 221. [56] Uncatalogued letters, Stokes Collection, NLI.
[57] Ibid. [58] Ibid.

of these interpretations point to her inability to find a visual register for representing or exploring sexual intimacy.

Themes of dissonance and resistance recur throughout Stokes's albums. Maryann Valiulis describes the Catholic hierarchy's construction of the ideal Irish woman as 'the self-sacrificing mother whose world was bound by the confines of her home, a woman who was pure, modest, who valued traditional culture, especially that of dress and dance, a woman who inculcated these virtues in her daughters and nationalist ideology in her sons, a woman who knew and accepted her place in society'.[59] Stokes was aware of the religious and patriarchal culture she inhabited, but her hobby provided her with the means to explore these themes and to have a sense of agency regarding her own representation. She resisted and undermined state and religious discourses of femininity in her photographs through a visual register which was constructed in dialogue with international images of leisure and femininity promulgated by the makers and sellers of photographic equipment. In her photographs of landscape, which remained within standard constructions of the picturesque while retaining a sense of knowingness about the spectacle she was part of, she also provided a reinterpretation of traditional images to explore her own perspective on state and nation. Using this set of images of people and places, she was able to create her own representations of alternative Irish womanhood and national belonging for her own consumption, and in so doing, create a space for her own self-expression, first through taking photographs, and again through placing them in albums. However, it is important to note that these sites of resistance were not only enabled, but also constituted and bounded, by the genre of snapshot photography—while this provided certain visual templates for depiction of her female friends, it provided no vocabulary for the exploration of her sexual relationships, which were always hidden or expunged.

James F. and the Poetics of the Japanese Parasol

Two photographs sit alone on an otherwise empty page, captioned 'Bunbeg. Aug. 1940'.[60] The first shows a young man sitting up on a blanket on a beach

[59] Maryann Valiulis, 'Neither Feminist nor Flapper: The Ecclesiastical Construction of the Ideal Irish woman', in Mary O'Dowd and Sabine Wichert (eds.), *Chattel, Servant or Citizen? Women's Status in Church, State and Society* (Belfast, 1995), 178.

[60] Public Records Office of Northern Ireland (PRONI) D4194/E/1, James F. photograph album.

clothed only in a vest and bathing trunks. His left arm is wrapped around his knees, while his right hand—incongruously—holds an oilpaper umbrella covered in an ornate floral pattern. In the second photograph, the same man now lies down on an inflatable mattress, again staring fixedly, seriously, at the camera (Figure 1.6). The two photographs, with their focus on naked skin, the contours of the body, and even the incongruous detail of the Japanese umbrella with its connotations of orientalism and romantic ritual, seem to reveal a snatched moment of intimacy, desire, and eroticism amongst the sand and grasses of Bunbeg beach. These two photographs capture the brief moments when this man and his unseen companion dragged their blankets away from other bathers on the Donegal shore to spend time alone together, and then took charged, intimate photographs of each other which reified their sexualized gazes. The positioning of the photographs within the album reinforces this sense of intimacy, distance, and alterity. They are the only photographs on an otherwise empty double page, with three blank leaves either side framing them and buffering them from photographs of more pedestrian aspects of life.

The album in which these photographs reside belonged to James F., the only son of a shoe shop owner and a national school teacher in Enniskillen, the market town of Co. Fermanagh.[61] F. was born in 1906, in an Ireland governed from Westminster. However, he came of age and his life was determined by his hometown's proximity to the border—a new political structure which was imposed on the landscape shortly after his fourteenth birthday. As Fermanagh Catholics, partition turned his family into a minority; a new social fact which had a determining impact on their life choices and experiences. Nevertheless, his parents' social aspirations for their son sent him south across the state boundary; first to Clongowes Wood College, one of the new Free State's most prestigious boarding schools, and then on to University College Dublin. He qualified as a solicitor in 1932, at which time he returned to Enniskillen, to practice law in the town.[62] F.'s role as a solicitor gave him a prominent public profile in his local community. He largely served the Catholic community of the locality, often representing them when accused of crimes which partition had created, such as smuggling tea and tobacco and driving with incorrect documents, and other minor misdemeanours such as fighting, serving alcohol outside licenced hours,

[61] 1911 census entry for James F. and family.

[62] *Fermanagh Herald*, 3 January 1970, 7.

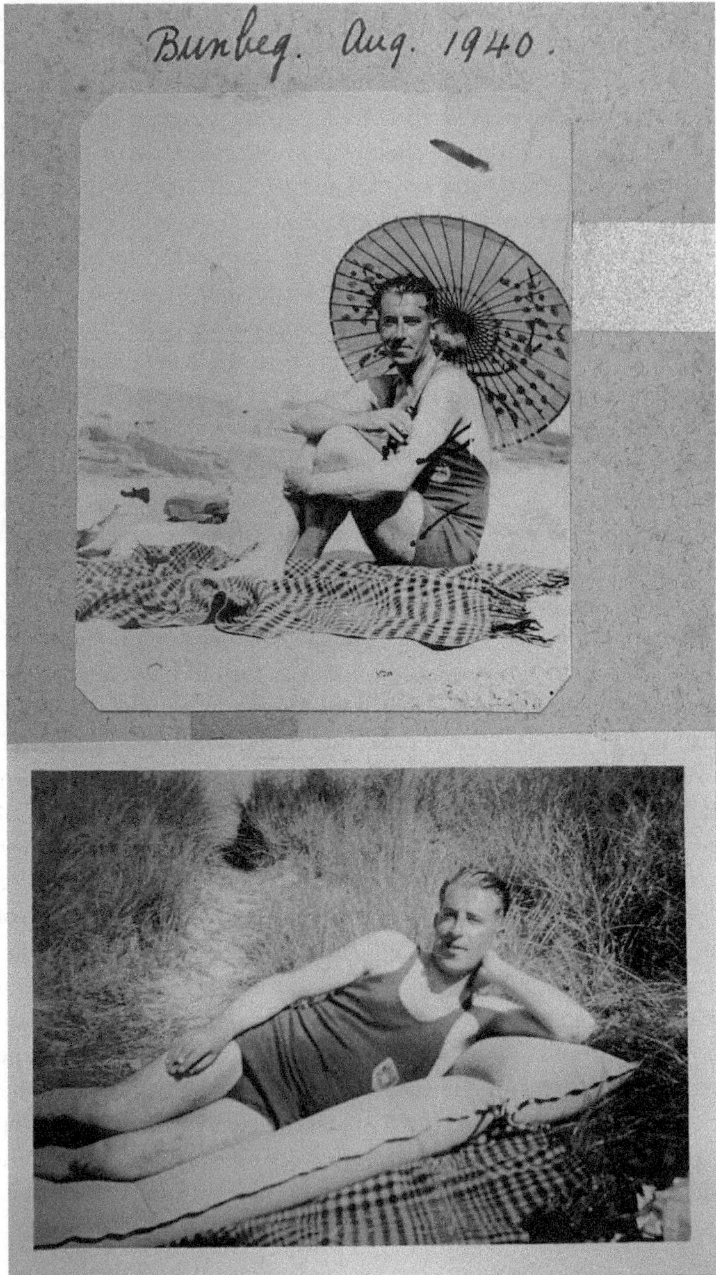

Figure 1.6 Bunbeg August, 1940. Image courtesy of the Deputy Keeper of the Records, the Public Record Office of Northern Ireland.

non-payment of rent, and poaching.[63] He frequently took up campaigns for the improved health and well-being of the minority including lobbying for the opening of a swimming pool, for a Catholic tennis club, and for improved rural housing.[64] Moreover, F. often appeared in the local press for his 'strongly national views', being an active worker in the Nationalist party in earlier years, a close associate of Cahir Healy, and one of the leading spokesmen in Fermanagh of the Anti-Partition League from its foundation.[65] Speaking at an Irish Union Association meeting in Boho, Co. Fermanagh, for example, he condemned the 'expedient of partition' as 'dividing up our country on account of a so-called religious distinction'.[66]

Between 1927 and 1942, F. kept a photograph album, which recorded his life in Enniskillen and excursions across Ireland in the early years after partition.[67] Through these images, he navigated the conflicting demands of his increasingly public persona as a prominent solicitor in a small town and the aspirations, and desires, of a young single man. F.'s identity as a visible professional in Fermanagh's principal town was largely structured and dictated by institutions: school, university, the various religious organizations, and local bodies, recorded in studio portraits by professional photographers. The album began with a statement of prestige and distinction, opening with a photograph entitled 'Graduation Day, Queen's University Belfast July 1931', which showed a university official in ceremonial attire accompanied by two women. Studio portraits of F. in his graduation gown and with his family followed this image.[68] Throughout the album, more of these sorts of image featured, including a photograph of F. amongst a class of Clongowes boys taken by the Dublin photographers Keogh Brothers, a photograph of fifty men, studying at Salamanca in religious attire, and an image of F. in glasses, with pen in hand, acting out his role as solicitor. While these studio portraits curated his public image, the snapshots he took himself recorded a very different story. These images recorded a life away from his public interests in justice for Fermanagh's Catholic community; instead it largely delineated a narrow social world where the upheavals of partition on the life of a Catholic man in a border town are unseen. These photographs show his continued crossing and re-crossing of the border as he continued to live

[63] *Fermanagh Herald*, 12 October 1940, 6; *Fermanagh Herald*, 18 March 1939, 5; *Fermanagh Herald*, 11 November 1944, 5; *Fermanagh Herald*, 28 August 1954, 5.

[64] *Fermanagh Herald* 10 July 1937, 5; *Fermanagh Herald*, 9 May 1945, 5.

[65] *Fermanagh Herald*, 3 January 1970, 7.

[66] PRONI D2991/A/3/61 press cutting.

[67] PRONI D4194/E/1, James F. photograph album.

[68] PRONI D4194/E/1, James F. photograph album.

his life without partition, depicting the fun and seemingly carefree life of a single and prosperous young man at leisure.

These snapshots display moments of charged transgression which were enabled by the presence of the camera. Paying attention to these brief moments when people huddled, posed, and smiled for a photographer can open up experiences which were not only represented, but also created, by the camera.[69] Across the pages of the album, cheeks meet cheeks and hands meet hands in dancehalls; men and women stride laughingly together arm in arm down metropolitan streets; and bare skin meets bare skin as couples clasp each other on windswept Irish beaches. A photograph entitled 'O'Conoll's [sic] Ballroom. July 1943' showed F. and a young woman embracing, flash blurring out their features and obscuring the background, contributing to a sense of a late-night relaxation of social conventions. A large number of photographs recorded F.'s trips to coastal resorts across Ireland, such as Ballybunion, Bundoran, and Courtown. These seaside resorts and, in particular, their beaches, played a role in F.'s life as ambivalent spaces where the normal boundaries of propriety were elastic, where playful bodily gestures could be experimented with, clothes discarded, and suggestive images captured.[70] An image entitled 'Courtown Harbour 1941 August' showed two men and two women reclining together, clothed only in swimsuits, with one woman's hand placed suggestively and proprietorially near to a man's crotch (Figure 1.7). At Tramore in 1938, he and another woman posed in swimsuits, arms around each other, holding a newspaper together, drawn together inside the narrow framing of the image. A third, undated, image showed a girl reclining on a beach. Despite being clothed in woollen bathing suit, her conscious awareness of her sexual potency was explicit in her adoption of a pose which evoked both pin-up and classical nude, but also in her shyness in being photographed, with an arm cupping her breasts and her hand partially obscuring her face (Figure 1.8).[71] These photographs are highly ambivalent—they took on their power through their dual interpretation: both as conventional depictions of a day at the beach while also reflecting more intimate and private moments.

[69] Elizabeth Edwards, 'Anthropology and Photography: A Long History of Knowledge and Affect', *Photographies* 8/3 (2015), 241.

[70] Ballybunion was noted as having a reputation for 'much public immorality and marriages of necessity'. Diarmaid Ferriter, *Occasions of Sin*, 178.

[71] Lynda Nead, *The Female Nude: Art, Obscenity, Sexuality* (London, 1992); John Berger, *Ways of Seeing* (London, 1972), 45–64.

Figure 1.7 Courtown Harbour, 1941 August. Image courtesy of the Deputy Keeper of the Records, the Public Record Office of Northern Ireland.

Figure 1.8 Courtown Harbour, 1937. Image courtesy of the Deputy Keeper of the Records, the Public Record Office of Northern Ireland.

The inside of the back cover contained a series of images of F. himself: a range of passport photographs, entitled 1927, 1933, 1938, and 1942.[72] Over these photographs F. aged—he purchased glasses and new suits; he put on weight and acquired new wrinkles; and he gradually morphed into the figure of the solicitor, becoming ever more comfortable in his professional attire. These concluding photographs are important. The album's principal protagonist, subject, author, and intended viewer were all the same person—James F. He appears on every page of the album, and in fifty-two of its images. The centrality of F. himself to the album's creation and purpose is reinforced by his use of annotations. The photographs are inscribed only with locations and places, without any names of the protagonists in these images. Displaying the life of a single man, the images were not placed in the album for the benefit of his grandchildren or future generations, but rather for himself, to narrate his own story of coming of age.[73] Indeed, captioning required choices about the album's continued life after it became detached from the narration of the person who made it, but F. had no intention of this album being rescued from the condescension of posterity. These choices were irrelevant for F., for whom the primary purpose of the photographs not so much in embedding nostalgia, but in the moments the camera created.

F. died in 1970 without having filled in this album's blank pages. The 1940s were a time of transition for him, both due to the war and to changes in his private life. While the war was largely absent in his portrayal of life in Fermanagh, at the end of the album it suddenly made an appearance. The back page shows a studio portrait of Father Willie Pilgrim, sombrely captioned 'Killed in day light air raid Sussex January 1943'. It was the last photograph he put into the album. This event was followed by his wedding in 1944, by the births of three children, and then by the early death of his wife. He added no photographs of this later phase in his life—this is a memento of youth, flirtation, and play, not the album of a father and husband. Indeed, it is telling that this album did not end up in a family archive, passed down through generations, but was instead bundled with the papers of the law firm in which he practised. This archival fact leads us to speculate that this album was kept in his office, rather than at home; it was part of the self-fashioning of a single man, who inhabited the public spaces of beach,

[72] PRONI D4194/E/1, James F. photograph album.

[73] Gil Pasternak, 'Taking Snapshots, Living the Picture: The Kodak Company's Making of Photographic Biography', *Lifewriting* 12 (2015), 431–46.

street, and dancehall, and so had no place within the domestic interior of the family home.[74]

This close group of (largely unnamed) friends clearly enjoyed playing and performing for the camera. These moments would have disappeared into the ether if not for these photographs. These images attest to intimate ephemeral moments shared in places like beaches and dancehalls where normal rules of propriety and distance barely applied, and where—usually—these discreet transgressions would recede into the unspoken. However, the photograph makes material and permanent something which would normally remain fleeting, ambivalent, and undefined; indeed, no other record remains of these brief moments, an archival fact which underlines again the crucial importance of reintegrating these sources in order to obtain a more rounded and complex understanding of how young people socialized in mid-century Ireland. However, the camera did not just record these fleeting flirtations, it also created these moments. In mid-century Ireland, where social conventions dictated formal and curtailed relations between unmarried people, here we witness this group of holiday-makers using Kodak conventions in order to socialize and perform on the beaches of Ireland. Indeed, the use of 'conventional' Kodak photography allowed these people a much greater freedom in terms of physical contact, and bodily gestures than would have been perceived as appropriate in any other context. As such, the presence of a camera on the beach opened up new spaces for expression and action. Indeed, photography did important work in creating, and then preserving, moments which would not have made it into the archive through any other route, and so shows how tensions of respectability and impropriety were navigated and negotiated by young people in mid-century Ireland.

William C. and Snapshots of Distance

A woman, two girls, and a boy perch on the side of a car in front of a grand stone house (Figure 1.9). The texture and brown-grey tones of the small image, the car, and the women's dresses locate this scene in summer, somewhere in the 1910s. The women and girls have their arms around each other; they are also visually united by the palate of the pastel-coloured dresses which all three wear. The boy sits to their left in a dark school blazer. He

[74] *Fermanagh Herald*, 3 January 1970, 7.

Figure 1.9 Family group (1918) (NAI).

is unsmiling, keeps his hands to himself, and looks awkward and perhaps unhappy, as if he is being photographed under duress. It is impossible to discuss a singular 'history' of this photograph, because it has multiple stories, with prints existing in albums belonging to members of the family.[75] The proliferation of this image indicates that this document was a key part of the visual economy which defined this family: this portrait of affluence, leisure, and unity was representative of how this family wished to imagine itself, and was embedded through the repetition, replication, and circulation of this photograph. The story of these photographs and these albums spills out from this day on the terrace in Dublin across Ireland, Europe, and empire, and provides a suggestive exemplar for a consideration of some important themes for Irish social history: among them the place of photograph albums in constituting the family, the role of things in maintaining affective relationships with those in the diaspora, the scales, materials, and processes through which both revealing and concealing operate.

The C.s were a middle-class family resident in south Dublin throughout the early twentieth century. The family business, supplying altar wine to Ireland, was successful throughout the early twentieth century, if sometimes subject to wry jibes for its canny combination of piety and commerce. As such, the family were part of Dublin's prosperous middle class who had profited from Britain's imperial connections; in the early years of the twentieth century they moved between houses in the salubrious suburbs of Rathgar, Killiney, and Donnybrook, purchased their first car in 1904, and took foreign holidays across Europe and North Africa, including frequent trips to the Alps to ski.[76] One of their markers of distinction was their use of photography—both studio portraitists and simple domestic cameras—to record the events of their lives. Alongside the family's personal and business papers, their photographic collection is now housed in the National Archives.

The beguiling ability of photograph albums to manufacture truths and cover over inconvenient stories is revealed by the album made during the 1920s by C.'s eldest son, William (1905–38).[77] He inscribed his album on the first page 'William C., . . . Killiney, Co. Dublin, 1st December 1923'. It contains images stretching throughout the 1920s, the final photograph being pasted into the album in July 1930. Despite the turbulent times in which this album

[75] This photograph is in both NAI 1182/15/1 and 1182/15/2; Rose, *Doing Family Photography*, 59–72 on the circulation of family photographs.

[76] NAI 1182/15/2 photograph albums.

[77] NAI 1182/15/2.

was begun, his initial focus was both local and domestic. The entire first page was taken up by a studio portrait of the patriarch, James C., staring out with the dignified, serious pose of a successful businessman. The following pages consist of a mixture of photographs taken during the 1920s. This included a studio portrait of his mother from 1921, an image of his younger brother at the age of six on Killiney Strand, and the image of C., his aunt, and sisters perched on their car in front of their house in Killiney. The images displayed the leisure time of a prosperous family in the wake of independence, including picnics in the garden, days out at the beach, and motoring adventures around Dublin and Wicklow. However, the album also displayed an unusual mobility, including several professional photographs taken on skiing holidays at St. Moritz, images of James C. in Tangiers in 1924, and photographs of Kenya.

Halfway through the album, a postcard of the SS Gloucester Castle marks a rupture, and is central to unravelling the album's—and C.'s—story. The image is labelled 'Left Tilbury Docks 2pm Friday 7 ~~January 1922~~ December 1923 Called Las Palmas Ascension & St Helena Xmas Day. Arr Cape Town 1/1/1924. Tonnage 7,999' (Figure 1.10).[78] This date, six days after the album came into C.'s possession, gives it an entirely new reading. In July 1922, after leaving Ampleforth, C. had started working at the family firm. However, after only eighteen months, he left this position, and Ireland, and made the long journey—on the boat in the image—to South Africa, taking a position farming at Bandelierkop, in the north of the country.[79] After three years there, he moved on to Kenya in 1927, first to Nairobi where he worked as a motor mechanic, and then to Eldoret, where, with the financial aid of his mother, he bought a coffee plantation.[80] This otherwise unremarkable postcard of SS Gloucester Castle was bought to commemorate this defining life moment. Despite the album's domestic focus, it was not compiled in Dublin, but in Africa. C. was no longer present when these photographs were being taken; rather the images were posted to him to illustrate family events which he had missed. Indeed, the fact that many of the images were reprints of photographs from his mother's collection indicates that the album was probably a leaving gift from his parents on his departure for his extended voyage to the British colony.

On a second viewing, and foregrounding C.'s distance from the family home, a different set of images and themes take on new significance.

[78] NAI 1182/15/2. [79] NAI 1182/1/41 family history. [80] NAI 1182/1/41.

Figure 1.10 Left Tilbury Docks 2pm (1922) (NAI).

This distance played a fundamental role in how the album took shape. While C. appeared in a few of the photographs as a child, there is not a single image of him which dates from after the album's beginning amongst the days out at the beach or parties in the garden; indeed, he was not to return to Ireland again for six years after his departure in 1923, and was simply not present when most of the photographs were taken. At a distance of thousands of miles, his siblings grew up; his brother grew into a round-cheeked schoolboy while his sister became a poised, fashionable woman who knew how to pose. A photograph of her on a veranda, criss-crossed by the shadows of the balcony, for example, replicated modern fashion photography in her severe pose, while on another occasion she displayed her modernity by being photographed beside a new car with a striking rectilinear bob. This distance also provides an explanation for the inclusion of some images which were often excluded from photograph albums. When C.'s father died in 1925, his mother posted him photographs of his father's grave, which showed both the inscription and the headstone in a broader context, sent to C. in substitution of his attendance at the funeral. Indeed, it seems that he worked over his grief for the loss of his father through the album. The studio portrait of his father on the first page had been initially captioned 'James J. C . . . . Killarney'. Added later, in a different pen, was a new inscription: '"Daddy" "Gone but not forgotten" His son'. In a third pen, added finally: 'DIED 19th March 1925'. A few pages later, another studio portrait of his father, titled 'Daddy' was re-captioned 'DIED 19th March 1925, Requiescat in Pacis His sorrowing son 28/3/28'. The inclusion of both the date of his father's death, and the date of C.'s 'sorrow' changed the image—it no longer commemorated just the loss of the father, but also the grief of his son, and in particular, the distance between the two dates gives an indication of his own geographical and temporal removal from familial mourning. This sense of distance only increased as C.'s time in Africa continued and the album progressed. When the C.s moved from the house in Killiney, in which C. had grown up, to a new home in Donnybrook, his mother again posted him photographs of the house they were leaving, which he illustrated with captions which displayed his knowledge of his former residence: he put an 'x' on his former bedroom and inscribed 'taken from path leading to strand' underneath, situating himself in his childhood garden. However, never having been to the place where his mother and siblings resided only increased his sense of distance from home. While the family in Dublin continued to post C. photographs to illustrate their activities, the captions C. wrote under the images became increasingly brief—often he simply did not know the people in the photographs, and so appended ambivalent labels such as 'Brenda and friend' or simply left photographs uncaptioned. Indeed, he moved from writing descriptions of people and places to simply stating the year under each image.

The focus of the album remained largely, overwhelmingly, on images of Ireland, even as C. travelled through Africa. He did not place any images taken in Africa until 1927, and in total only thirty-four of 173 images were taken on the continent—indeed, there are so few that on first glance they might appear to have been taken on a holiday, or sent back to Dublin by a relative. While the photographs from Ireland were closely trained on the intimate details of family life, C.'s African photographs were very different, recording the landscape as a wide open space with few people or signs of modernity—a fitting perspective for a man who had come to farm and to colonize. An outlet for a new type of photographic tourism was provided, however, in spring 1928 when his mother went to visit C. to 'settl[e] him on his Coffee Estate'.[81] They took turns to take each other's photograph in the dusty landscape of Soy Road in Kenya's Rift Valley, and took visits to local beauty spots, such as Selby Falls. After he purchased his coffee plantation, images of Kenya were increasingly frequent, including 'tractor ploughing', 'cattle branding', and 'building my huts'.[82] These images display the proprietorial nature of image making, and recorded his own attempt to control and civilize the African landscape; however, the landscape he recorded was always unfinished; providing a view of management in process and control in formation. James Ryan has explored how 'photographic practices and aesthetics...express and articulate ideologies of imperialism'.[83] These photographs, however, show something very different; they provide images of empire which are ambivalent, and display the instability, anxiety, and incompletion of the imperial project. It is notable, however, that unlike images drawn on by Ryan, such as the Royal Geographic Slides or Sam Alexander's *Photographic Scenery of South Africa* (1880), the images C. sent back from Africa had a narrow circulation, and were perhaps seen only by a few people during their movements through imperial networks. As such, these images received in the post in correspondence between Africa and Europe shaped domestic and familial understandings of empire in dialogue with public iconographies sponsored by state and commerce.

[81] NAI 1182/2/1 note relating to William's finances. [82] NAI 1182/15/2.

[83] James Ryan, *Picturing Empire: Photography and the Visualization of the British Empire* (Chicago, 1998), 13.

Despite the activity displayed in these images, C.'s time in Kenya was not a success. The farm did not work out as planned, and soon after purchase began to drain money rather than produce a profit. A note left with his mother's papers concerning him records a total of £2,663 spent on him over the period between 1927 to 1929, including £1,850 to purchase the farm cabled at his request on 15 December 1927, a description of how she had 'gone out in March 1928 to Kenya, paid all his debts, bills, living expenses, and left him nearly £100 to credit in Standard bank when leaving in May 1928'.[84] Even after this maternal intervention, however, C. could not make the farm work; a telegram to Dublin asking for a further 3,000s on 2 March 1929 recorded starkly: 'crop failed coffee dead'.[85] On 23 May 1929 she replied to this request, 'Impossible to do any more', to which his solicitor responded to say that he would communicate this information 'at an appropriate occasion' due to C. being 'in hospital here, undergoing a very severe bout of fever'.[86] Shortly after this exchange she received a cable telling her that the 'doctor orders me home chronic malaria... my health gone send money'.[87] C.'s experiences of Kenya were in line with the fortunes of many European emigrants attempting to make a living in east Africa during the 1920s; the land was difficult to farm, global economic instability meant that investments were unstable, and, despite the colony's myths and reputation as 'Happy Valley', life was often very difficult for those who settled in the country.[88] Terminating C.'s African sojourn, the family's accounts record the £55 his mother paid for his passage back to Ireland, with C. finally returning to Dublin in December 1929.[89]

C. only remained at home for seven months. The photograph on the last page of the album shows him uneasily perched on the deck of a ship, beside a second photograph of his mother in the same position, captioned, 'On board tender beside SS Melita Belfast Lough 19/7/30'.[90] The shipping list records his departure that day en route to Quebec, aged twenty-five, listing his profession as farming, with his country of intended future permanent residence registered as Canada. With his mother to wish him off, he travelled alone, the only person on board from the Irish Free State.[91] Despite his

[84] NAI 1182/2/1 memo. [85] NAI 1182/2/1 telegram from William, 2 March 1929.
[86] NAI 1182/2/1 letter. [87] NAI 1182/2/1.
[88] Will Jackson, 'White Man's Country: Kenya Colony and the Making of a Myth', *Journal of Eastern African Studies* 5/2 (2011), 345; John Lonsdale, 'Kenya: Home County and African Frontier', in Robert Bickers (ed.), *Settlers and Expatriates: Britons over the Seas* (Oxford, 2010), 74–111.
[89] NAI 1182/2/1 memo. [90] NAI 1182/2/1 memo.
[91] TNA Shipping List, https://www.archives.gov/research/immigration.

stated intention to again pursue a career in farming, after arrival in Canada he spent two years working on the Trans-Canada Highway near Boufield, in the north of Ontario.[92] However, his time there was cut short by another personal disaster. On 9 April 1932, a telegram sent by his uncle, resident in Winnipeg, to his family in Dublin read: 'William seriously injured fractured spine...nuns have written [to his mother] but do not wish to tell her how serious he is.'[93] Another telegram stated: 'William very bright but doomed doesn't know' and recorded the arrangements he had already put in place for the funeral.[94] After these terse telegrams, a letter finally arrived in Dublin explaining that C. had been sitting under an overhanging ledge when it had collapsed, crushing him forward, breaking his spine, and paralysing him from the waist down.[95] However, despite medical prophecies to the contrary, confined to a hospital bed in North Bay, C. kept living. He died slowly of his injuries in September 1938, six years after medical opinion agreed that he should have passed away. A postcard kept by his mother, showing the institutional architecture of St. Joseph's Hospital, North Bay, Ontario records simply 'Hospital North Bay where C. died 8–9–38. Six years ill fractured spine.'[96] This mass-produced postcard is the only visual record of his time in Canada.

C.'s albums reveal all the complexities and nuances of unpacking photographic practice. The album contains multiple authors, reprinted photographs which had already appeared in other places, and was made and re-made over a decade—a stretched chronology which is made manifest in the gradual deterioration of C.'s handwriting from the day in 1922 when he began the album to his obvious difficulty in writing while in hospital in Canada. Sending images was, for the C. family, an important part of maintaining affective relationships across large distances. Indeed, the family in Dublin were active in shaping their perception in the diaspora by both posing for, and then choosing, images to send to C. However, C. did not merely passively receive these photographs, but played his own part in the story of home through choosing, sequencing, and labelling images. Over a distance of many thousands of miles he told a story he did not wholly know; excluded from the day-to-day squabbles and anxieties, he created a family of his own imagination. He was an unreliable narrator, filling in the silences between letters and photographs with couplings of images and captions of his own choosing, creating a warm, unified, and idealized family in distant Dublin.

[92] NAI 1182/1.41 family history.
[93] NAI 1182/2/1 telegram, 12 April 1932.
[94] NAI 1182/2/1 telegram.
[95] NAI 1182/2/1 letter.
[96] NAI 1182/2/1 postcard.

This process of engaging with images through making, touching, and labelling was an important part of enacting his belonging to a family unit thousands of miles away. Indeed, the capacity of photography to freeze a moment was crucial to how the album constituted ideas of home for C. while he was in Africa. From the fact that many of the photographs were re-captioned, it seems as though C. looked at these images over and over again, and that the sometimes trivial moments they recorded became a key part of how he viewed his family's history after his departure.

The story of C.'s life contains many areas of silence. A newspaper clipping kept by his mother records that C. also moonlighted as 'Safari', setting the chess puzzle for a Dublin newspaper, a fitting profession for a man who seems to sit uneasily both in his time and in his nation. In the column beside his puzzle, he was described as 'A great African traveller, [who] spent some seven years in all in the heart of the Dark Continent, where at one time he owned and supervised a coffee plantation for a period of two years'.[97] This model of imperial masculinity was, however, not borne out by C.'s communications with his mother. A note appended to C.'s correspondence in the family archive, written from his mother to his younger brother, reads, 'I kept these family papers re poor C. as a matter of interest to you and to let you see the anxieties I had in his case. You may as well tear them up when you go through them – they are sad reading. He was a perfectly charming and fine looking fellow, afflicted with "Wanderlust"'.[98] This note indicates the silences—even secrets—which C.'s mother concealed from the rest of the family. His siblings had only been small children when he left for South Africa; the implication of this note is that they had barely known their older brother, and known even less about his personal difficulties and long-term illness. William's mother did not tell her children the entire story of what had happened to him. Writing from Canada, William's uncle did not tell his mother how serious her son's illness was. C. presented himself to the world as the swashbuckling imperial adventurer when he struggled both medically and financially in Africa. Part of all this was his photograph album. On first glance, it looks like the album of a prosperous and happy middle-class family who made occasional journeys to various parts of the empire. However, on closer inspection it becomes something else: C. assembled this 'family' album while alone in the empire from photographs and postcards he had been posted by his family. In so doing, he reconstituted this key locus of family at a distance. He brought it with him to Canada, and as he sat in his

[97] NAI 1182/2/1 cutting. [98] NAI 1182/2/1 note Christmas 1948.

hospital bed waiting to die, he went over the images, reinterpreting them, adding new captions, and adjusting the dates as his memories changed. These difficulties, shifts in meaning, and movements of people are all hidden by the content and form of the album, which foreground familial unity and leisure. After his death, it was probably his uncle who posted the album back to his mother, alongside his other meagre possessions. And so the album was returned to the C. family home in south Dublin, the site in which the majority of the photographs had been produced.

A loose photo of C., tucked into the back of the album, shows him emaciated, his belt pulling in an oversized shirt and trousers across his thin body, smiling grimly in a pith helmet in front of a thatched cabin (Figure 1.11). The photograph makes painful viewing; the financial, physical, and emotional difficulties of life on the farm underneath the Kenyan sun is written across his thin limbs, and clothes which no longer fit his thin frame. There are traces of the vulnerable awkward boy, unwilling to pose for the camera on a summer day in 1918, in this photograph of C. as a man. A black band across the lower right-hand corner indicates that at one time this photograph had resided within another album, but at a certain point it had been removed, and his image had been tucked away into the back of his photograph collection, alongside the other traces of his life. As this photograph attests, C. has been detached from the variety of narratives used to make sense of historical figures. He had a difficult story and a difficult past that did not fit easily into the repetitive rhythms of weddings, births, and funerals which make up his family story. Similarly, C.'s life does not fit into the national narrative: he was one of the multitudes of Irish men and women who went to seek their financial or personal reward in the empire, and who have been largely forgotten.

C.'s album shows just how many different stories can reside within a photograph album. If we look solely at the images, examine their content, and explore how their authors used lighting, tone, and composition, we discover a story of how a family represented itself in the early years of the Irish Free State. However, making sense of C.'s album, and exploring all the historical uses it can be put to, requires an exploration of so much more than the form and content of the images. A very different story lies in tracing the trajectories of people and things. The social biography of both the individual photographs and the album as a whole is key to making sense of their significance, and using these objects to explore C.'s life fully. As Edwards has stated, photographs 'cannot be understood through only one moment of their existence but are marked through successive moments of consumption

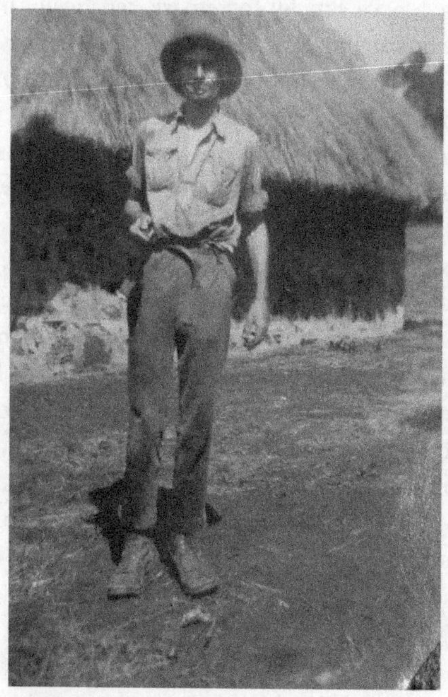

Figure 1.11 William C. (NAI).

across space and time'.[99] In the captions written and rewritten, the gradual deterioration of C.'s handwriting across the years, the many hands each individual photograph passed through, and the movements the album underwent from Dublin, to South Africa, Kenya, and Canada, we discover a story of loss, silence, and longing across great distances. Indeed, it is the dissonance between the narratives created by these two divergent methods—the aesthetic and the material—that give the album its resonance.

The convention witnessed in these albums continued throughout the twentieth century, latterly as slides or in colour, but with relatively little adaption, allowing Maeve Binchy to remark caustically in 1968, 'is there anything more frightening than the cry: did I show you the pictures of my holiday?'[100] However, Binchy is unfair on her contemporaries, and there is far more to snapshot photography than immediately meets the eye. So what can we make of these three differing photograph collections? How can we draw together their similarities, make sense of when to weave them into conservation with the themes of the Irish twentieth century, and know when to respect their distinctiveness and individuality? Conventions constructed by Kodak and other multi-national photography companies pushed the album makers towards new registers of depicting self, social world, and landscape, with the central theme being sunlit leisure away from both home and work. However, despite Binchy's assertion, the replication of convention only took the photographer so far, and seeking convention can only take the historian a certain distance. Repeated handling and close looking shows that both through photographs and album each photographer discussed in these pages created very different images of their lives. Indeed, the real excitement of these albums lies in how a critical and attentive turn to visual culture can open up themes and narratives wholly absent in work on the private life of the individual in modern Ireland. These beach photographs may look familiar, but they simply do not fit within a social historical corpus focused on institutional archives and which has explored social transgressions largely through their construction by those in authority. Spaces such as beaches, dancehalls, and cars are those which usually only appear in historical writing as subjects of moral panics; they are, however, depicted by these photographers as everyday places.[101] For both Stokes and F., we witness instances where the camera and photographic registers opened

[99] Elizabeth Edwards, 'Objects of Affect: Photography beyond the Image', Annual Review of Anthropology (2012), 222.

[100] *Irish Times*, 5 November 1969, 6.

[101] Ferriter, *Occasions of Sin*, 178–9.

up spaces of action and performance which would otherwise have been understood to have resided on the boundaries of propriety.

However, there are significant absences in these photograph albums, which raise a range of questions for historians about how we approach the things we do not know, and how we can pay attention to spaces deliberately left in the archival record by our historical subjects.[102] Even within the defined worlds of affluence and leisure, what was depicted was always partial. These albums are unusual as each is accompanied by (differing, fragmentary) textual records, which provide an indication of strategies of revealing and concealing in which the photograph operated, and each photographer made conscious choices about what to include and what to exclude. Stokes did not include any reference to her female lover, F. used his snapshots to record a life away from his professional persona, and C. constructed an image of Ireland and family which largely elided his own situation in Africa. Unhappiness, homosexuality, and financial hardship, among other themes, did not fit within the pages of these albums. While photography and photograph albums allowed for self-fashioning, this process was always undertaken with reference to social and national norms. In the dissonance between textual and visual sources, we witness secrets in the process of formation—lives constructed in one medium, or knowledge shared with one group of people, which was kept from others. Here we witness the fluidity through which social, moral, and national discourses operated in practice. These photograph albums show how people like F., Stokes, and C. allowed different information to be shared by different groups, discreetly transgressed social norms in certain fora, and had a profound sense of both the limits and extent of their own agency in how they situated themselves as part of a family, community, and nation.

[102] Alison Light, *Common People: The History of an English Family* (London, 2015), 252.

2

Clasped Hands and Clear Complexions

Studio Portraits and Respectability, 1922–60

A photograph of a couple standing side by side is rendered in greys (Figure 2.1). It is their wedding day. She is wearing a long white dress, a cloche hat, and pearls, while he is dressed in a suit and tie, with a white chrysanthemum in his lapel. They are standing together, but they are not too demonstrative in their affections; she clasps her hands in front of her, while he holds his behind his back. Both of them look uncomfortable. They are awkward, slightly hunched, as if they aren't used to posing in this way. Behind them a window, vase of flowers, and elaborate cornicing are painted on to a background, forming a distinguished, if flattened, domestic scene.[1] This pair was probably only one of a dozen groupings that arrived in the portrait studio on this unremembered day somewhere in the first half of the twentieth century; these newly-weds were dressed in similar clothes, and took similar expressions and poses to their neighbours, who also frequented the studio and posed in front of identical backdrops and props. This image is hard to read; although the flowers and pearls indicate that the photograph was taken to commemorate the wedding of this couple, the image does not give much else away. Moreover, these individuals are depicted divorced from their home, their possessions, and their profession, the key markers social historians would normally use to understand this couple's place within the narrative of the Irish century. This sense of distance and anonymity is increased by the apparent heavy editing of the faces of the man and woman in front of the camera, smooth and clear in the light of the photographic studio, with traces of individuality and personality seemingly removed or minimized. This combination of signs, props, gestures, and smiles is characteristic of studio portraiture in Ireland, with these features

[1] Waterford County Archive (WCA) Brophy Collection (BC), from Brophy's Weddings exhibition, Christ Church Cathedral (2008).

Snapshot Stories: Visuality, Photography, and the Social History of Ireland, 1922–2000. Erika Hanna, Oxford University Press (2020).

DOI: 10.1093/oso/9780198823032.001.0001

Figure 2.1 Wedding photograph. Waterford City Archive (WCA).

repeating with small deviation in hundreds of thousands of photograph frames and family archives across Ireland.

Today, boxes and boxes of these studio photographs remain in archives throughout Ireland, but they are tricky documents. Often when we search records and papers for photos of relatives and historical figures, we do so because we want to experience a connection between ourselves and the lives of our forbearers, but studio portraits seem to offer none of that tantalizing glimpse of human connection across the decades. They are unforthcoming. These figures seem distant, formal, and cold, with stiff bodies and blank inexpressive faces; detached from their home or workplace they seem to reveal little about the lives of those staring out of the frame, let alone tell us anything bigger about Irish culture. The archive disappoints. To compound these problems, the sources which accompany these studio portraits can also be difficult and uncommunicative. The day books which accompany these images merely reproduce long lists of names, noted down without dates or prices, while any correspondence associated with these studios seems to have been lost.

In Ireland, low ownership of cameras in the first half of the twentieth century meant that the photographer's studio remained a key part of the social rituals of town and countryside. So, despite the problems of these sources, it is nonetheless crucial that we take these material remains seriously, and develop research questions and methods to adequately understand them. Rather than trawling through thousands of studio portraits seeking rare moments of technical innovation or artistic flair, here I instead follow the disarmingly obvious questions suggested by the archive. Indeed, the problems of the archive can be worked with, rather than pushed against. Reading along the collection, and exploring the repetitions, rhythms, and deviations which constitute the average photographic portrait, is more illuminating than viewing photographs in isolation in providing evidence of visual customs and conventions surrounding studio portraiture. Moreover, the photograph's physical, yet invisible qualities—marks on the negative, cropped edges, and traces of chemicals—can allow us to make sense of how the image was adapted after it was taken in order to ensure an appropriate finished product. This close reading of the photographic image, combined with an attentiveness to the practices of photography, can provide us with an opportunity to consider the self-fashioning of individuals and families from outside the elite, how they conceived of conventions around appearance and dress, but had a sense of their own distance from these norms.[2]

[2] Geoffrey Batchen, 'Dreams of Ordinary Life: Cartes-de-Visite and the Bourgeois Imagination', in J. J. Long, Andrea Noble, and Edmund Welch (eds.), *Photography: Theoretical*

Here in these images resides an intimate and compelling story of the social and personal aspirations of people from across Ireland, emotional lives which have often remained outside the purview of historical study. Indeed, displaying moments of individual, familial, and communal importance, such as weddings, and communions, these images seem to suggest a source for writing an affective history of the small towns and countryside, if only we look closely and find new ways to read these sources.

In particular, these studio portraits provide us with a unique window into the operation of respectability in Irish culture. Respectability is hard to define—it is a shifting quality which varies from decade to decade and place to place; however, most people know almost instinctually who has it and who hasn't. During the twentieth century in Ireland, it was characterized by a combination of economic pragmatism, studied cleanliness, sexual morality, and religious observance—a set of social practices which bound the individual closely to the community.[3] Indeed, the pursuit, performance, and maintenance of respectability, enacted through attendance at church, memberships of sports clubs and religious associations, and appearances at social engagements, were key parts of the social order and large parts of familial labour. Respectability was fundamental to how communities understood themselves in the twentieth century and became a way of making sense of power and influence within close-knit communities. Indeed, the performance and maintenance of familial respectability was in essence an economic activity, as it had a direct relationship to a family's access to markets and networks.[4] In the words of Gavin Foster, 'whatever the historical forces and factors that explain Ireland's intense status consciousness, the elaborate and heterogeneous nature of this "world of hierarchies" that existed at the time requires close attention to discourses, values, attitudes, perceptions,

Snapshots (Abingdon, 2008), 81; John Tagg, *The Burden of Representation: Essays on Photographies and Histories* (London, 1988), 37; Val Williams, *Women Photographers: the Other Observers 1900 to the Present* (London, 1986), 158; Elizabeth Edwards and Janet Hart (eds.), *Photographs, Objects, Histories: On the Materiality of Images* (Abingdon, 2004); Christopher Pinney and Nicholas Peterson (eds.), *Photography's Other Histories* (Duke, 2003); Heike Behrend, 'Love á la Hollywood and Bombay in Kenyan Studio Photography', *Paideuma* 44 (1998), 139–53; Liam Buckley, 'Studio Photography and the Aesthetics of Citizenship in The Gambia, West Africa', in Elizabeth Edwards, Chris Godsen, and Ruth B. Phillips (eds.), *Sensible Objects: Colonialism, Museums, and Material Culture* (New York, 2006), 61–86; Elizabeth Cameron and John Peffer (eds.), *Portraiture and Photography in Africa* (Indiana, 2013).

[3] Catriona Kennedy, 'Women and Gender in Modern Ireland', in Bourke, Richard and McBride, Ian (eds.), *Princeton History of Ireland* (Princeton, 2016), 373.

[4] Joanna Bourke, 'The Best of all Home Rulers: Economic Power of Women in Ireland, 1880–1914', *Irish Economic and Social History* 18/1 (1991), 34–47.

behaviours and material culture over more quantifiable socioeconomic phenomena.'[5] But respectability was not only a prized commodity, it was also constantly under threat. While this was particularly in evidence in the immediate post-independence years when elites, power, and belonging were contested and in flux, this heightened awareness of respectability continued through much of the century.[6] From the 1930s into the 1960s, the many local newspapers which served the towns and regions reported not only on births, marriages, and deaths, but also on the proceedings of the courts, the emigration of individuals and families, who had bought a new car, where people were taking their holidays, and which families had relatives visiting. This microscopic social politics of the newspaper merely reflected the broader value of social information within local communities, the visibility of people in small towns on narrow shopping streets, and the operation of gossip as neighbours visited each other to exchange news. The scrutiny of these social forums meant that the performance of the public self was both detailed and insistent. Indeed, the significance of discourses of respectability to Irish culture can also be observed through the criticisms of the small sector of Ireland's artistic elite, who saw the politics of respectability as fundamental to the disappointment of the independent state. In 1940, for example, Seán Keating described Ireland as 'dull and respectable'.[7] In Seán Ó Faoláin's novel, *Bird Alone* (1936), the misfit anti-hero Corney Crone observes of Cork's inhabitants, 'They're all out to get money and be rich and respectable. *They think of nothing else but what's going to be thought and said of them.* It's all pretence and sham and fear and cowardice.'[8]

Respectability was a profoundly visual trait. Simon Cordery has described how 'to be respectable was the same as appearing respectable; it was a matter of conforming in dress and outward behaviour to certain standards'.[9] This often meant a tidy, clean, and understated appearance, with a better suit on Sundays. In a society where clothes were expensive, and many occupations could be hard on them, this could often be a time-consuming task, involving pressing, brushing, and washing, and begging letters to family in Britain and America asking for coats and boots to be bought and posted home.[10]

[5] Gavin Foster, *The Irish Civil War and Society: Politics, Class, and Conflict* (London, 2015), 18.

[6] Foster, *The Irish Civil War and Society*, 115.

[7] *Irish Press*, 17 December 1940, 7; Frances Flanagan, *Remembering the Revolution: Dissent, Culture, and Nationalism in the Irish Free State* (Oxford, 2015).

[8] Seán Ó Faoláin, *Bird Alone* (Oxford, 1985, first edition 1936), 291.

[9] Simon Cordery, 'Friendly Societies and the Discourse of Respectability in Britain, 1825–75', *Journal of British Studies* 34/1 (1995), 37.

[10] See, for example, letters of Evans family, NLI MS 46,681/1-16.

However, the labour which underpinned this visual respectability succeeded most profoundly when it was invisible, and when dress and comportment appeared effortless. These invisible efforts of respectability were central to women's work.[11] In an era when 'legislation ... progressively eroded women's position in public life', the regulation and dissemination of the family's respectability was a key way in which the female members of the household could increase the family's social capital within a small community.[12] Indeed, the commercialization, commodification, and dissemination of respectability across Ireland throughout the twentieth century is fundamental to understanding how society functioned, and, in particular, excavating the often unseen role that women played within it. The composed bodies and neat clothes presented in the studio portrait provide an ideal way in to tracing the tone of respectability, and also allow us to explore the processes through which this quality was constructed, maintained, and disseminated.

Portrait Studios in Ireland

The studio photograph came to Ireland as part of the wave of innovations of the nineteenth century which transformed life across Europe. Soon after the invention of the daguerreotype in Paris, photographic studios began to appear in Ireland, with the first opened in Dublin by the British photographic entrepreneur Richard Beard in 1841, while in October of the following year, Francis Beatty opened his daguerreotype establishment at 22 Castle Street, Belfast.[13] While these early businesses were slow to establish themselves and turn a profit, trade increased and new studios opened after the invention of the wet collodion process in 1851.[14] Indeed, in common with other European nations, the photographic trade boomed in the latter part of the nineteenth century and, as Stephanie Rains has shown, became part of the commodity culture of the prosperous metropolitan middle class.[15] William Lawrence,

[11] Clair Wills, 'Women, Domesticity and The Family: Recent Feminist Work in Irish Cultural Studies', *Cultural Studies* 15/1 (2001), 33–57.

[12] Kennedy, 'Women and Gender in Modern Ireland', in Bourke and McBride (eds.), *Princeton History of Ireland*, 373; Tony Fahey, 'Housework, the Household Economy and Economic Development in Ireland Since the 1920s', *Irish Journal of Sociology* 2/1 (1992), 42–69.

[13] W.A. Maguire, *A Century in Focus: Photography and Photographers in the North of Ireland 1839–1939* (Belfast, 2000), 5.

[14] Maguire, *A Century in Focus*, 9.

[15] Stephanie Rains, *Commodity Culture and Social Class in Dublin 1950–1916* (Dublin, 2010), 129–68.

who opened his studio on Sackville Street in 1865, is probably the best known of this first generation of Irish photographic entrepreneurs. In the words of Justin Carville, he was 'a new breed of photographic capitalist' who mingled various aspects of the pleasure culture of spectacle in his Great Bazaar and photographic galleries, which included an archery gallery and a toy shop.[16] Lawrence's views of Dublin and provincial Ireland have become a well-known record of how the country looked on the eve of upheaval, war, and partition. However, the studio's principal trade was always portrait photography; alongside his principle rival Lafayette, they dominated the trade in images of children, individuals, and family in nineteenth-century Dublin.[17] In 1900, for example, Lawrence advertised in the *Irish Times*: 'Get your photograph taken. Cabinet portraits. 12s per dozen. Enamelled and finished in best style. Lawrence's studio. 5,6,7, Upper Sackville Street. No extra charge for children.'[18]

While the first photographic establishments were clustered in Dublin and Belfast, from the late nineteenth century studios began to open and chemists began to do portrait work throughout the small towns of Ireland. In 1930, for example, there were ninety-three photography shops and photographic studios listed across Ireland in the *Thom's Directory*. These enterprises were also part of the spectacle and economy of the emerging tourist industry, so provincial studios often clustered in scenic locations such as Bundoran and Killarney.[19] However, there were also studios located in many market towns, including Mohill, Mullingar, and Roscommon, which catered to the photographic needs of the local population.[20] For example, Franz Hazelbeck, born in Manchester to German immigrant parents, photographed public events, political conflict, and family groupings in Limerick for much of the twentieth century.[21] Yann Guiomard came to Galway from Brittany during the 1940s, working as a freelance photographer before setting up Yann Studios in 1959.[22] Herbert Cooper arrived from London to set up a studio in Strabane in 1913.[23] William Allison and his cousin Herbert came from Yorkshire to establish a photography studio in Belfast during the 1890s.[24] From there

[16] Carville, *Photography and Ireland*, 27.

[17] Carville, *Photography and Ireland*, 22–7; *Thom's Directory*, 1911.

[18] *Irish Times*, 2 January 1900, 4. [19] *Thom's Directory*, 1930.

[20] *Thom's Directory*, 1930.

[21] Patricia Haselbeck Flynn, *Franz Haselbeck's Ireland* (Cork, 2013).

[22] *Tuam Herald*, 30 May 1959, 5.

[23] Maguire, *A Century in Focus*, 77; Public Record Office of Northern Ireland (PRONI) D2886 Allison papers.

[24] Maguire, *A Century in Focus*, 70.

they expanded across eastern Ulster and beyond, opening studios in Dundalk, Armagh, Newry, and Warrenpoint during the early twentieth century.[25]

During the revolutionary period, studio photographs were used in a variety of ways by those on both sides of the conflict to spread news, elicit sympathy, and display the respectability of their cause.[26] Perhaps the most significant studio photographers of the nationalist movement were John and Brendan Keogh. These brothers set up their studio, Keogh Bros, in the house they lived in with their parents at 75 Lower Dorset Street in 1906, before opening another branch on St Stephen's Green in 1917. The brothers photographed nationalist, socialist, and feminist organizations, including the Irish Women's Workers' Union on the steps of Liberty Hall, the O'Donovan Rossa funeral committee, and Fianna Éireann.[27] Their photographs also recorded a heady urban modernity of crowds, visually orchestrated protests, and fractured landscapes in the wake of the 1916 Rising: an image of Dublin as a site of excitement and flux, and where the street was the crucible of cultural and political change.[28] Moreover, the brothers' business also became an important part of the formulation of a republican aesthetic during this era. The Keoghs photographed the leaders of the revolutionary movement in a highly effective manner, depicting them as masculine fighters overlaid with the iconography of a Gaelic tradition.[29] However, this was not the only way in which Keoghs attempted to further the cause of Irish nationalism. In 1920, the firm had both their St Stephen's Green and their Dorset Street offices raided by soldiers and auxiliaries; they took away some order books and a notebook, presumably on the assumption that the firm's clientele corresponded to those involved in republican organizations.[30] The Keoghs also used the legal structures of photographic rights in order to further their nationalist sympathies. In March 1922, the Protestant Truth Society published a pamphlet entitled 'Rome behind Sinn Fein', and the Keoghs, alongside Wilson Hartnell and Co., Lafayette Ltd., J. Cashman, and C. P. Bryan, took the organization

[25] Maguire, *A Century in Focus*, 70–1.

[26] Orla Fitzpatrick, 'Portraits and Propaganda: Photographs of the Widows and Children of the 1916 Leaders in the *Catholic Bulletin*', in Godson, Lisa and Brück, Joanna (eds.), *Making 1916: Material and Visual Culture of the Easter Rising* (Liverpool, 2016), 82–90.

[27] National Library of Ireland (NLI) KE 204 Members of the Irish Women Workers' Union on the Steps of Liberty Hall; NLI KE181 O'Donovan Rossa Funeral Committee; NLI KE210 Fianna Éireann Scouts Engaged in Medical Field Training.

[28] NLI KE224 Funeral of Dr. Walsh; NLI KEN6 Crowd in Attendance at an Election Rally in St. Stephen's Green; NLI KE122 Crowds at Entrance to Pearse Station to Meet Released Prisoners; NLI KE 115, Abbey Street Corner after the Easter Rising.

[29] Aidan Beatty, *Masculinity and Power in Irish Nationalism* (London, 2016).

[30] *Irish Times*, 16 November 1920, 5.

to court for violating copyright by reproducing their photographs without their consent.[31] Today the Keoghs' images have become embedded in historical practice in Ireland, as their images of figures such as Michael Collins, Countess Markievicz, and Éamon de Valera are endlessly reproduced across historical works and public sites, and have come to define an image of the key personalities of the revolutionary period.

For the majority of studios, however, the mainstay of their work was of a more parochial significance. With their foreign proprietors and exotic names, and selling a wide range of products and services, they brought many of the trappings of modernity and a certain sense of glamour to the small towns of Ireland. These firms also traded in the materials of domestic photography including frames, films, and photograph albums, as well as selling a wider range of accoutrements of the early domestic technological revolution, such as cameras and gramophones, to the regional middle class.[32] For example, Cooper, a canny entrepreneur, not only sold photographs, but was also owner of the Palindrome, Strabane's first silent cinema, where he played the violin in accompaniment to films, and then later opened a second cinema, the Commodore, to play films with sound. During the revolutionary period, this commerce brought him briefly into conflict with the Strabane Boycott committee, who took exception with his trade with Belfast, and only allowed him to play the new Charlie Chaplin picture if they took half the earnings from the evening.[33] The businesses also served as an important point of modern commerce and a node mediating the relationship between the town, the nation, and the global diaspora. The windows of Hughes and Co., located on Waterford's The Mall, displayed examples of their work including a portrait of a lady in the character of the 'Colleen Bawn' and views of the countryside around Waterford.[34] Poole's studio nearby also produced expensive souvenir collections of images of the town's buildings for visitors.[35] The extensive plate glass windows of Cooper's studio in Strabane—pictured in Figure 2.2—greeted customers arriving at the town's large railway station with images of the local landscape. In these windows, these businesses translated and displayed images of Ireland drawing on longstanding motifs, reinterpreted and repackaged for a tourist market, teaching locals and tourists alike how to see the picturesque in the surrounding landscape. Moreover, through their studio portraiture they

[31] *Irish Times*, 22 March 1922, 3.
[32] *Strabane Chronicle*, 25 August 1917, 2.
[33] PRONI Cooper papers; *Strabane Chronicle*, 2 April 1960, 1.
[34] *Munster Express*, 2 December 1911, 5.
[35] Like NAI Alb 399 Mrs Day.

Figure 2.2 Cooper's, Strabane. Image courtesy of the Deputy Keeper of the Records, the Public Record Office of Northern Ireland.

provided a crucial mechanism for individuals and families to construct a sense of identity, which could be both displayed in the home, in the local press, and disseminated throughout an extended family network resident across the Irish world. It is this visual economy to which we turn next.

Positive and Negative in Waterford

Two complete archives of portrait studios survive from Waterford, providing us with an exemplar of how the photographic trade operated in the market towns of provincial Ireland. The city is clustered on the southern bank of the River Suir, rising steeply away from the quays, first in sturdy and steep-walled eighteenth-century traders' houses and warehouses, and then in smaller pebble-dash cottages.[36] Like other towns of its size, the nature of both Waterford landscape and society was determined by the prominent physical and social position taken by religious and state institutions, including the De La Salle School, the Sisters of Mercy Convent, the Barracks, and the Sisters of Charity school all located near to the quays, with hospitals, asylums, and more schools situated on the arterial roads to the south of the city.[37] In 1946, its population was approximately 28,000, composed primarily of shopkeepers and traders servicing the harbour and its Munster agricultural hinterland.[38] The city had a reputation for being restrained, a quality which has been presented as both a virtue and a drawback; for example, the author of the city's municipal guide wrote approvingly that he 'found in Waterford an air of quiet' and 'a sense of proportion' and described the people as being 'undemonstrative'. He added that 'they do not lack intelligence or amiability, they just have them implicit'.[39]

The city's earliest, and most distinguished, photographic business was owned by the Poole family.[40] The founder of the photographic dynasty, Arthur Henri Poole, was born in 1857 in Taunton.[41] He married the Waterford local Elizabeth (or Lily) Moran, sister of the editor D. P. Moran, and with

[36] Town Clerk's Office, *Waterford: A Municipal Directory* (Waterford, 1955), 5.

[37] *Waterford City and County Official Guide* (Dublin, 1954), 85.

[38] Census of Ireland 1951: https://cso.ie (accessed 28 June 2017).

[39] *Waterford: A Municipal Guide*, 5; see also Eibhear Walshe, *Cissie's Abattoir* (Cork, 2010), 7 for a less favourable assessment.

[40] For more on the Poole collection, see Margaret O'Brien Moran 'The Curious Case of George Tooth', NLI blog, 23 July 2013: https://blog.nli.ie/index.php/2013/07/26/the-curious-case-of-george-tooth (accessed 4 August 2018).

[41] *Munster Express*, 4 October 1946, 7.

her ran a shop abutting Reginald's Tower on the Quays.[42] On 30 June 1884, he expanded this business into photography. He began with photographing local people and news scenes; his first day's commissions included photographs for Patrick Muhen in New Ross, Maggie Haines on William Street, and a photograph of a child for Mrs Connolly on the Quays.[43] This trade was increasingly successful throughout the late nineteenth and early twentieth centuries, with his commissions extending throughout the south east. After the retirement of Arthur Poole, the business was taken over by his elder son; alongside photography, Bertram Poole had an interest in Irish antiquarianism, writing frequently on the archaeology and built remains of Munster for the *Cork Examiner*. Bertram's brother, Vyvyan, was also involved in photography. He moved to Dublin, where he became a well-known society and celebrity photographer, with his photographs of drinks and dinners at the Shelbourne and the Gresham hotels appearing in the society pages of newspapers and magazines such as the *Irish Tatler and Sketch*.[44]

In 1922, a few streets away from the Pooles, Annie Brophy set up a portrait studio. Born in the city in 1899, Brophy had displayed an early artistic flair while at St Otteran's School, encouraged by Mother de Sales Lowry, an early pioneer of Montessori teaching in Ireland.[45] Like many women who worked within the photographic industry, her career began as an assistant at the age of sixteen, when the local photographer George Hughes called to the convent to ask for a girl to work with him.[46] His business advertised itself as 'art photographers for the highest class work'. The studio undertook many types of experimental photography, including sepia 'Russian vignettes', 'sketch portraits in colour', and 'photo Christmas cards'.[47] With this firm, Brophy learned the processes of photography, brush-work, retouching, and tinting. However, unlike other women working as photographers' assistants, the alignment of national political upheavals and local circumstances meant that she was not to remain in Hughes's employment indefinitely. In January 1920, Hughes had his Ford motor-car thrown into the river at the ferry landing-stage for defying the Waterford motor picket.[48] He left Ireland shortly after, and when the photographer Frank Phillips took over his

[42] On Lily Poole: Pat McCarthy, *The Irish Revolution 1912–23: Waterford* (Dublin, 2015), 12.
[43] NLI Poole 363 Day Book 1884.
[44] *Munster Express*, 11 October 1946, 6; Eamonn McEneaney, 'Social Studies', *Irish Arts Review* 23 (2006), 92–5.
[45] *Munster Express*, 10 October 1986, 7.
[46] *Munster Express*, 9 December 1911, 4; *Munster Express*, 10 October 1986, 7.
[47] *Munster Express*, 14 October 1911, 2.
[48] *Munster Express*, 24 January 1920, 6.

premises, Annie Brophy set up on her own.[49] Her studio was on the ground floor of her home on 9 Barker Street, where she conducted the bulk of the studio portraiture while her brother helped with developing and processing, and carried out much of the outdoor work. Building from a slow start during the 1920s, the Brophys' trade increased during the 1930s and peaked during the 1940s when they took on an average of 1,800 commissions a year.[50] Their customers were overwhelmingly residents of the small terrace houses of Waterford's inner suburbs. As Annie Brophy's fame increased in tandem with interest in photography, she increasingly received commissions from across the south east, from places such as Kilkenny, Dungarvan, and Carrick-on-Suir.[51] The siblings were Waterford's best-known photographers for more than forty years, until their eventual retirement in the late 1970s.

As the Poole and Brophy photographic collections show, studio portraiture played a vital part in the construction and self-presentation of society for those who resided in the south east. Through a range of photographs, Poole recorded the events which set the wealthier sector of society apart from the other residents of the locale. This included events such as a hunt meet riding out of the gate of Mount Loftus, the Beagle Ball held at Waterford City Hall in 1935, and elaborate picnics on days out to the beach at Rosslare.[52] He also recorded family groups in his studio, displaying contented patriarchs surrounded by their families and their sons in uniforms of schoolboys, soldiers, and priests. More wealthy clients tended to be pictured at their houses, reinforcing through imagery the economic and social basis of their power. During the 1920s and 1930s, the Dowley family of Tinvane, the Power family of Belvedere, Tramore, and the Power family of Suir View were all pictured on the steps in front of their homes.[53] One of his frequent clients was the Prittie family, who lived between Tipperary and London, and frequented portrait studios both at home and abroad. Their eighteenth-century Kilboy House had been burned in 1922 and was slowly,

[49] *Munster Express*, 10 October 1986, 7.

[50] Waterford City Archive (WCI) Brophy Collection (BC), Index Book 3, 1940–8.

[51] Based on a sampling of the 120 addresses listed under 'C' in her logbooks for the years 1922–32 and 1956–60.

[52] NAI Poole WP4079 Hunt Meet: Commissioned by Miss Patricia Loftus, Mount Loftus, Goresbridge, Co. Kilkenny; NAI Poole WP4073 Beagle Ball Group, Flashlight Photo Taken at Townhall; NAI Poole WP 1686 Party Group Rosslare.

[53] NAI Poole WP3641, Family Group, Commissioned by Mr. Edward Dowley, Tinvane, Carrick-on-Suir, 4 August 1929; Poole WP3287, Family group commissioned by Mr. Richard Power, Belvedere, Tramore, 13 June 1925; NAI Poole WP 3645, Family group commissioned by Mr. Frank Power, Suir View, Waterford, 1 September 1929.

painstakingly reconstructed during the 1920s, before being reduced to a single floor in 1955.[54] The house was at the heart of the family; however, its maintenance and upkeep during a time of familial and national insecurity put a strain on older and younger generations alike. After failing to manage the farm in the years after independence, the Prittie family moved to Britain, wistful about the locality they had left.[55] Despite the upheaval and instability of their position in the early years of the state, the photographs supplied by Poole implied permanence and rootedness. In 1933, Poole recorded the extended family dressed in tweeds, standing on the steps of Kilboy House, arms folded and hands in pockets, satisfied and self-consciously proprietorial (Figure 2.3).[56]

Brophy's clientele originated from a less elevated social world. Her studio on Barker Street was close to the city's commercial thoroughfares and the town's market at Ballybricken. The core of her business consisted of photographing family groupings and milestones for the shop owners of Waterford and small farmers of the city's hinterland, and here she was near to the terraced homes of her clients. In the first years that she operated, her studio portraiture was very much an adult affair: the majority of her images consisted of women in their best dresses, men in professional attire, and couples on their wedding day. Single young women also used their disposable income to have themselves photographed in new dresses and before local dances. In an era when women have been cast as increasingly subjugated by economic and religious constraints, in these studio portraits they dressed up, made themselves glamorous, and stared boldly at the camera, evoking Hollywood icons and displaying their youthful attractiveness. From the 1940s, however, this adult way of framing the external self-image of the household shifted, gradually replaced by images of children as symbols of the family's success. By the 1960s, photographs of new babies, first communions, and portraits of children had instead become the staple of Brophy's work. But throughout the fifty years that Brophy's studio operated, even as fashions in family portraiture changed, the organization of the nuclear family's presentation to itself and its networks remained the task of

[54] Teresa Byrne, 'The Burning of Kilboy House, August 1922', Master's Thesis, National University of Ireland, Maynooth (2006): http://eprints.maynoothuniversity.ie/5234 (accessed 10 May 2018).

[55] Lord Dunalley, *Khaki and Rifle Green* (London, 1940); Terence Prittie, *Through Irish Eyes: A Journalist's Memoirs* (London, 1977).

[56] NLI Poole WP4008 Coming of age of Lord Dunally's son, the Hon. Desmond Prittie, commissioned by Lord Dunally, Kilboy, Nenagh, Co. Tipperary, 14 October 1933.

Figure 2.3 Dunalley Family, Kilboy (1933). Image Courtesy of the National Library of Ireland.

the female head of the household, who booked sessions in the studio, marshalled family members to attend, inevitably prepared their best clothes, and paid for prints and reprints.[57]

Individuals pulled themselves into their freshly pressed suits and, in newly polished shoes, climbed up the steep cobbled steps to Brophy's studio. Once inside they skimmed wrinkles on skirts with the palms of their hands, neatened cuffs and collars, tugged at ties, and smiled nervously under the heat of the tungsten lamp. In these images families appeared clothed in their best suits and coats, with best handkerchief in pocket ('more show than blow' in contemporary parlance), clutching gloves and handbags. In contrast to the performance of intimacy of snapshot photography, these images displayed the family as they would be seen on Broad Street on a Sunday afternoon, sartorially presented for acquaintances, rather than dressed in the clothes of the home. Mr and Mrs Gough were pictured in suits and coats, with Mrs Gough holding a clutch bag; Mrs Murphy was pictured in a long coat with a large fur trim and a cloche hat; the Murphy family were portrayed with the father in a suit, mother in a smart dress, and boys in matching sailor suits.[58] What they chose to wear, and to hold, was significant. In the words of Gavin Foster, 'clothing remained a widely accepted marker of social identity and a means by which people modelled the differences in outlook and material circumstances that distinguished various class and sectors of Irish society from one another.'[59] Indeed, their carefully staged bodies—tucked-in arms, folded hands, crossed legs, standing near family members, but with restrained affection—reinforced this sense of formality and distance. Ireland was a society where the hard labour and heavy lifting of agricultural or industrial work meant that by middle age many had a stooped comportment; Pierre Bourdieu has shown how these bent and work-weary bodies were 'marked by the social stamp' and were often the subject of shame.[60] Inversely, a straight back and composed shoulders became a hallmark of modern presentation and middle-class occupation, an aspirational physicality which was displayed by the upright positioning of men and women in these images.[61] This emphasis on the modern body

[57] As an indication, the listing for 'A' in the period 1922–32 contained only sixteen men out of sixty-seven listings and, in the period 1966–72 listed only seven men from forty names.

[58] WCA BC Gough 10,658; BC Murphy 10,673; BC Murphy 216.

[59] Foster, *The Irish Civil War and Society*, 88.

[60] Pierre Bourdieu, 'The Peasant and his Body', *Ethnography* 5/4 (2004), 585.

[61] Sander Gilman, '"Stand Up Straight": Notes Towards a History of Posture', *Journal of Medical Humanities* 35/1 (2014), 57–83.

was reinforced by Brophy's composition which pulled back to include the full height of the sitter within the frame, providing an emphasis on suits, ties, gloves, handbags, and posture rather than the face (Figure 2.4).

The customers presented the best version of themselves in their newest suits, straightened their backs, and smiled. But Poole and Brophy were also able to draw on a range of techniques of their own after the shutter closed to help present these groups in their best light. An important skill of the studio portraitist was the adaption of the negative after the photograph was taken, but before printing, to ensure that the sitter was depicted in the most flattering way possible. This meant treating the image with a primer before darkening certain areas of the negative with a pencil, lightening others with a scalpel, and hiding defects with masking fluid. Due to the inverse nature of the negative, pencil marks came out lighter and scalpel marks darker when the film was eventually printed. While the basic skills of this process were the same across all studio portraitists, the way they deployed their techniques—from how they flicked their scalpel to the use of pencil and masking fluid—mean that each of Ireland's photographers developed a different and recognizable photographic idiom.

These scrapes and darkened patches are almost invisible on negatives, and entirely invisible on the final print. However, they reveal a wealth of detail about the visual constitution of respectability in mid-century Ireland. In 1958, *The Lens*, the magazine of the Photographic Society of Ireland, published tips in retouching and finishing for the benefit of its readers which gave explicit advice on how to flatter their clients:

> According to the lighting, the breast-bones of thin ladies are often more or less conspicuous; if so, the shadows about them may be well filled in with soft led (on the negative) but if the lights are too insistent it is necessary to reduce them with the knife. Ladies do not like to look scraggy and it is quite legitimate to correct the exaggerations of over-strong lighting, but it is a moot point whether one is entitled to 'fillet' the bones. The arms, if bare, show the veins most prominently when hanging down; the vaccination mark may show, or moles and other kinds of spots. The arms, then may be smoothed up generally. The hands of all sitters may be smoothed out according to age or sex.

Brophy and Poole both followed the advice of the PSI. Miss Flaherty, who came in to Brophy's studio in her Irish dancing costume, had her face softened

Figure 2.4 Wedding (WCA).

and her skin clarified.[62] A middle-aged woman holding a photograph album had shade added to her nose and chin to give her face added definition.[63] Another woman, photographed in profile in an evening dress, had her double chin removed.[64] Poole also made similar adaptions. For example, in a photograph dating from 1928 showing a wedding group of four, commissioned by Alec Tringey, the bride has had the lines around her mouth and her eyes smoothed out.[65] Also pictured in 1928, Mrs Prendergast was seated with her husband, holding a Greek primer. She had an extra piece of fringe added across her forehead, perhaps to disguise a scar, and also had the roughness of her hands disguised with masking fluid.[66] Mr and Mrs Maurice Ferguson were photographed together on their wedding day in 1940. Mrs Ferguson's appearance was considerably adapted—her neck was slimmed, and shadows around her cheeks, eyes, and neck were reduced.[67] In the photograph of Mr and Mrs Liam Swift, of 10 John's Hill, Waterford, pictured on their wedding day in 1948, Mrs Swift had the wrinkles around her mouth and under her eyes smoothed out.[68]

The adaptions of pencil and scalpel ensured that the final printed image conformed more closely to ideals of respectability than the person who had presented themselves in front of Brophy's practised gaze. Wrinkles, lines, and dark skin under the eyes were removed in order to make faces appear more youthful and more middle class. Removing marks on hands and lightening the skin was also a way of hiding signs of aging or hard work. Clean and smooth hands had long been associated with 'virtue, femininity and ultimately resources', while rough hands were an obvious marker of hard work.[69] As the PSI guidance suggested:

> There is character in the hands; one can tell at a glance a hand marked with age, rheumatism or manual labour, while some apparently have nothing else to do but keep frequent appointments with the manicurist. Therefore pay attention to the hands, temper justice with mercy in the case of the

[62] WCA AB80 Miss Flaherty, Gracedieu.

[63] WCA 5781 [no name].

[64] WCA Brophy 5766 Burke.

[65] NAI Poole WP3583 'Wedding, Group of Four: Commissioned by Mr A. Tringey, Moran's Hotel, Dublin', 17 October, 1928.

[66] NAI Poole WP3204 Group of Two: Commissioned by Mrs Prendergast, Kealfoun, Kilmacthomas 1924.

[67] NAI Poole WP4349 Mr and Mrs Maurice Ferguson Standing, 1940.

[68] NAI Poole WP4596 Mr and Mrs Liam Swift, 10, Johns Hill, Waterford, standing, *c.*1948.

[69] Kate Smith, 'In Her Hands: Materializing Distinction in Georgian Britain', *Cultural and Social History* 11/4 (2014), 489.

poor who must work; they would like their hands to look decent if only photographically.[70]

Indeed, in a society such as Waterford, where the distinction between women who had to do hard physical work and those that didn't was always fragile, the economic status signalled by soft clean hands was always unstable, making it especially important that the photographer paid attention to this area when cleaning up the print.

The line between flattery and erasure was both fine and subjective. In 1926, the journalist J. J. Matthews suggested that 'what a girl wants in a photograph is not the unprejudiced eye of what the camera observes, but what a myopic lover with soft focus spectacles would see in her. The professional photographer has spent years learning how to give her that. He knows that what the sitter wants is not justice, but mercy.'[71] Matthews's description of the professional photograph as replicating the gaze of 'a myopic lover with soft spectacles' is an apt metaphor for the way that studio portraiture softened and flattered the sitter. But these adaptations could go too far. In a manual for aspiring studio portraitists published in 1937, Herbert Williams provided a sober assessment of the problems and possibilities of doctoring images.[72] While Williams considered this a legitimate exercise in softening the effects of harsh studio lighting, he warned against the removal of character which came with overzealous correction: 'those smooth, insipid, empty faces from which all traces of character and individuality had been painstakingly removed.'[73] Indeed, there were moments when both Brophy and Poole seemed to have slipped from gentle flattery into the erasure of character as described by Williams, with sitters' faces instead rendered indistinct, shiny, lacking in any trace of individuality, and seemingly unrealistic. To be sure, these images certainly seem to be lacking in the psychological complexity which is seen within art history to be the epitome of portrait photography and which usually characterizes the presentation of artists and writers.[74] In photographs taken to commemorate weddings, both men's and women's faces were adapted to make them appear younger, at a time when men and women tended to marry later in life. However, adaptions were much more interventionist on women's faces, leaving them

[70] *The Lens*, February 1958, 2.

[71] *Irish Independent*, 13 May 1926, 6.

[72] Herbert Williams, *Portrait Photography* (London, 1937), 63.

[73] Williams, *Portrait Photography*, 61.

[74] Clarke, *The Portrait in Photography* (London, 1992); Naomi Rosenblum, *A World History of Photography* (New York, 2008), 555.

more 'attractive' and more youthful, but also with less individuality and personality, especially when compared with the weather-worn skin of the men standing beside them. Moreover, some photographers were more skilled at achieving the desired balance between personality and presentability than others. Indeed, Brophy's use of priming fluid was often visible around the faces of her subjects, leaving a pale halo effect, while her editing of the face could be heavy-handed, leading to the shiny, blank effect described by Williams. Poole's commitment to glass-plate negative meant that his negatives were easier to cleanly adapt, and as such his amendments were often more subtle than Brophy's; however, his materials were also considerably more expensive than hers. The appearance of verisimilitude was an expensive commodity.

While the social function of studio portraiture was certainly important, to read these images solely in this way would be to do their complexity and meaning a disservice. Indeed, in 1920s Ireland, the logical extension of adaptations around staging and retouching were put to use by some consumers, who used deviations from the photographic index to produce an aspirational image. The elastic and playful relationship between the negative and the printed photograph was particularly apparent in clients' repurposing of their own family photograph archives. Indeed, a whole range of technologies were available for updating and modernizing photographic images. Cooper advertised a 'wonderful' new style of photography called the 'Sepia Electrograph' which would update 'old or fading photographs': 'If you have a dear departed friend or relative, why not have one made to behold his face as in life?'[75] Photographs taken of deceased relatives at the end of the nineteenth century were frequently brought into the studio to have backgrounds updated, in order to adhere more closely to contemporary visual conventions. For example, Mr Hally, resident of Kilmacthomas, Waterford, brought in a photograph of an older man in a heavy black suit and hat, and woman, in a thick black woollen shawl to Poole's studio. On his instruction they were cut out of their domestic surroundings and reprinted on to a more contemporary, and more neutral, background.[76] In 1926, Catherine Daly of Drumnakilly, Co. Tyrone, employed Frank McGuire to enlarge and reproduce a photograph of her with her dead husband, eliminating a fur necklace, while 'the lady's hair was also to conform to the more modern mode than

[75] *Strabane Chronicle*, 25 August 1917, 2.

[76] NAI Poole WP3368, Group of two: commissioned by Mr. N. Hally, Kilmacthomas, 8 May 1926.

the style that was prevailing at the time the original photograph was taken.'[77] When Miss McCarthy of Thomas Street, Waterford, had a reprint made of a Victorian relative, she had it adapted so that the woman's bare shoulders looked like they were under a shawl.[78] Chris Pinney has described these sorts of adaptions as 'surprising', as 'one might anticipate that in the attempt to recover the individual as a permanent visual trace one would relinquish indexical traces last of all.'[79] However, Pinney noted that the supposed indexicality of photography does not function the same way in all places and periods, rather the photographic image forms part of a 'semiotic democracy'.[80] He described studio portraiture as existing outside understandings of realism, conforming more to what is often dubbed a 'hyper reality': a solidification of certain features and the diminution of others.[81] Following the philosopher Nelson Goodman, he described realism as 'a matter of habit', with the 'correctness' of a picture within any system dependent 'upon how accurate is the information about the object that is obtained by reading the picture according to that system.'[82] These Irish examples have much in common with Pinney's reading; here we see that the factors which normally determine cultural understandings of photography—authenticity, indexicality, the trace of presence—had little traction in the composition or use of these images. Rather, the residents of Waterford had their own measure of photographic success based on the image's ability to narrate stories of belonging and identity.

Circulation of Images

In the Ó Faoláin short story 'Hymeneal', set in 1929, the main character went into the study of his detested, recently deceased brother-in-law, Mr Failey, and described the scene:

> there was no doubt whose room he was in. The wall above the fireplace was covered with black-framed photographs of Failey, massed shoulder to shoulder and head to tail. Failey, with a face like a boy's, dressed in cap and gown, holding a scroll. Failey wearing a barrister's wig. Failey in a cutaway

[77] *Ulster Herald*, 31 October 1931, 3. [78] WCA AB528 McCarthy 818.
[79] Chris Pinney, *Camera Indica: The Social Life of Indian Photographs* (Chicago, 1998), 138.
[80] Pinney, *Camera Indica*, 138–9. [81] Chris Pinney, *Camera Indica*, 140.
[82] Chris Pinney, *Camera Indica*, 140; Nelson Goodman, *Languages of Art: An Approach to a Theory of Symbols* (Indianapolis, 1976), 38.

> coat, holding a grey topper in the crook of his left arm, standing beside Molly in a wedding dress whose train curved in a white stream about her feet. Failey as parliamentary secretary for Minister for Roads and Railways opening a factory. Failey as Minister for R and R opening another factory. Failey as Minister for Education opening a new school. Failey grinning on the golf course. Failey addressing Rotary. Failey in a Franciscan robe with a white cincture roped around his belly recalled the press announcement of his death... There were at least a hundred of those black edged pictures. Vanity? Or just a cool awareness of the value of publicity?[83]

As Ó Faoláin's description shows, these photographs played an important role in establishing the status of individuals and families, even if Failey took these conventions too far, belabouring the point unrespectably. Photographs of defining life moments were framed and hung on walls. Studio portraits of families often appeared in the local press. New brides frequently sent in their wedding images to magazines that circulated nationally, such as the photographs, taken by Brophy, which appeared in the February 1957 edition of *Women's Life*.[84] These photographs also played an important role in maintaining long distance relationships as families dispersed across the world. Women returned to Brophy's and Poole's studios on multiple occasions to order reprints of their favourite photographs, which they then posted to their extended families living across the Irish world. In turn they received photographs from their extended families who were making their lives abroad. Indeed, these photographs often came more frequently from the side of the family who had emigrated, living in places where domestic Kodak cameras were more readily available and more affordable.

One of these families was the Minihans, who recorded their life in studio portraits for a century from the 1890s. Their family was prosperous, middle class, and respectable. They were first based at Kill, Co. Kildare, where John Minihan (1875–1953) was in the Royal Irish Constabulary (RIC).[85] Family lore has it that John resigned from the RIC in 1921, prompted by an attack on the family house. Shortly after, the family moved to Ramsey, Huntingdon in

[83] Seán Ó Faoláin, 'Hymeneal', in *The Collected Short Stories of Seán Ó Faoláin*, Vol. 3 (Edinburgh, 1983), 44.
[84] *Women's Life*, 2 February 1957, 2.
[85] 'Minihan Family Photographic Collection 1890–1980: A Descriptive List Prepared by Galway County Council Archives', available online at file:///C:/Users/eh2804/Chrome%20Local%20Downloads/GP8%20Minihan%20Photographic%20Collection%201890-1980.pdf (accessed 15 September 2018).

England, before returning to Ireland—first to Caherhenry near Loughreagh, then moving to Galway, eventually settling in Nuns' Island around 1930. The family were educated and distinguished, with sons taking up positions as priests and teachers across Ireland and further afield. In common with many families across Ireland, their lives were structured by institutions—after the RIC, schools, monasteries, hurling clubs, and the priesthood. These institutions also formed a key backdrop to their identity. Up to the 1970s, the family never owned its own camera. Instead they ventured to studio portraitists to mark important family occasions, or bought copies of images where a professional photographer had been dispatched to schools and seminaries. The sturdy mass of the RIC barracks at Kill was recorded, with four officers and two bicycles—the photographer having to step back a considerable distance in order to get the whole building in the frame, showing the centrality of the organization to the photographers' intention, and rendering the men almost indistinguishable to any viewer who did not know where they had been standing on that day.[86] Men were recorded when they obtained their degrees, and when they entered religious orders. Fr Michael Minihan, Redemptorist and inhabitant of the Philippines, was rendered glossy, wrinkle-free, and entirely unnatural by a photograph taken on a visit home by Dublin's Keogh Brothers.[87] These photographs were set in cardboard borders, framed, hung on the walls of houses, and posted to family members across the Irish diaspora.

For the Evans family, sending letters between the family farm in Tipperary, the south Dublin suburbs, and New York, and New Zealand from the 1930s to the 1950s, the politics of exchange of images became part of the emotional economies of long-distance familial relationships. Their letters were full of requests for photographs, and affirmative comments each other's appearances; in 1936, for example, Ellen wrote to her sister Margaret, 'If you write which I trust in god you will send me a snap of the boy. If you do I'll send you snaps of all here', while again in 1943 she wrote, 'I am enclosing a snap of Jimmie when he was home last summer...Send me a snap of your son sometime.'[88] As they arrived, these photographs were framed and hung up, alongside other pictures of those who had emigrated or died.[89] As Hugh Brody noted, the 'pictures of the new generation making its life abroad' on the walls of the parlour played an important role in displaying 'the success

[86] GP8/16. [87] GP8/29.
[88] NAI MS 46,681/12 Letter from Ellen Feehan to Margaret Evans 22 November 1943.
[89] Conrad Arensberg and Solon Kimball, *The Irish Countryman* (Gloucester, Mass., 1937).

of the family'. However, the parlour was rarely used apart from tea with visitors from out of town or the priest, and as such this room became 'completely a symbol', with an ambivalent dual message; the photographs around the room displayed both the forces which 'worked their changes on Irish family life and the absence of a generation for the future'.[90] But even in marking the successes of those who had left the locality, these photographs—and the micro-geographies of their placement in the house—could cause family friction. Writing autobiographically in the 1950s, Margaret Evans wrote that she had given 'Molly William's photo but she kept it in her bureau drawer the Hackett's children were kept on her dresser in red leather frames for everyone to see'.[91]

Finding meaning in mass-produced images

As the twentieth century progressed, the magical other-spaces of the portrait studio slowly lost their aura. Prices of domestic cameras dropped, ownership moved beyond the wealthiest segment of the population, the numbers of snapshot images produced increased, and significant days moved from being marked by professionals to family members. Studio portraits were replaced by photograph albums and the luminous colour of the slide show as the key ways of recording and disseminating images of family milestones.[92] During this time, many studio portraitists ceased trading. Famous names that had dominated the nineteenth century closed, including Lawrence's in 1943 and Lafayette's in 1952, while new types of operation began to replace the portrait studio such as Slattery's, Ilford, and Gevaert, which sold imported equipment to the amateur market. The same trends were also visible outside Dublin; for example, Allison's of Armagh was sold in 1952, and Cooper's of Strabane shut its doors in 1960.[93] While the Pooles had operated a successful and prestigious enterprise in its first years, it went through less positive times. The patriarch Arthur Poole went missing in November 1928.[94] In 1955, Bertram was evicted by his landlord, the Trustees of the Holy Ghost

[90] Hugh Brody, *Inishkillane: Change and Decline in the West of Ireland* (Harmondsworth, 1974), 130.

[91] NAI MS 46,681/11 Autobiography of Margaret Evans, *c.*1950s.

[92] Jennifer F. Eisenhauer, 'Next Slide Please: The Magical, Scientific, and Corporate Discourses of Visual Projection Technologies', *Studies in Art Education* 47/3 (2006), 198–214.

[93] *Strabane Chronicle*, 2 April 1960, 1.

[94] *Irish Times*, 27 October 1931, 5; *Munster Express*, 30 October 1931, 7.

Hospital, from the premises he had lived and worked in since 1890, with the owner accusing him publicly of failing to maintain the building.[95] His antique furniture, silver, and plate were sold by auction by Stokes and Quire on 7 September 1955.[96] After this, the photographic business closed and Bertram Poole left Ireland, retiring to England.[97] From the high-water mark of the 1940s, Brophy's business also slowly declined. Indeed, her final index book records an average of only 427 orders a year for the 1970s, and she and her brother finally retired in 1978.[98] She did, however, begin to obtain recognition of a different sort in the city shortly before she died, with an exhibition of her photographs held at the Garter Lane Arts Centre in Waterford in October 1986.[99] Today her 65,000 photographs are frequently exhibited and form markers of belonging for Waterford's older residents.

Local Waterford families—such as the Goughs, the Murphys, and the Flahertys—all had very different positions within the town, family histories, and family secrets, and a wide spectrum of differing relationships to nostrums of respectability. They returned again and again to Poole's and Brophy's studios, and had their families photographed in clothes and poses which underplayed or even elided these distinctions. Neat suits, straight backs, and smart gloves and handbags were repeatedly portrayed to present an image of understated affluence and respectability. Within this carefully constructed register, small deviations and details did give some sense of the differences between these groupings. For example, in a wedding photograph from this period, the skin and nails of a mechanic stained permanently with oil reveal a kind of roughness; however, they lie unhidden in the centre of the frame, perhaps also denoting the prosperity that went alongside a modern skilled trade. A Miss Geraldine Farrell was also depicted staring at the camera in a cloche hat and a sleeveless dress, a pose and styling which reinforced her sense of affluence and modernity.[100] However, while we can seek out these moments of distinction, the overwhelming impact of these collections taken in their entirety is instead one of conformity. Studio portraitists across Ireland produced these images in order to give their customers what they wanted, an image of themselves where individuality was minimized, and which instead focused on the portrayal of the public self.

Studio portraits turned individuals into public figures, and preserved them behind glass. This process relied on multiple moments of selection:

[95] *Munster Express*, 29 April 1955, 8.
[96] *Munster Express*, 19 August 1955, 7.
[97] *Munster Express*, 10 April 1964, 18.
[98] WCA BC, Index Book 8, 1973–8.
[99] *Munster Express*, 10 October 1986, 7.
[100] WCA BC 5781 Farrell.

people selected themselves for this treatment, and then selected what they wore, what they carried, how they posed, and where the images were displayed and posted after they were developed. A close attentiveness to these processes of selection can tell us much about contemporaneous visual practices and the desires and expectations of sitters. Looking across Waterford and its hinterland serviced by Poole and Brophy, these archives do not present a comprehensive view of the community. Many people and themes were excluded, or only made a rare appearance, including those in poverty, suffering from a disability, and the large population of Ireland who inhabited institutions. In terms of those who did present themselves in front of Poole and Brophy's backdrops to be recorded, small details were also removed in order for these people to adhere physically to societal standards. Read in this context, the soft focus, masking fluid, and anonymous surroundings of the studio portraitist may obscure some of the texture of the sitters' features, but in so doing it reveals a wealth of detail about the values and norms of Irish society at mid-century. Rough hands, rough faces, thick waists and double chins were all removed in order for the town's residents—in particular, women—to comply with normal physical standards. But these moments of erasure leave a trace. Remains of pencil and scratches of the scalpel are revealing of a shared consciousness between photographer and sitter of how people failed to live up to public standards. Reading along the grain of the archive provides us with a sense of a shared vocabulary of respectability as it was understood at mid-century, the intimate relationship between individual and community, and the complex emotional landscape of pride and shame these relations underpinned.

In *Another Way of Telling*, John Berger recounts the story of a farmer called Marcel who came to see him and asked to have his photograph taken. Marcel had been spending the previous few weeks being followed as he went about his work by the photographer Jean Mohr, as part of a documentary project on Europe's declining peasantry. Every day he was photographed in his working clothes, covered in dirt, as he laboured with his hands in fields and barns. On this day he was dressed differently. He was wearing his best suit, had his face washed, and his hair brushed. He posed in front of Berger, hand on hip, back straight. When the image was developed and he saw his portrait, 'in which he had chosen everything for himself, he said with a kind of relief: "And now my great grandchildren will know what sort of man I was."'[101] Marcel and Mohr were in conflict about what it

[101] John Berger and Jean Mohr, *Another Way of Telling* (New York, 1982), 37.

meant to depict a person authentically. In the studied and composed world of the portrait studio, the image also has a photographic realism, but a realism based on an alternate schema of success, where the individual was rendered as an idealized type. The anecdote of Marcel and the photograph was repeated across Ireland throughout the twentieth century. Individuals composed themselves in the studio and in the frame, with their Sunday-best self visible not just on Main Street, but also across space and time: posted to relatives across the world and preserved and passed on as heirlooms.

3

Dark Rooms and Developing Fluid

Amateur Photographers, Photographic Clubs, and the Irish Landscape, 1945–70

In 1940, Mrs Djerassi was concerned about the activities of her upstairs neighbour. Living at 38 Upper Mount Street with her husband Dario Djerassi, a good address of well-kept Georgian houses set between Merrion Square and the Pepper Cannister church, she observed the solitary gentleman leave the house daily, and remain out all day. 'It is believed,' she told the authorities, 'that he spends the greater part of his time in taking photographs of the Army and Military barracks etc.' When this neighbour got home he 'he remains up at his apartments to a late hour each night. The water taps [were] heard to run continually during the time that he is up.' The final straw came when 'the landlady at the house had altercation with him concerning the spilling of some chemical substance on the floor, which injured the floor covering'.[1] Not only was this man acting suspiciously, but Mrs Djerassi had other reasons to have reservations about his character. This neighbour was believed to be a German national, and keeping company with an Irish girl.[2]

The guards came to investigate this suspicious scenario reported by Mrs Djerassi. They corroborated the account with other neighbours, who had seen this stranger who 'was always seen to carry a camera with him' in many parts of the city. Although he was never observed taking photographs that contravened the provisions of the Emergency Powers restrictions on photography, 'it was considered likely that he might take these photographs and afterwards make improper use of them'.[3] They searched the property and found a camera, photographs, an Irish girl, but no German. Instead they discovered Giorgio Favilla, a naturalized Italian citizen who had

[1] National Archives of Ireland (NAI) 2011/25/19 An Garda Síochána Metropolitan Division 'F' District, 28 August 1940.
[2] NAI 2011/25/19 An Garda Síochána Metropolitan Division 'F' District, 28 August 1940.
[3] NAI 2011/25/19 An Garda Síochána Metropolitan Division 'F' District, 28 August 1940.

Snapshot Stories: Visuality, Photography, and the Social History of Ireland, 1922–2000. Erika Hanna, Oxford University Press (2020). © Erika Hanna.
DOI: 10.1093/oso/9780198823032.001.0001

arrived in Ireland in 1927, working as a marble importer and erector. However, Favilla denied any improper purpose. He told the authorities that he had the intention of holding a photographic exhibition of 'Dublin views and Dublin life with a three-fold aim: Pictorial, Artistic and Architectural, and Social.'[4] His photographs were seized and inspected, and found, as Favilla had protested, to be 'purely of an artistic nature. Some of them were bordering on being indecent, but generally all could be described as being consistent with those taken by a person who intended having a photographic exhibition.'[5] There were none of Army or military property. Favilla heard nothing more of it for three months until, on 25 November 1940, two detectives again called at his home, asking him to surrender his camera for the duration of the war, 'failing which proceedings would be taken' against him for the nine photographs in contravention of the Emergency Powers. Favilla pointed out that his camera was an essential part of his business as a marble importer, and moreover that he was contemplating taking up photography due to his lack of business because of the war.[6] His protestations got him off with a warning.

With the onset of the Second World War in Europe, photography in Ireland became more restricted. In Northern Ireland, photography was restricted by Control of Photography orders, which included ports, military posts, and war damage, and made provision for permits for photo journalists.[7] Similar regulations were also extended to the southern state. Under the Emergency Powers (Restrictions on Photography) Order of 1939, it became illegal to 'photograph, plan or sketch' any defensive work, battery position, signal station barracks, arsenal, factory, magazine or munitions store, dockyard, or harbour—including lights, buoys or aids to navigation, power stations, air craft, troops, or ships.[8] The problem with these regulations was not only that they encompassed a large proportion of the Irish landscape, but moreover, that their stipulations often encompassed the sorts of locations which formed the repertoire of the picturesque.[9] As bombs fell across Europe,

[4] NAI 2011/25/19 Letter from Giorgio Favilla, to the Assistant Commissioner An Garda Síochána, 14 September 1940.

[5] NAI 2011/25/19 'Search of flat occupied by Giorgio Favilla', 3 October 1940.

[6] NAI 2011/25/19 Letter from Giorgio Favilla to the Minister for Justice, 25 November 1940.

[7] Public Record Office Northern Ireland (PRONI) CAB/9/CD/213/1 Control of Photography Order, 1940.

[8] NAI 90/119/2 Emergency Powers (Restrictions on Photography) Order.

[9] Donal O Drisceoil, *Censorship in Ireland 1939–1945: Neutrality, Politics, and Society* (Cork, 1996); Peter Martin, *Censorship in the Two Irelands 1922–1939* (Dublin, 2006); Robert Cole, *Propaganda, Neutrality, and Irish Censorship in the Second World War* (Edinburgh, 2006).

Irish men and women on blustery walks by the coast came under suspicion for taking their cameras out. During field exercises of the local security force at Balbriggan, on Sunday 15 September 1940, a guard found a man using a camera 'from a position in bushes 100 yards from the sea and adjacent to the Great Northern Railway Line at Hampton at 4pm'. He was Robert O'Doherty, of 5 South Frederick Street, a solicitor with 'a keen interest in photographing trains'. His film was seized.[10] Dr Bradlaw, of Brighton Road, Rathgar, also had his cine-film seized, containing shots of both trains and a dockyard.[11] In 1941, Laurence Sharkey, of 101 Pearse Street, and Annie Longmore, from Sandymount, were detained for taking photographs at Ringsend which included the anti-aircraft battery.[12] Clarke, of 22 Palmerston Gardens, was stopped while attempting to compose a classic image of Dublin life, showing the Custom House and some Guinness's vehicles.[13]

These snatched and fragmentary stories of enthusiasts having their cameras seized and their films inspected on bracing walks by scenic stretches of coast and viaducts are revealing of the invisible boundaries that surround photography. All the evidence indicates that all of these people were just seeking to pursue their hobby, to record their days off, and perhaps to flirt through striking poses and framing images. However, they were not viewed this way by others. Through letters written to the government, and men and women who fetched the guards, we see that some people were more likely to be viewed suspiciously than others, such as people who were thought to be foreign, people who were thought to be having improper sexual relationships, and people whose character was in doubt. In the unfortunate case of Mr Favilla, the very act of turning a camera on 'social' issues, scenes which were not familial or picturesque, but rather 'bordering on being indecent', was enough to render him worthy of suspicion. Indeed, turns of phrases in these papers suggest that these implicit, gossipy views were commonplace in the neighbourhood. Mrs Djerassi's use of the passive voice—'it is believed', 'the taps are heard to run'—suggests that this was not just a fancy of Mrs Djerassi on her own, but a concern that had been worked through, and worked up, in conversation with her neighbours.

The war ended, and photography once again became a viable hobby. Europe was rebuilding, and Ireland was also changing in ways which were

10 NAI 90/119/2 Memorandum Film seized at Hampton Balbriggan on Sunday, 15 September 1940.

11 NAI 90/112/2 Memorandum, 10 January 1941.

12 NAI 90/112/2 Memorandum, 7 July 1941.

13 NAI 90/112/2 Man found taking photographs at Custom House Quay, 29 April 1942.

both in and out of step with broader continental shifts. As the restrictions of war ended, new technologies entered the market, and photography was increasingly taken up as a hobby for the leisure time of Ireland's urban middle class. Men and women travelled out of the towns and cities in cars and on bikes at the weekends, and sought out suitable landscapes to compose and record. While studio photography focused on the domestic realm, the club photographer distinguished himself or herself in a range of ways. Pictorial photography was a photography that had to be *mastered*. This was not a case of the familiarity and assurance of Kodak's advertising that photography was easy and straightforward. In self-conscious differentiation, this was a photography which needed time, diligence, and commitment to learn, allowing these skilled amateurs to display their affluence and cultural capital. It also needed time to undertake: places were viewed over and over again in order to find the right angle, while committed photographers swapped stories of just how long they waited for just the right chink in the clouds. As such, photography was like fishing for carp, an activity that took time and patience; in the phrasing of Bernhard Rieger, it 'served as an antidote to the pressures of everyday life under the conditions of modernity, offering a welcome release, especially from the professional and economic dictates of the workplace'.[14] With its emphasis on looking, photography enabled its protagonists to carve out a niche for introspection in busy and crowded lives, and became a conduit for emotional expression in a society where masculine emotions were often denied or suppressed.[15]

Moreover, this was a photography which was both enabled and limited by the culture and conventions of the club. In the 1960s, Pierre Bourdieu explored the social dynamics of the photography club and the values of those who regularly attended.[16] He stated:

> the range of that which suggests itself as really photographable for a given social class (that is, the range of 'takeable' photographs or photographs 'to be taken' as opposed to the universe of realities which are objectively photographable given the technical possibilities of the camera) is defined by implicit models which may be understood via photographic practice and its product, because they objectively determine the meaning which a

[14] Bernhard Rieger, *Technology and the Culture of Modernity in Britain and Germany* (Cambridge, 2005), 221.

[15] Rieger, *Technology and the Culture of Modernity*, 207.

[16] Pierre Bourdieu, *Photography: A Middle-Brow Art* (Stanford, 1990), 1.

> group confers upon the photographic act as the ontological choice of an object which is perceived as worthy of being photographed, which is captured, stored, communicated, shown and admired. The norms which organize the photographic valuation of the world in terms of the opposition between that which is photographable and that which is not are indissociable from the implicit system of values maintained by a class, profession or artistic coterie, of which the photographic aesthetic must always be one aspect even if it desperately claims autonomy.[17]

Throughout post-war Europe, photography became newly available to the expanded middle class, and a key part of understanding and valuing their newfound leisure time. As Bourdieu avers, there is nothing natural or innate about what was photographed. The conditions of the modern photographic club, and the formal conventions of club photography, meant that photographers made conscious choices about what to include and exclude in their photographs. These choices were intimately bound up with conventions of class and taste which structured middle-class cultural life, and as such, conventions of photographic value or pictorial distinction can tell us much about how this society perceived itself and wanted to be seen.

This chapter takes Bourdieu's assertion seriously. Through an examination of the photographic output of photographers associated with the societies, and the newsletters and minutes of a range of photographic clubs, this chapter considers these questions of photographic culture, community, and practice. Through teaching, exhibiting, and practising photography, these club photographers played an important role in constituting and disseminating visual regimes of Ireland as they were remade at mid-century. Technology, genre, composition, and subject combined to create a formalized and recognizable visual rhetoric of Ireland which was always selective and partial. This chapter provides an examination of how these images were formed, how the 'photographable' was understood, and a close reading of what was both visualized and rendered invisible at a moment when photographic technologies and conventions were being transformed.

These dynamics of making visible and making invisible were most apparent in the way that club photographers focused their gaze and their lens on the landscape. Landscape is a shifting, plural term for the environment around us and how it is viewed, which 'shuttle[d]' between social,

[17] Bourdieu, *Photography*, 7.

economic, and physical 'fields of reference'. Indeed, 'the power of landscape resides in it being simultaneously a site of economic, social, political, and aesthetic value, with each aspect being of equal importance.'[18] Landscape has been a crucial constituent in debates about power and possession in Ireland. Indeed, the Irish landscape not only was a 'locus for artistic inspiration', but also played a key role in the construction of a discourse and a semiotics of national identity.[19] Writing on the Irish landscape in the 1950s, Robert Lloyd Praeger epitomized a popular strain of thought when he celebrated the 'the lovely verdant undisturbed countryside with its refreshing greenness, starry wildflowers, limpid brooks, health-giving atmosphere and golden crops', and compared it favourably to the 'the present-day city model—incessant hurry, incessant noise and glare and excitement, and especially the deplorable craze for ugliness which is rapidly on the increase'.[20] Praeger's simple and comforting dialectic between a bucolic Irish past and a noisy, dirty, urbanizing present was, of course, overly simplistic. Despite this, his celebration of the countryside can be understood as part of a dispensation whereby landscape, culture, and political consensus were entwined and inextricable. In Irish visual culture, this often meant the erasure of objects, people, and places that did not chime with these themes, and the construction of a way of seeing that privileged certain vistas.

During the 1950s, images of the Irish pastoral, rendered in intense and brilliant colours, became formalized, solidified, and were globally disseminated on postcards and international photo-magazines. But despite the bucolic and serene images which characterized the output of many club members, the Irish landscape was contentious to record, document, and photograph, and these images can be read as sitting on the cusp of multiple points of change within Irish society. The photographs were a product of photographic technologies newly available and affordable on the Irish market at this time, combined with a particular vision of landscape which was highly selective and produced through a way of seeing and a way of moving through place created by the motorcar. Indeed, as Eric Zuelow has shown, the Irish Tourist Association, Bord Fáilte, and local authorities actively worked to shape

[18] David Matless, *Landscape and Englishness* (London, 2001), 12.

[19] Sighle Breathnach-Lynch, *Ireland's Art, Ireland's History: Representing Ireland, 1845 to Present* (Creighton, 2007), 74; Stephen Daniels, *Fields of Vision: Landscape Imagery & National Identity in England and the United States* (Cambridge, 1993), 1–11.

[20] Robert Lloyd Praeger, *The Landscape of Ireland* (Dublin, 1953), p. 7; also Emyr Estyn Evans, *The Personality of Ireland: Habitat, Heritage, History* (Cambridge, 1973); Matless, *Landscape and Englishness*, 74–8.

Ireland's physical environment for both native and touristic visual consumption during this period.[21] As part of this, local government worked hard to force farmers to clear their fields of detritus to maintain picturesque views for the appreciation of tourists. But just as these new technologies were enabling new forms of looking, rural Ireland was at a moment of social and economic crisis. Emigration, population decline, and diminishing profits meant that the rural society was increasingly under pressure.[22] It is significant that during this period, photographers focused on rolling hills and productive land rather than boggier or bleaker landscapes, and, in keeping to the mid-distance, tended to obscure markers of change or modernity. These landscape images, which entirely elided the problems of the countryside and the exigencies of the working landscape, played their own ideological role in the creation of rural Ireland at a moment of profound crisis. Indeed, the timelessness of the scene was part of the unseen work of the image.[23] The operation of these differential tensions in tandem can help us understand the nature of Ireland's emergent modernity during this axial period.[24] The dissemination of this hyper-real mid-distance photography can be read as part of an increasingly stratified Ireland where a new urbanized, motoring, camera-owning population saw the landscape as an object of consumption through photographs and postcards, and was distant from the concerns and experiences of rural communities. Indeed, these images were part of a process whereby the structural shifts to the economy and landscape were rendered invisible.

Camera Clubs in Ireland 1945–75

Photography clubs had existed in Ireland from the inception of the medium. Indeed, the Photographic Society of Ireland, founded in Dublin in 1854, claims the distinction of being the second oldest photography club in the world, predated only by the Royal Photographic Society.[25] But the popularity

[21] Eric Zuelow, *Making Ireland Irish: Tourism and National Identity* (Syracuse, 2009), 178; Michael Cronin and Barbara O'Connor (eds.), *Irish Tourism: Image, Culture, and Identity* (Buffalo, 2003), 11.

[22] Dermot Keogh, *The Lost Decade: Ireland in the 1950s* (Mercier, 2004): Mary Daly, *Sixties Ireland: Reshaping Economy, State and Society 1957–73* (Cambridge, 2016), 87–100.

[23] Raymond Williams, *The Country and the City* (London, 1973), 149.

[24] Matless, *Landscape and Englishness*, 16.

[25] The Royal Photographic Society was founded as the Photographic Society of London in 1853.

of the camera soon spread across Ireland. Munster Camera Club was founded in 1891; it had only been in existence only a few weeks when it filled the lecture theatre of the Crawford Municipal Schools of Science and Art for a demonstration on taking photographs with Kodaks.[26] During the twentieth century, in line with the increasing availability and affordability of cameras, these institutions transformed themselves from distinguished scientific bodies into organizations geared towards the leisure time of a mass membership. Many photographic clubs were attached to factories and, because of this, the north east of Ireland saw a faster expansion of photographic clubs than the rest of the island. In 1911, the Central Camera Club of the Central Presbyterian Association was founded in Belfast, and continued to meet throughout the subsequent decade despite many of its members departing for the Great War and restrictions on photography.[27] In 1923, the Queen's Island Photographic Society was founded with a membership exclusively drawn from the employees of the shipyards, with its club headquarters at the Harland and Wolff employees' recreation grounds at Pirrie Park, while Short Brothers, the aircraft manufacturer, had a camera club associated with the factory.[28] The membership of Dublin Amateur Camera Club was also drawn largely from Dublin's skilled working class, with many of its stalwarts drawn from Guinness's, Jacob's, and Córas Iompair Éireann (CIÉ). It was founded and refounded on several occasions across the early part of the twentieth century, with its most recent incarnation dating from 1945. The number of clubs increased considerably during the 1950s when these photographic bodies were joined by new societies, with a marked increase in Ireland's provincial centres. Clubs were founded in Enniskillen, Derry, Portadown, Galway, Limerick, and Strabane during the decade.[29] Although some of these clubs were fairly short-lived, the concentration of clubs in Ulster persisted. The photographic enthusiast Hugh Doran estimated that in the 1950s, Northern Ireland had around thirty clubs, in comparison with the south's three, due to photography's association with manual trades, and factories often providing dark room space and equipment.[30]

The photographic societies attracted a cross section of amateurs and professionals. Many of the men who became involved in photography were

[26] *Irish Examiner*, 12 November 1891, 3.

[27] PRONI D4005/1 Minute book of the Central Camera Club, 1912–1923.

[28] *The Camera*, September 1923, 86.

[29] *Amateur Photographer*, 111 (1956); PRONI D3479/1/A/1 Minute book of the '57 Club, Strabane, 1957–1966.

[30] Irish Architectural Archive (IAA) 2005/023.1/3/12(i) Hugh Doran Lecture notes.

from manual occupations. Matt Boylan joined Guinness's in 1922, and began taking photographs in the early 1930s, working in the photographic department. From there, he started taking pictorial images, and joined the PSI in 1950.[31] Hugh Doran also worked for Guinness's, joining the printing department in 1941 at the age of fourteen, and starting to take photographs shortly after. Reginald Wiltshire owned the Green Studio along with his wife Elinor, which focused on industrial and technical outputs. In common with other professional photographers, he tended to work within a more artistic and studied style in his work with the PSI. But the nature and personnel of clubs shifted in the post-war period, as they adapted to the potentials of new technologies. Japanese industrialization brought newer, cheaper cameras onto the market during the 1950s, while increased car ownership provided new opportunities to travel and photographically capture the picturesque. This was accompanied by a new and marked fetishization of equipment during a period when photographic technologies available in Irish shops—and so visual possibilities—were expanding rapidly. In 1958, the sales catalogue of the Camerashop on Grafton Street showcased the range of products available for the discerning amateur with deep pockets. It exhibited the enormous range of cameras on the market, from Brownie box cameras for snapshooters to 35mm cameras aimed at the growing market for colour photography, and Rolleiflex cameras for serious amateurs and professionals. It also sold an extensive range of sundry apparatus associated with this trade for people who wanted to perfect their technique and could spend large amounts of money, including flashes, films, slide projectors, and books to teach basic technique and improve style.[32]

The clubs' primary activity was teaching technical skills and composition enabled by the new equipment, in classes on pictorialism, portraiture, colour, and still life with the end products of these classes were displayed in monthly competitions and in an annual exhibition. Indeed, the standards and conventions of these classes played an important role in the perceptions of photography as a past time. The new availability of cameras both bolstered the membership of photography clubs while also threatening the qualities that defined their practice. In terms that echoed the ambivalence of Walter Benjamin's discourse on art in modernity, in 1961 the PSI explored the shifting nature of photography during an era of affluence and newly demotic cultural forms. In its journal, it described photography as 'unique as an

[31] *The Lens*, July 1967, 11.

[32] *A Guide to Photographic Equipment* (Dublin, 1958).

Art-Form' because it could be indulged in 'by a tremendous amount of people'. However, the new accessibility of photography was not a universal good. 'Its very availability puts into jeopardy the standards required of it as an Art Form. The artist has always been in the minority in all civilizations and though millions of people can, for the first time use his tools the number of arts produced by this involvement will not increase.' Instead, 'the serious photographer must accept the responsibility imposed by his medium and apply as rigorous a standard to it as a musician would to his music. Where there are in existence societies devoted to furtherance of photography then their function should consist in making known these aims and insuring that they are adhered to rigidly.'[33]

These photographers spent the weekends of the drier, brighter, summer months exploring the Irish landscape on club-run trips. In 1960, for example, the Central Presbyterian Association Camera Club's trips included 'a weekend at Ballyedmond Castle, Rostrevor; visits to Barnett House, North Antrim, including at Corfield factory at Ballymoney, a treasure hunt finishing at Bangor; a Saturday excursion through Gilford and Tandergee to Rostrevor, and a September weekend to Ballycastle'.[34] The PSI's trips included Achill, Lambay, and Wicklow. On a drizzly Saturday in August 1960, the members of the PSI set off for Luggala via Enniskerry, stopping en route at an 'extremely attractive cottage' on a back route. 'A pair of Leica "fans", blasé about all this pictorial stuff, happily rigged their own pictures with an iron work gate, an old yard brush and a nicely textured white wash wall.'[35] Later, at Aghavannagh, they sighted 'an interesting looking field of cut corn in the distance with nice long shadows from the evening sun... but alas after surmounting ditches, a marsh and barbed wire, three breathless optimists arrived in the cornfields just as the sun disappeared for good behind clouds'.[36]

When winters drew in and the days became too wet and dark for successful photography or enjoyable outings, the activities of the clubs instead were focused around a programme of evening lectures showcasing new products or the photographic output of individuals. While these lectures were sometimes based on the works of well-known photographers, more often club stalwarts volunteered to show their latest photographic outputs, which were largely photographs taken on holiday in Ireland and across continental

33 *The Lens*, September 1961, 2.

34 PRONI D4005/1 Annual Report of the Central Presbyterian Association Camera Club, 1961.

35 *The Lens*, September 1960, 2.

36 *The Lens*, September 1960, 2.

Europe. The rural places visited in the summer light formed the subject matter of many evening lectures during the winter season. Mr Weir, for example, had 'an enthusiasm for Irish scenery and folk-lore... Whether he is pursuing the pilgrims up Croagh Patrick or studying the ruins of the pre-historic forts of Caherconree, he can find something of interest and something of beauty and he has a gift of expression which enhances the value of his slides and a fund of anecdotes to enliven his lecture.'[37] Indeed, many of these new opportunities were associated with new forms of travel impelled by a dynamic Catholic church embracing the demands of the post-war world. In the approach to summer of Holy Year 1950, Kodak advertised heavily in the Irish press, announcing 'Rome 1950: A great occasion for a Kodak.'[38] One of the people who took up this combination of tourism and pilgrimage was Hugh Doran, who made his first trip out of Ireland that year. He joined a '500 strong Augustinian pilgrimage by surface travel staying overnight in both Paris and Lucerne before going on to Rome', taking his camera with him and photographing the sites en route.[39] Jimmy Murphy travelled to Fatima during the Marian year (1953–4), having purchased an 'elderly and massive Ford motor car with an immense thirst for petrol and water' for the purpose. He told the lecture hall that 'one realizes just how valuable a hobby photography can be, not merely for its own sake but as a tool and a notebook of personal history.'[40] The title, 'Holiday rambles with a camera' was 'the only Victorian thing about' Julian Rowntree's lecture in November 1956, which showcased his 'ramblings' in a Jaguar Mark VII accompanied by a Leica M3, loaded with colour film and with a coupled exposure meter. His journey took him from Ireland to England, Belgium, Germany, France, Switzerland, Italy, and back through France 'in the space of one month.'[41]

As these journeys and events suggest, Irish photography was inherently outward facing. Once every two years, the PSI organized the Irish Photographic Salon, which received entries from across Europe, Asia, and America, and from both sides of the iron curtain. Club members also entered competitions in Britain and on continental Europe. Indeed, throughout Ireland's seemingly introspective post-Second World War period, photographic clubs were always international, in terms of materials,

[37] *The Lens*, May 1956, 21. [38] *Irish Press*, 29 May 1950, 3.
[39] IAA 2005/023.1/3/12(i) Lecture notes. [40] *The Lens*, January 1957, 63.
[41] *The Lens*, February 1956, 6.

photographic genres, and professional and artistic networks.[42] Despite the intense localism of much of the subject matter, it was conceived and conveyed through pictorialism—in a genre which was reproduced and readable across the photographic world, the subject to which we turn next.

Photographing Rural Landscape

Ireland's rural landscape has been depicted through many styles, genres, and traditions, from military maps, to historical painting, and caustic cartooning. At mid-century, pictorialism dominated the output of the photography clubs. This genre developed across Europe and America from the latter decades of the nineteenth century as photographic enthusiasts attempted to differentiate themselves from 'snapshooting' amateurs on the one hand and from the status of photography as auto-mechanical reproduction on the other. However, the term 'pictorialism' was not coined until the end of the First World War, as the style began to lose its dominance.[43] Indeed, it rapidly fell out of fashion in much of Europe and America from the end of the war, reflecting a new urgency to find artistic forms through which to explore the difficulty and uncertainty of life in the post-war world. In Ireland, however, the style remained, in particular within amateur practice.[44] In its choice of subject matter—pastoral landscapes, empty beaches, soft and perfected feminine beauty—it was an aesthetic code which combined with the way of seeing Ireland of both nineteenth-century colonialism and twentieth-century tourist postcards.

In the photography of Ireland at mid-century, this tone was most often a serene, nostalgic look at the Irish countryside. The pictorial work was epitomized by the photographic output of the *Capuchin Annual*, characterized by its conservative and Catholic ethos, but which was one of the few journals which published the work of Irish photographers during the 1950s.[45] In 1956, it published a photo essay entitled 'Beneath the Light of Irish Skies'

[42] Kim Sichel, 'Pictorialism: An International Phenomenon', in Stacey McCarroll, *California Dreamin': Camera Clubs and the Pictorial Photography Tradition* (Boston, 2004), 10.

[43] Paul Spence Sternberger, *Between Amateur and Aesthete: The Legitimization of Photography as Art in America 1880–1990* (Albuquerque, 2001), 34.

[44] Orla Fitzpatrick, 'Photographic Modernism on the Margins: William Harding, *The Camera* and the Irish Salons of Photography 1927 to 1939', *Irish Studies Review* 26/3 (2018), 361–73.

[45] Róisín Kennedy, 'The *Capuchin Annual:* Visual Art and the Legacy of 1916, One Generation On', in Lisa Godson and Joanna Brück (eds.), *Making 1916: Material and Visual Culture of the Easter Rising* (Liverpool, 2016), 154–63.

featuring images by Arthur Campbell, Arthur O'Callaghan, and Father Browne.[46] The photographs in this collection largely occluded both markers of poverty and modernity, revealing Ireland instead as a timeless agricultural economy. Ireland's ancient Christian heritage, farming, and landscape formed the primary subject, in a country where the sun constantly shone. Whereas these barren, rugged landscapes have received many interpretations, as indicative of a land from which people have had to emigrate, and a colonial economic system which leached wealth from Ireland, these images contained none of these overtones. Formalized and balanced composition, mid-tones, and an image plane located largely in the middle-distance created a visual language of harmony which represented this peaceable community. Moreover, the photo-essays of this magazine reveal Irish pictorialism at mid-century to be not so much an aesthetic as an approach to visual knowledge; where complex or negative readings of images were possible, captions served to direct the eye and to pre-empt the readings the images provided. These included 'Cosy homestead', 'Attractive Farmstead', and 'A secluded corner of Cork city', all turns of phrase which evoked a calm and peaceful rural community in line with the broader political ethos.[47]

The field trips organized by photography clubs were focused on seeking out the pictorial in the Irish landscape. This often meant the use of ladders, wellies, and patience. It also meant handbrake turns and diversions up boreens to chase light and a fleeting view. One member's 'car made its way by a side road along the very edge of the shore towards Rostrevor' when:

> we suddenly spotted a lovely pictorial scene, not unlike the one which carried off the Gevaert Cup at this year's exhibition, and a somewhat chaotic few moments ensued during which we called on the Hon. Registrar to halt and reverse his automobile (along a narrow country road!) while trying to disentangle our gear which had been packed away but eventually we got our cameras out and the scene was duly recorded (after all that panic let's hope that the shots were worth it!!).[48]

Indeed, finding the pictorial was a key way in which the beauty of the Irish landscape was understood. Ballyfin House, a boarding school for boys in Co. Laois, was set in an 'extensive demense which was immensely pictorial'.

[46] 'Beneath the Light of Irish Skies', *The Cappuchin Annual 1956–7*, 79–94.
[47] 'Beneath the Light of Irish Skies', *The Capuchin Annual*.
[48] *The Lens*, October 1963, 7.

The house was full of architectural detail, while the flowers, trees, and a man-made lake also provided ample opportunities for photography: 'never before has your editor seen such an astonishing variety of potential pictures in one place.'[49] According with longstanding traditions of the representation of landscape derived from painting, pictorial scenes like these were thought to be enhanced by a well-placed figure in the middle distance. However, the figure was to be 'appropriate and harmonious'.[50] When Mr Nutt showed his slides of Ireland, he explained how he had wanted a figure in the foreground of his image, 'Lakeland scene', but 'after waiting quite a while no figure appeared, so he went and drove a cow into the correct place from five fields away, of course returning it afterwards!'.[51]

This focus on pastoral scenes was combined with an attentiveness to the emotional resonance of the image. In 1926, David Hogg, a professional photographer working in Belfast, gave a lecture on pictorial photography to the Belfast CPA which was reported in the *Amateur Photographer*: 'The pictorialist should look beyond the surface to the spirit of his subject, and find it rather in the play and gradations of light and in the mysteries of atmosphere, than in the outlines and shapes of separate objects' as 'each picture must have a specific sentiment'.[52] As Hogg's discussion implied, pictorial photography put its emphasis on the photographer's ability to convey mood and emotion, in contrast with an earlier emphasis on the scientific or factual function of photography. As Jimmy Murphy recorded in the *Lens* in 1964, 'All photographers who produce great pictures have a definite feeling for their subjects: a feeling of love, hate, sympathy, but never indifference. Before one can produce pictures which are emotionally stirring one must have a strong emotional response of some kind to the subject. Otherwise it would be impossible to arouse a similar emotion in the viewer. Subject approach must be governed by interest and feeling.'[53]

One of these enthusiasts was Charles Jones, a keen motor-tourist who took landscape photographs influenced by the pictorial tradition throughout the 1950s. Living in south Dublin, he was a professional photographer, and an active member of the PSI, taking part in exhibitions and competitions during the 1940s and 1950s.[54] He also experimented with new photographic techniques, showcasing cine-film, colour, and 'talkies' as part of talks and

[49] *The Lens*, September 1963, 6.
[50] *The Lens*, November 1956, 49.
[51] *The Lens*, April 1965, 6.
[52] *Amateur Photographer*, 15 December 1926, 62/1988, 531.
[53] *The Lens*, March 1964, 3.
[54] In 1950 he also became a founder of the Irish Professional Photographers' Association.

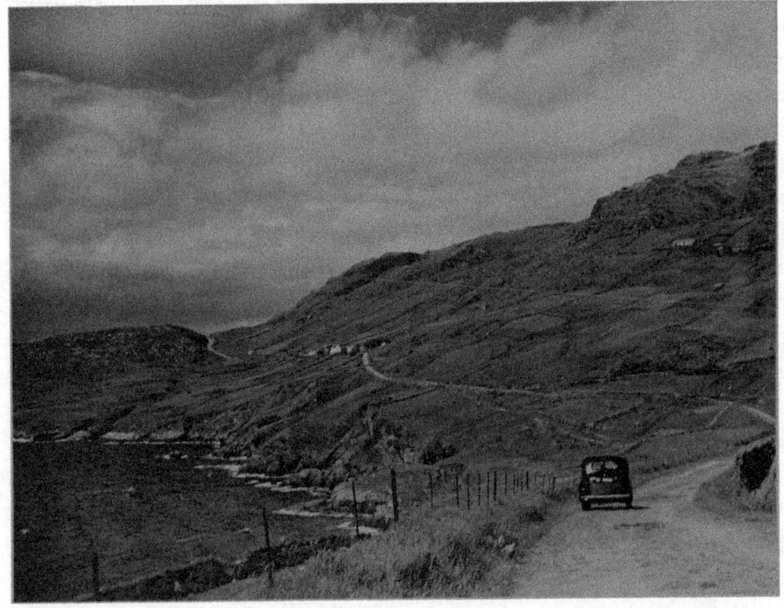

Figure 3.1 Charles Jones Killybegs album. Image Courtesy of the National Library of Ireland.

demonstrations to the society. During the 1950s, he took photographs in locations along Ireland's western seaboard. In blistering summer sun, he recorded the coasts and mountains of these locations. His motoring mobility was central to how he experienced landscape, framed these locations in line with notions of the picturesque, and indeed, how he displayed his own affluence, success, and masculinity.[55] He constructed the west as a location empty of people, settlements, farming equipment, or the things and objects of emergent post-war modern domesticity, while his car was ever present at the centre of the picture (Figure 3.1). This was a way of seeing more commonly associated with the external gaze of British and American travellers, but the view from the driver's seat also framed how city dwellers constructed Ireland's underdeveloped areas.[56] Indeed, this was a reading of these locations encouraged by the Irish Tourist Association, which, in its 1948 guide to Connacht, described the journey into the province: 'In centuries past, to cross the Shannon was to cross into Terra Incognita', but 'for those who tour by bike or car the roads of Connacht provide endless miles of easy travel'.[57] Pictorial standards and the status and mobility of the modern motor car combined to refashion longstanding themes of the picturesque for a new era.

Photographing in Kodachrome

The new availability of colour film was the biggest photographic shift of the post-war era, as the hyper-real blues, greens, and reds of Kodachrome and its rivals became available to skilled and unskilled amateurs alike across Ireland. Through the work of the Trinity scientist James Joly, Ireland had been at the forefront of developments in colour photography during the nineteenth century.[58] However, this rate of technical innovation was not sustained, and during the twentieth century these domestic experiments with colour were overtaken by products from America and continental Europe. Kodachrome was introduced in America in 1935. It

[55] Zuelow, *Making Ireland Irish*, 210.

[56] Lynda Nead, *The Haunted Gallery: Painting, Photography, Film c. 1900* (New Haven, 2008), ch. 4.

[57] Irish Tourist Association, *Connacht: Galway, Mayo, Sligo, Leitrim, Roscommon* (Dublin, 1948), 11.

[58] John Nudds, 'The Life and Work of John Joly (1857–1933)', *Irish Journal of Earth Sciences* 8/1 (1986), 84–5.

was not widely available in Ireland until the 1950s; but during this decade a wide range of products entered the market to cater for the demands of the colour enthusiast.[59] However, processing these new products remained expensive, complicated, and confined to professionals. In 1955 alongside the international firms Kodak, Ilford, Agfa, and Gevaert, only Wiltshire's Green Studios, O'Loughlins of Mullingar, and Ricky Stevens of Wicklow Street were equipped to print colour prints of studio photographs.[60] As the evolution of colour technology opened up new possibilities during this period, it became a locus of debate regarding shifts in depictions of place and landscape.

The combination of technical expertise, modern equipment, and experimentation that colour processing demanded appealed to a certain sector of the membership of the PSI. Lyall Smyth began experimental work on colour films in 1928, and around 1949 was approached by the Agfa Film Company of Germany with the proposal that he should undertake the processing of Agfa coloured film in Ireland. This also led to his processing colour work from the eastern bloc countries.[61] Reginald Wiltshire experimented with colour processes throughout the 1950s, and worked with Trinity College Dublin to produce the first collection of colour slides of the Book of Kells in 1962.[62] The PSI's colour group was increasingly popular during the latter 1950s. Indeed, during this period, many people were coming into photography 'via colour', and as such the clubs felt compelled to adapt in order to entice these new photographers to join.[63]

One of these new enthusiasts was Alfred Ternan, a housing architect with Dublin Corporation. As a young man, he had compiled albums showing his young family and the young state developing in tandem: images of family days out interspersed with images of war damage to Dublin's landmarks (see chapter 1). After a break of twenty-five years, the purchase of a new camera revived Ternan's interest in photography, and from 1958 he set about once again documenting Ireland's development and his family's place within it, now in the bright Kodachrome colours and luminous modernity of the slide machine.[64] In line with his career as an architect, this often focused on the new edifices of the state, such as the new buildings of Ballymun and Dublin Airport during the 1960s. In the 1970s, he photographed the new

[59] *The Lens*, November 1956, 8.
[60] IND/22/19 Report of a Meeting regarding Processing of Colour Films, 17 August 1965.
[61] IND/22/19 Report of a Meeting regarding Processing of Colour Films, 17 August 1965.
[62] *Irish Independent*, 3 October 1962, 8.
[63] *The Lens*, April 1964, 7.
[64] National Photographic Archive (NPA) Ternan collection.

shopping centre on Oscar Traynor Road, and the modern, post-Vatican II church in Donneycarney. This new Ireland existed in colour, and these colours were central to how he used photography and how he framed the emergent modernity of the new state. His photographs were almost always taken on sunny days, when the strength of the light made the colours of the city rich. The play of these bright colours was central to all his compositions; in the yellow flowers of Glendalough against the brown gorse and blue skies; the myriad of greens and greys of Co. Galway (Figure 3.2); and in his wife's red coat against the green hills of West Cork. These slides were densely labelled with details of the dates they were taken, the buildings and their history, which provided him with a script for his slide shows. Indeed, through his photography he became a collector of the history of the country. Civic rituals, new buildings, and new technologies were documented photographically, and then labelled, given a number, and indexed in a catalogue, which provided a history of the state from his point of view. In later years, with restricted mobility, he kept up this practice of documenting the grand civic occasions by taking photographs of the television screen as RTÉ displayed historic events, recording the inauguration of President Hillery, the death of Éamon De Valera, and the pope's visit to Ireland in this fashion.

When these new enthusiasts inserted colour film into their cameras, they generated new ways of looking and new forms of composition which foregrounded the colour palate of the Irish landscape. As Mr Deegan told the PSI:

> the colour photographer must learn to see in colour. Most experienced photographers tend to assess subjects in monochrome and this habit must be discontinued, for which reason it is impossible to mix colour and monochrome photography on the same outing. But even without this acquired barrier, people do not really look at colours. For example, everyone knows that grass is green, so they take it for granted that it is always green—but if they really looked at it they would find that it changes colour according to the lighting conditions.[65]

Mr Cuffe echoed these sentiments, arguing that 'colour slides had on many people the peculiar effect of giving them an increased awareness, so that they

[65] *The Lens*, February 1957, 68.

Figure 3.2 Slide of Ballyvaughan Bay viewed from Co. Galway. (1960). Image Courtesy of the National Library of Ireland.

looked on a familiar scene with a fresh outlook much as a foreigner might do'.[66] Moreover, colour also changed the way that pictorial work was framed. It meant that composition now had to be considered as the relationship between three variables: colours, shapes, and tones. This provided new opportunities for playing with colour, in particular on bright summer days. In Mr Deegan's experience, 'the ideal conditions for outdoor colour photography were blue skies with plenty of white clouds which resulted in full colour saturation because the strength of colour depends upon the strength of light shining upon it.'[67] In this spirit, in 1964, members of the PSI drove along the Atlantic coast in perfect weather. 'Blazing sunshine in the sky, not of clear blue, but with light white, fleecy clouds, just right for pictorial effects...On one beach a young lady in a Kodachrome swim suit became considerably alarmed when a horde of photographers pursued her all over the sands!'[68]

Despite these seductive qualities, colour was not without its detractors. G. H. Gray, the art critic of the *Irish Times*, editor of the *Pictorial*, and fierce critic of the Irish middlebrow, 'likened most colour photographers to a child with a box of paints who insists on using the lot'.[69] Unlike Mr Deegan, Mr Ryan warned photographers against the luminous unreality of photographing in colour on bright days, arguing instead that colour photography needed to develop a more muted palate. As he told the PSI:

> pictures could be made successfully using three, two, or even varying shades and densities of one colour. On this line Mr Ryan dealt with colour as taken by the manufacturer's rules. Flat lighting in full sunlight gives harsh, sharply defined colours. It is much better to shoot in subdued light, such as when a cloud covers the sun. This gives pastel colours which are restful and more pleasing to the eye, and much more attractive together. The most effective pictures are made with side or back lighting although colour is almost removed one or two colours at most remaining. This is also completely against the manufacturers' instructions.[70]

However, it was not only that these colours were too bright, but also that their brightness was unrealistic. Most film could not yet authentically reproduce the colours seen by the eye or through the lens, leading to the hyper-real opaque colours now uniquely associated with images from the

[66] *The Lens*, April 1957, 79.
[67] *The Lens*, February 1957, 68.
[68] *The Lens*, August 1964, 8.
[69] *The Lens*, March 1957, 74.
[70] *The Lens*, March 1961, 3.

mid-twentieth century. In the words of one enthusiast, 'Nature had a long way to go to catch up on Kodachrome.' This was due to its pinkish colour cast which gave 'a warmth and brilliancy to most subjects which is very flattering'.[71] On the other hand, a material like Agfacolor, which gave colder tones was, in the opinion of its Irish distributor, ideal for photographing the 'soft pastel shades' of the Irish countryside caused by the 'water vapour in the air'.[72] Indeed, this palette of brassy and unrealistic colours had undertones of the simplistic, condescending American gaze, which had replaced the British perspective as the principle architect of an external view.

But the tones and hues of colour film were not the only things that were perceived to be inauthentic about colour photography; this valuable commodity was also compromised by the techniques through which images were developed. Colour was complicated to process and tended to be beyond the expertise of all but the most technically minded of amateurs. Most colour films instead had to be developed professionally, while Kodachrome, the most popular brand, had to be sent to Harrow for processing, taking two weeks to return the images. As a group of purists wrote to the *Lens*:

> A photographer worthy of his name would rather be seen dead than send his precious monochrome films to the D&P station to be processed but once he is caught by the colour craze he too often becomes a mere button-presser, leaving the processing of his films to the manufacturer, even when using material that can be home processed. We feel that colour transparencies so produced—no matter how beautiful—cannot satisfy the creative urge in us or give us the same feeling of achievement and pleasure that we get from the production of a first-class enlargement or lantern slide from a good monochrome negative.[73]

These photographers saw a link between the individual and the entire creative process, from composition to developing and printing, which was fractured by the use of commercial processing. Moreover, the complexity of developing colour film, for both professionals and amateurs, made it very hard to perform adaptions. This meant that the ideas of emotion, representation, and artistry, which were central to understandings of the pictorial tradition,

[71] *The Lens*, February 1957, 68. [72] *The Lens*, February 1957, 68.
[73] *The Lens*, February 1956, 1.

did not translate across easily to colour work.[74] In a lecture to the PSI in 1961, Mr Ryan said 'that the main jib at colour photography was that it was snapshotting, as there was no control possible in the process'.[75] This ambivalence surrounding the authenticity and artistry of the colour image became a point of contention in debates surrounding colour entries to PSI competitions. At the members' exhibition in 1956, trade-processed colour transparencies were banned for the first time, and so work made on Kodachrome and Ilfochrome was excluded.[76] In 1960 this rule was reversed, when trade-processed colour transparencies were accepted at the Irish Salon of Photography, although they were shown in their own class.[77]

This wary gaze towards the work of foreigner photographers is suggestive. In this period, colour-saturated images of green fields, blue skies, and red hair became a key part of the global visual economy of Irishness. John Hinde's first Irish postcards were printed in 1957, defining scenic views and creating images of holiday destinations. The American photo-magazines—such as *Time*, *Life*, and *National Geographic*—visited Ireland several times. Dorothea Lange's well-known photography essay on the culture and customs of Co. Clare was published in *Life* magazine as 'Irish Country People' in 1955.[78] An article in *Holiday* magazine caused a minor storm both in Ireland and in the Irish-American community when its beguiling colour-saturated landscape photographs were accompanied by a text by Frank O'Connor eviscerating Irish mentalities.[79] These images were accompanied by Technicolor films such as *The Quiet Man* (1952), which rendered Irish landscapes in intense and brilliant hues. These themes were taken up by the amateurs who were turning to colour across Ireland during the 1960s. But while opening new ways of seeing, colour photography also confined others. Colour disrupted the link between photographer and image, while also working through tropes which foregrounded the verdancy and abundance of the countryside. While these new technologies reinforced political rhetorics surrounding the persistence and value of rural society, they had little capacity to reflect critically or with nuance on its reality. Rather, these charming images are more representative of the increasing detachment of Ireland's urbanized and affluent middle class from the exigencies of rural culture.

[74] *The Lens*, September 1959, 2. [75] *The Lens*, March 1961, 3.

[76] *The Lens*, July 1957, 94. [77] *The Lens*, February 1960, 2.

[78] 'Irish Country People', *Life* 21 March 1955, 135–43; Linda Gordon, *Dorothea Lange: A Life Beyond Limits* (London, 2009), 370–3; Gerry Mullins and Daniel Dixon (eds.) *Dorothea Lange's Ireland* (Boulder, 1998).

[79] NAI TSCH/3/S14716/A; Zuelow, *Making Ireland Irish*, xxvi.

Photographing Buildings

While many photographers drew on longstanding traditions of the rural idyll in their photography of Ireland, others moved closer to the buildings that studded these places. Like rural landscapes, the depiction of the buildings of Ireland was redolent with meaning; indeed, the ruins of medieval civilization, the defensive fortifications of the early modern period, and the elegant proportions of the big houses of the eighteenth century all have complex associations alongside their long histories. Hugh Doran compiled one of the most comprehensive photographic records of the Irish built landscape in the latter half of the twentieth century, recording a unique and fleeting moment in big house life, suspended between previous prosperity and terminal decline.

Doran was an amateur photographer who spent his working life in the printing department of the Guinness brewery. Beyond this occupation, he was a perpetual autodidact. As education was 'encouraged' by Guinness's, he went to evening classes in the technical college, spending much of his time at the student debating society, while he also joined the Old Dublin Society in 1959. His photography reflected these interests. He obtained his first camera during the 1940s. It was, in his words, 'the era of pre-war second-hands obtained through the photo-ads in the *Evening Mail*.'[80] In this period he graduated quickly through cameras, from a 12a Conway box camera, to a Zeiss Ikonta, to, in 1952, a Rolleiflex, which cost him £63, or 'about 8 times a printer's wages.'[81] Alongside his photographs, he also taxonomized his life through assiduous and obsessive diaries, recording the time he got up, what he ate, how warm his bath was, and concerns shaped by the camera including the angles at which he saw buildings and the quality of the light. Desmond Guinness, president of the Irish Georgian Society (IGS), came across Doran's images in 1958 when they were exhibited as part of a Bord Fáilte photography competition on eighteenth-century Irish architecture.[82] Subsequently, Guinness wrote to Doran, explaining that the IGS was planning on holding its own exhibition on the Irish eighteenth century in the summer of 1959, to correspond with a visit to Ireland by the American Society of Architectural Historians, and asking Doran to take the photographs for it. This was soon followed by a telegram inviting

[80] IAA 2005/023.1/3/12(i) Lecture notes. [81] IAA 2005/023.1/3/12(i) Lecture notes.
[82] Erika Hanna, *Modern Dublin: Urban Change and the Irish Past, 1957–73* (Oxford, 2013), 67–83.

Doran for tea. So, as Doran's notes record, 'on the following Sunday, a cold December day, I drove to Leixlip and its castle.' This was the beginning of a relationship that would last half a century.[83]

Using a Linhof camera bought for the purpose, Doran spent much of the spring of 1959 photographing the eighteenth-century architecture of Ireland, alongside Desmond Guinness's wife, Mariga. They began in Dublin, where they photographed sites including the Rotunda Hospital, Powerscourt House, Charlemont House, and Aldborough House. Their commitment to discovering the appropriate vantage point led them into confrontation with the city's poorer inhabitants, who now occupied many of these buildings. After shooting close-up photographs of the Bluecoat School:

> Mariga thought it would be a good idea to get a picture of Blackhall street with the Bluecoat school closing the vista. I was all on for shooting from ground level but M insisted that it must have an elevated viewpoint, so up we went the stairs of the first tenement, but the floor tenant was out. I hoped she would call it off but no! Up the stairs of the tenement next door. This time the top floor was in. M did the talking – Georgian architecture exhibition in BT [Brown Thomas], and we were invited in. While I shot the picture we got a short history of the family and their plight in this room. The paid 6/6 per week for it, to a lady from Killiney, who personally collected it every Monday ('if you wait she will be here any minute!') the roof leaked on to the bed where three kids sleep.[84]

Here the camera allowed for Doran and Guinness to access places which otherwise would have been outside their usual paths through the city; however, it also created a situation in which they were both intruders and wholly dominant in the exchange between visitor and resident as it unfolded. This dynamic can also be read in the view he captured. The resulting image shows an elevated view of the street, empty apart from a couple of cyclists and women gathered around a cluster of prams on the pavement, small viewed from the top floor and against the backdrop of the towering eighteenth-century houses (Figure 3.3).[85]

From Dublin, Doran's journeys radiated across the country, taking in the country houses of Ireland, sometimes on his own on a motorbike, and

[83] IAA 2005/023.1/3/10 Georgian Adventure 1959.
[84] IAA 2005/023.1/3/10 Georgian Adventure 1959.
[85] IAA HD902. Blackhall Place viewed from Blackhall Street.

Figure 3.3 Blackhall Street, Dublin (1959). Hugh Doran Collection, Irish Architectural Archive.

sometimes in the Guinnesses' Citroën. These journeys were a mixture of getting lost, searching woodland, and improbable encounters in decaying country houses. Indeed, from both photographs and the accompanying diaries, there emerges a sense in which Doran saw himself along with the Guinnesses as 'discovering' lost houses, lying unknown and forgotten in the Irish landscape. Some, like French Park, were already derelict, pictured by Doran as an empty shell, with its roof off and garden untended.[86] Hazelwood House, in Sligo, was at that time a psychiatric hospital. 'When the official appeared it looked as though there would be no photography but M did some fast talking and I was allowed to shoot the interior of the hall which is like Bellinter with its niches and fireplaces. I tried to shoot through the open door which shows Ben Bulben' (Figure 3.4).[87] The hallway was largely empty of decoration and sparsely, institutionally furnished. He largely avoided the traces of this in his photography, apart from a telephone by the principal entrance, and he avoided institutional unmatched furniture, light switches, and strip lighting which had been more recently installed.[88] The house's situation, in the shadow of Ben Bulben, was still highly picturesque, and 'the first time I have ever shot a picture from the middle of a ploughed field with the rain running down my neck.'[89] Doran sought out the ruins of Dunmore House, which, according to the vague notations of his Esso map, were located approximately half way between Abbeyleix and Durrow. However, finding the house was not this simple. He stopped in Abbeyleix and 'asked the local police if they knew a house, with wings, with or without curved curtain walls, halfway between Durrow and Abbeyleix. We had quite a chat, with some of the locals being called in to rack their brain.' However, 'it was no good.' Instead Doran drove three miles and stopped, asking a local farmer ploughing nearby, who—finally—knew where the house was located. It was 7pm when he finally arrived, saying 'prayers of thanks when I found the light right.'[90] In bright evening sun he photographed the house with the roof off, grass growing out of the walls, with an impromptu doorway having been smashed through masonry, presumably to enable the old stately rooms to be used for storage.[91]

[86] IAA 2005/023.1/3/10 Georgian Adventure 1959; IAA Roscommon photographs French Park.

[87] IAA Diary 1959.

[88] IAA Sligo photographs: Hazelwood.

[89] IAA 2005/023.1/3/10 Georgian Adventure 1959.

[90] IAA 2005/023.1/3/10 Georgian Adventure 1959.

[91] IAA Laois photographs: Dunmore House.

Figure 3.4 Hazelwood House, Sligo (1959). Hugh Doran Collection, Irish Architectural Archive.

His camera gave him a reason to cross social thresholds, bringing him into intimate contact with the draughty ancestral halls of Anglo-Irish society. At the centre of this world was the Guinness family. Leixlip Castle was 'a cross between an antique shop and a refrigerator', a constantly rotating carousel of activity and big personalities all 'weighted down with plenty of wine of course'.[92] This conviviality, however, was often matched by Doran's sense of unease at being socially out of his depth. He often spent dinners at Leixlip Castle with the Guinnesses and their friends in silence, listening to them speak about 'things [he] knew nothing about'.[93] Breakfast was no less complicated. One morning he breakfasted with Mariga, and 'asked for some milk for my tea, very non-U I think'.[94] On another occasion he came down to breakfast to find 'an old French lady' already at the table; the 'conversation was in French, with me catching every tenth word'.[95] For all his discomfort, his association with the Guinnesses opened doors both literal and metaphorical. As Doran recalled, 'In the 1960s it was possible to drive up to a mansion, say that Desmond Guinness sent me, and be allowed to shoot.'[96] For example, the owner of Bridestream was 'a large amiable man named Prat McMahon', who, 'after hearing our piece about the exhibition, immediately invited us in for a drink'.[97] Belview was 'a discovery of Maurice Craig's'. However, the owner was not so excited as many other owners to make their acquaintance. 'When we arrived there was a car at the front door but nobody around so we waited for half an hour until the owner did appear, leading a horse. His name is Frank Boland, he did not mind us shooting his house, and he drove his car out of the picture. Unfortunately he did not invite us in, in fact he neatly dismissed us by saying that he knew we were busy people and he would not delay us.'[98]

On more familiar territory, Doran continued to photograph Dublin throughout his life, with a particular focus on the streets and buildings of St James's Gate and the Liberties, near to where he lived and worked.[99] During the 1960s, he finally relinquished his aversion to colour photography, and began to take slides, first in Ferraniacolor and later in Kodachrome. Living locally, he would visit a site several times in order to ensure that he caught it in the best light, and free of cars. He also photographed the city

[92] IAA 2005/023.1/3/10 Georgian Adventure 1959. [93] 2005/023/1/1/5/1 Diary 1959.
[94] 2005/023/1/1/5/1 Diary 1959. [95] 1959 Diary Georgian Adventure.
[96] IAA 2005/023.1/3/12(i) Lecture notes.
[97] IAA 2005/023.1/3/10 Georgian Adventure 1959.
[98] IAA 2005/023.1/3/10 Georgian Adventure 1959.
[99] IAA 2005/23.1/3/2 A Photographer looks at Dublin.

largely without people, a favourite technique instead to photograph a single old man, head down, reading a newspaper, giving the image a silent, sleepy, and intimate air. Presenting lectures on his photography of Dublin during the 1960s, he used his images in order to remark on how much the city had changed since he started taking photographs; indeed, his photography provided a way for him to make sense of a disparate series of urban changes which might otherwise have gone unnoticed. His shot of Ormond Quay would have been complete 'if I had a Guinness barge in it but the barges had gone by the time I began shooting colour slides'.[100] The Irish House Pub was 'gone', its bas-reliefs housed instead in the Guinness museum. The Canal Basin had 'lost its water…this branch of the Grand Canal is being filled in and at the moment this part is like a ditch as the water has almost entirely evaporated revealing the debris of 2000 years'. Weavers Hall was also gone, 'as indeed have all the old guilds;. The buildings of St Michael's Hill and Winetavern Street were also gone, 'including Mr Young and his hats'.[101]

For Doran, the camera transformed the way he looked at and experienced Ireland. His camera began a journey of exploration around the country, where old buildings were 'discovered' and collected like specimens. He cleared tables and chairs, telephone wires, got owners to move their cars, in order to record this architecture in a way which was designed to seem timeless. While the encroaching ivy and broken masonry of Ireland's new ruins could provide a wistful narrative to his photography, he shied away from including the traces of new institutional uses. This process was only reinforced in the areas he knew best, around St James's Gate, where his proximity allowed him to visit and revisit churches, halls, and residential architecture until he captured them at the perfect moment, again with few cars and people on the street. Central to all this was the light, with delicate shafts of pale winter light illuminating eighteenth-century streets captured with skill and sensitivity, like a butterfly catcher.

Photographing Industry

Belfast had its own distinctive visual tradition, defined by civic and industrial pride and which has focused on the strong structural forms of industry and the glistening metals of the docks. Harland and Wolff dominated the

[100] IAA 2005/23.1/3/2 A Photographer looks at Dublin.
[101] IAA 2005/23.1/3/2 A Photographer looks at Dublin.

landscape of east Belfast and the social and cultural life of the northern industrial city. The company was founded during a nineteenth-century shipping boom related to the increased trade of emigration. Its fate in the later twentieth century was, however, more mixed, enduring the bombs of the Second World War, experiencing a final fevered period of prosperity emerging from post-war reconstruction, and after this, undergoing long slow degradation in trade during the 1960s and 1970s.[102] Through both boom and bust, the shipyard has been central to Belfast's image in the world and the city's image of itself, and as such throughout its existence it has been extensively photographed.[103] During the late nineteenth and early twentieth centuries, the photographer Robert Welch recorded its early history in well-known glass-plate images. His pictures of groups of tough men with strong hands and thick arms staring unsmilingly at his camera against a backdrop of heavy dark machinery almost define an image of prelapsarian working class unity for Belfast.[104]

Bert Martin worked at Harland and Wolff during the 1950s and 1960s, and was a keen amateur photographer. On his days off he went walking and cycling around Ulster with friends, taking black and white photographs of the province and taking pleasure in the craft of composing images and in the journeys and encounters his camera led him to. In the context of the new buildings, infrastructure, and society of the post-war dispensation, his eye sought out people, things, and places that were seemingly disappearing from view in the province. In Fermanagh and Donegal, he took ethnographic photographs which gazed at a disappearing world: a man and a donkey pulling a cart on a track through the bog between Pettigo and Donegal town (Figure 3.5); the lock-keeper at Shaw's Bridge; a farm labourer leaning over a half-door at Rathfriland.[105] These were rural scenes populated by old men: strong with wizened faces and skilled hands, bending over antiquated farming machinery, working slowly and silently. In Belfast, his photographs also turned towards disappearances, but these were places rather than people: the last tram, an empty site on Rowland Street where terrace housing used to be, the destruction of nineteenth-century buildings on the High Street in preparation for modern structures.[106] Here the Victorian

[102] Kevin Johnston, *In the Shadows of Giants: A Social History of the Belfast Shipyards* (Dublin, 2008), 299.

[103] Vivienne Pollock and Trevor Parkhill, *Made in Belfast* (Stroud, 2005).

[104] Michael McCaughin, *Steel Ships and Iron Men: Shipbuilding in Belfast 1894–1912* (1989); Colin Graham, *Northern Ireland: 30 Years of Photography* (Belfast, 2013), 88.

[105] Ulster Folk and Transport Museum (UFTM) Martin collection.

[106] UFTM Martin.

Figure 3.5 Road to Pettigo from Donegal town, through turf bog (Bert Martin). Image courtesy of National Museums Northern Ireland (Collection Ulster Museum).

city was being demolished rapidly and raggedly to make way for the new spatial forms of social democracy; as such, both excitement and nostalgia animated his images of loss and renewal. His photographs of Harland and Wolff, however, were in a different register. Here he was neither nostalgic nor ethnographic but instead displayed an intense enthusiasm for the workmanship and achievement of the shipyard. He photographed new types of boats which were supplying the needs of the post-war settlement, such as cruise-liners, oil tankers, and car ferries. He stood far back in order to get the entirety of the massive hulls into the viewfinder. In his framing they were white, gleaming, sculptural, and hulking. This composition meant that the dockworkers were tiny, reduced to flecks of black standing on the dockside beside these massive ships, emphasizing by their minuteness the power and engineering prowess of these constructions (Figure 3.6).[107] With hands in pockets and thick wool jackets, they looked up in awe.

Like others who photographed the north of Ireland, the province took on its own distinctive visual profile for Martin. Uniting the fields of Donegal with the shipyards of Belfast was a sense of the manual skill and hard work of the people of Ulster, and a heightened sense of the passage of time and the changing years. Indeed, Martin's ethnographic depiction of the slow days and ancestral skill of the men in the fields created an imagery of the last traces of a declining social world. While elegiac, this was not a pessimistic picture, as these older patterns of home and labour were replaced by the infrastructure of modernity and the vitality of a prosperous Belfast.

Club photography debated

During the late 1950s, photography took on a new excitement in Ireland. The leading department stores began to stock the new models, camera shops opened to cater for the needs of enthusiastic amateurs, and a whole range of new clubs were set up to cater for their interests and needs. This moment was characterized by a marked fetishization of equipment during a period when the possibilities of photographic technology were expanding rapidly. Indeed, this was matched by the values of the club which privileged formalized notions of the pictorial and demonstrations of technical skill in the way that they judged and valued images. In tours in new hire-purchase motor-cars, the newly affluent of Ireland's principal cities set off to discover

[107] UFTM Martin.

Figure 3.6 'Southern Cross' at launch (Bert Martin). Image courtesy of National Museums Northern Ireland (Collection Ulster Museum).

light on water, verdant landscapes, and wooded valleys which reflected longstanding notions of Ireland and which largely effaced both the new landscapes of modernity and the problems of rural life. After some initial scepticism, these tendencies were bolstered by the emergence of colour, which was handled in a way that often reinforced pre-existing models of the depiction of landscape. New consumer goods and new mobilities combined to structure a new middle-class gaze on landscape.

The boundaries of the 'photographable' became increasingly contentious during the 1960s, as Irish society modernized and European photographic practice shifted. In the post-war era, the studied and careful compositions of the club practitioners were increasingly out of step with international photographic cultures and changes to Ireland's social and economic profile. During the 1960s, the PSI witnessed battles regarding the linked concerns of the boundaries of the social and the nature of aesthetic practice in contemporary Ireland. In 1961, a frustrated member wrote to *The Lens* under the pseudonym of 'Layman' to express disappointment at the nature of Irish photographic practice. Posing the questions 'How does work of its members compare with that of photographers in other countries? How conscious are they of the demands of their Art-Form?', he responded that 'the answer to both these questions is depressing'.[108] Although Irish photographers were as technically accomplished as their contemporaries in other countries, they fell down in other aspects:

> Again and again one sees the 'Monarch of the Glen' type of pictures; the harbour and yacht and tranquillity approach, the mawkish and unnatural children in contrived postures, fossilised 'Jack Tars', the 'Tussaud' like portraits. One could say 'excellent' to this work thirty years ago or even twenty years ago but one cannot continue saying it indefinitely. The world is not as the majority of these photographers would have us believe, in a state of bemused apathy. People suffer, fear, rejoice, hate, love and think. These emotions and natures can be depicted. They are known to us all and when re-presented by the artist they become universally significant things. The photographer should stir us to awareness of them as a Mozart does, not present us with a gratuitous imitation of ourselves full of false values and emotions. The world has come a long way from the relaxed and halcyon days of the twenties. Irish photographers would have us believe we are still

[108] *The Lens*, September 1961, 3.

> in them. But their world is dead and gone and has little meaning for us to-day. Freud, Einstein, Hitler and Stalin have insured this transformation. We must accept it, believe it and photograph it.[109]

It is significant that in the assessment of 'Layman', the photographers of the PSI were lacking not in technical skill, but rather in the imagination or inspiration to see beyond a narrow set of visual tropes. Indeed, the way of seeing given materiality through the photography of the PSI was one in which social change, poverty, and the trials—as opposed to romanticism—of rural life were unseen. While a new dispensation—personified by 'Freud, Einstein, Hitler and Stalin'—had reshaped the global order and everyday life across the world, the photographers clung to the security, and the narrow field of vision laid down and formalized in aesthetic codes during the nineteenth century. But despite these criticisms, many within the PSI had a problematic relationship with both documentary traditions and abstract art photography, preferring instead the photographs produced by its members to reflect the traditional skills and topics of the pictorial movement. An anonymous correspondent to the *Lens*, entitled 'The Irish Salon – An Ulster View' reported with regard to the 1964 Salon that:

> I do not think there is a place in a Salon for prints of bald-heads, children with running noses, legs without bodies, in skirts or bathing-costumes, goggles and leather jacket, motor-cycles, owls, dogs and cats. Aiming a camera through a hole in a wall at miserable poverty is unfair and although this and the others may be excused as examples of a wide range of subjects they are either undignified or inartistic. Nor did I see Art in enlarged heads showing pores and blemishes, still and stilted poses excused by such titles as 'Angry Mood' and puzzle pictures such as 'Enigma' or in a snap of a ballet-dancer perched on a ledge out of doors.[110]

Indeed, the role that pictorialism played in policing the boundaries of photographic practice is notable. Through a resistance to the forms, composition, and concerns of the documentary tradition, the correspondent also resisted its potential for radicalism, and its ability to make visible the more problematic or difficult aspects of Irish life. Indeed, in his condemnation of photographs of 'children with running noses', 'pores and

[109] *The Lens*, September 1961, 3. [110] *The Lens*, October 1964, 2.

blemishes', and contemporary photographers' tendency to aim 'a camera though a hole in a wall at miserable poverty' he constituted an aesthetic argument which was also a plea for keeping demotic artistic practice well within social boundaries. Despite these reservations, in response to the type of criticisms expressed by 'Layman', in 1962 the Society launched a new 'Experimental' section for its annual exhibition, to extend to work which was 'original in conception or which employ[ed] unusual techniques or treatment'.[111] Perhaps providing an indication of a certain artistic pessimism around contemporary national culture within Ireland in the early 1960s, *The Lens* introduced the section by stating that it gave 'an opportunity to anyone which wishes to experiment to see old things in new ways, to widen the photographic horizon and to see whether we can find anything fresh in this country which will be a contribution to photographic art as a whole'. However, 'The section' was 'in no way a threat to the more conventional modes of pictorial photographic in which the society excels'.[112]

For a brief moment, Ireland's photographic clubs captured the mood of Ireland's post-war modernity, providing a hobby which combined consumption, leisure, and triumph over the landscape for Ireland's prosperous urban residents. However, this was not to last. By the end of the 1960s, there were some efforts to move beyond the relatively arid debates of the *Lens*. In 1966, the PSI organized an exhibition of the 'Contemporary Scene', entitled 'The Irish Image', at Arnotts on Henry Street, as an attempt to breathe new life into images of Ireland.[113] However, the shifts occurring within photography would have a corrosive effect on these photographic clubs, as their structures proved impossible to adapt to the changing photographic landscape. The '57 Camera Club closed its doors in 1966, having been in existence less than a decade.[114] The Central Camera Club ceased to operate in 1967.[115] The PSI also endured constant battles for members and money throughout this period. In an Ireland which was changing, these organizations could not offer a way of understanding photography which chimed with the needs of Ireland's new generation of photographers. However, collective activity and photography would play an important role in Ireland in the later twentieth century, in a very different guise. Indeed, as the debates within the PSI already presaged, by the end of the 1960s, club photography in Ireland and

[111] *The Lens*, January 1962, 1. [112] *The Lens*, January 1962, 1.
[113] *Irish Image*, 1966 exhibition catalogue.
[114] PRONI D3479/1/A/1 Minute book of the '57 Club, Strabane, 1966.
[115] PRONI D4005 Minute book of the Belfast Central Camera Club 1967.

elsewhere had a bad reputation for being staid, conservative, and unresponsive to the challenges of post-war society. From the end of the 1960s, a new generation of photographers emerged who bypassed photography clubs in their entirety, and found new fora for learning photography, taking photographs, and using their images.

Even if this sort of hyper-real, technicolour image of the landscape was rejected by new photographers coming of age in the 1970s, more recently they have come back into fashion. Today, these colour photographs are popular again, and have come to embody a sense of loss for Ireland's emergent mid-century modernity. This is epitomized by the ongoing popularity of John Hinde's images of donkeys and red-haired children, but is also replicated in private slide and photograph collections across the country. Kodachrome photographs of blissed out summer days, vermillion green hillsides, azure blue seas, and cherry-red picnic boxes create a sense of loss for a past when colours were intense and brilliant and embody a relentless optimism through their glossy opaque tones. But colour prints are far more unstable than black and white, and after half a century these images have often faded to blue. In these images, photographic allegories of the distance and loss of our near-past take on a photographic materiality, even as older black and white photographs remain crisp and clear.

4

Community and Representation

Empowerment, Activism, and the Image, 1970–90

On a summer evening in June 1985, the poet Macdara Woods got on the number 13 bus heading north from Dublin city centre. The journey was evocative for him, retracing the route his grandmother had taken when she had moved from East Wall to Ballymun, 'an area she remembered from country walks of her childhood'. He was on his way to see an exhibition of photography by nine teenagers at Base 10, Ballymun Community Arts Centre. The photographic display included video installations, photographic essays on life in Ballymun, and portraits, images which had a striking impact on Woods:

> The skills involved are not confined to using a photographic enlarger... when it comes down to it they are about the quality of life itself as we see it and experience it and understand it. Communication on this level is self-perpetuating, it spreads out into all aspects of existence and it reaffirms identity by making us clarify for ourselves and others who and what we are.

But for Woods, the most telling words of the night came from a girl speaking on one of the videos, who said that art 'has to do with everything you see'. The power of this deceptively simple phrase had a profound impact: 'the potential for an ever-expanding consciousness and awareness behind those eight words is shaking.' On the bus home, he meditated on the ideas of the exhibition, and the way that vision, consciousness, and power intertwined in the images he had seen. Indeed, reflecting on these words led him to return to his own memories, and Louis MacNeice's eulogization of the quotidian in his adage that the best place to see a city was from the top of a double decker bus. Along the route home, memories of childhood journeys were 'swinging into focus': the Cross Guns pub, the valerian along the railway tracks, the silhouette of Mountjoy, Findlater's church, the far-away view

Snapshot Stories: Visuality, Photography, and the Social History of Ireland, 1922–2000. Erika Hanna, Oxford University Press (2020).
DOI: 10.1093/oso/9780198823032.001.0001

of mountains—'it was all there, all as clear as it ever was, as starling and immediate as a new print coming up out of the developing fluid.'[1]

This photographic activism in Ballymun was part of a broader community arts movement. Community arts initiatives had developed across European and American cities from the 1970s, with the aim of nurturing and harnessing the creativity of groups outside the formal art world. Their roots were in the new left activism of the 1970s, new interest in community politics, and developing understandings of ideas of well-being and creativity. Building on this lineage community arts took a range of forms—including theatre, murals, and dance—as schemes burgeoned in urban locations during that decade.[2] The movement also spread across Ireland's towns and cities, combining local activism with transnational cultural politics and practices.[3] One of the first workshops was the Grapevine Project, founded in 1973 by Sandy Fitzgerald in City Quay (renamed the City Arts Centre in the 1980s). The North Centre City Community Action Project was set up in 1975 and ran a range of artistic workshops, alongside campaigning for improved housing and local amenities in central Dublin.[4] Waterford for All was set up by Combat Poverty Waterford in 1979, and led to a variety of visual and performative arts initiatives in the city.[5] Neighbourhood Open Workshops was formed in 1978 in Belfast, initially running children's activities before expanding into collective art projects and performances.[6] Due to this organic growth and diverse array of participants, there was no unified definition of what community arts was; writing on Ireland in 1989, Ciaran Benson of Arts Community Education (ACE) reported that they had 'had difficulties with the adjective "community" as it qualified the noun "arts". And we also had difficulties with that same use of "arts" as a noun.'[7]

[1] *Irish Examiner*, 25 June 1985, 10.

[2] Sam Wetherell, 'Painting the Crisis: Community Arts and the Search for the "Ordinary", in 1970s and '80s London', *History Workshop Journal* 76/1 (2013), 235.

[3] Sandy Fitzgerald, 'Community Arts', in Andrew Carpenter and Paula Murphy (eds.), *Art and Architecture of Ireland* 3 (Dublin, 2015), 420–4.

[4] Ronan Sheehan, 'The Press and the People in Dublin Central: Ronan Sheehan Talks to Tony Gregory, Mick Rafferty and Fergus McCabe', *The Crane Bag* 8 (1984), 44–50.

[5] Sandy Fitzgerald, 'The Beginnings of Community Arts and the Irish Republic', in Sandy Fitzgerald (ed.), *An Outburst of Frankness: Community Arts in Ireland – A Reader* (Dublin, 2004), 11; Lilian Chambers, Ger FitzGibbon, and Eamon Jordan (eds.), *Theatre Talk: Voices of Irish Theatre Practitioners* (Dublin, 2008), 169.

[6] Sandy Fitzgerald, 'The Beginnings of Community Arts in the Irish Republic', in Fitzgerald (ed.), *An Outburst of Frankness*, 11.

[7] Ciaran Benson, *Art and the Ordinary: Report of the Arts Community Education Committee* (Dublin, 1989), 13.

Community photography had its own articulation due to the properties of the camera and cultural lineage of the photographic image. It was pioneered and championed by the Half Moon Photography workshop, set up in Brixton in 1972, but soon spread to Ireland; during the 1970s and 1980s, community and church halls across Ireland were repurposed for dark rooms and exhibition spaces for groups to learn, practise, and display photography. For example, the Shankill Photographic Workshop was set up by Buzz Logan in 1979.[8] Derry Camerawork was set up by Trisha Ziff in 1982.[9] In 1983, Sean McKernan organized the exhibition 'Belfast Exposed', which drew on the photography of local groups and amateurs, and which then led on to the foundation of the Belfast Exposed workshop and exhibition space.[10] In 1993, Kate Horgan was appointed photographer in residence to run a community photography project in some of the newer estates of Dublin, including Coolock, Ballyfermot, and Ballymun.[11] In 1996, an international festival of community photography was held in Balbriggan, organized by Fingal County Council. As Woods's reflections indicated, community photography developed at the intersection between community politics, ideas of empowerment, and a heightened sense of time and change in the city.

The 1970s and 1980s were a time of political disarray and economic challenges, and when the relentless violence of the Troubles disrupted daily life for many and dominated the mood and the atmosphere across the island.[12] Indeed, it has been remembered as a period of crisis, disillusionment, and anxiety both north and south of the border. These trends were particularly egregious in Ireland's cities. As factories shut and docks and ports downsized and containerized, the centres of Dublin, Belfast, Derry, and Cork became places of high unemployment and associated social problems as the trades and workplaces which had sustained these communities closed their doors. Moreover, the problems of deindustrialization were compounded by heavy-handed urban renewal.[13] Ambitious and

[8] *Hibernia*, 17 May 1979, 25. [9] *Irish Press*, 21 October 1982, 6.

[10] Mathilde Bertrand, '"A Tool for Social Change": Community Photography at Belfast Exposed', *Revue LISA/LISA e-journal* (2015).

[11] 'Report No. 190/1992: Additional Grants Under the Arts Act 1973' *Reports and Minutes of Dublin Corporation* (Dublin, 1993); Dublin City Council, *Fotofest '93: Dublin Public Libraries Festival of Photography* (Dublin, 1993).

[12] Diarmuid Ferriter, *Ambiguous Republic: Ireland in the 1970s* (London, 2014); Tim Pat Coogan, *Disillusioned Decades: Ireland 1966–1987* (Dublin, 1987); Brian Girvin, 'The Origins of Contemporary Ireland: New Perspectives on the Recent Past', *Irish Historical Studies* 38/151 (May 2013), 385–8.

[13] Paul Thompson, 'Community and Creativity: A Life Stories Perspective', *Oral History* 37/2, (2009), 34–44.

unsympathetic town planning schemes were introduced to overhaul these places, but frequently stalled due to bureaucracy and lack of money, meaning that these old neighbourhoods were transformed into barren landscapes of vacant sites, demolished housing, and boarded-up factories. These domestic problems were part of global trends. During this period, 'inner city' became a byword for all the failings of modern society the locus of media anxieties and social science studies. As Otto Saumarez Smith described: 'The inner city was both exemplified by particular places, but was also understood as a sinister and creeping malady, "a strange and foreign land set apart and ignored by society", a social concept made concrete in physical locations.'[14]

From their bases in arts centres, community photographers engaged in island-wide discourses surrounding the politics of visibility. As Tanya Kiang asserted in 1988, during the decade, many photographers 'tried to come to terms with the fact that Ireland is often simply "visual fodder" for the visiting photographer's lens.'[15] This discourse—of visibility and invisibility, exclusion and empowerment—was reproduced across various arenas of Irish activism. In particular, 'inner city' communities became loci for anxieties about social and economic change. Inner-city residents and activists were united in their belief that their communities were subject to negative national and international portrayal, whether that was negative images of unionist culture, sensational images of terrorism, or depictions of the inner city as a place of crime and decay. For example, when his book was launched in Dublin, Logan stated, 'I wanted to show that the Shankill Road is the same as anywhere else that has suffered from media coverage. That all the people there are not warring lunatics, but ordinary people suffered from the "Give a dog a bad name" syndrome, trying to build up a place that owes more to bulldozers than to bombs for its destruction.'[16] Similarly, the first issue of *IC*, a community magazine run in Dublin's inner city declared, 'The North city has been the victim of media misreporting. People have read reports and article in the National Press about their area in disbelief…the intention in bringing out this magazine is to provide a clear and independent voice that inner-city inhabitants will recognise as their own.'[17]

[14] Otto Saumarez Smith, 'The Inner City Crisis and the End of Urban Modernism in 1970s Britain', *Twentieth Century British History* 27/4 (2016), 579.

[15] Tanya Kiang, 'Dublin Time Capsule, Dublin Civic Museum 17 May – 10 June', *Circa* 41 (Aug–Sept 1988), 30.

[16] *Evening Herald*, 31 May 1979, 11.

[17] *IC*, 23 June 1983, 3.

These participants in community photography intervened in this visual landscape to provide instead what they saw as an authentic and sympathetic reading of the inner city. These readings took a variety of forms. Activists and community groups worked together to develop an imagery for depicting their neighbourhoods, which responded to negative imagery and instead portrayed them as hardworking, united, and 'ordinary'. Moreover, through the production of photographic catalogues of older buildings and residents and collecting and archiving older photographs, they re-established the identity of urban communities at a moment when they seemed to be profoundly under threat. But these practices and images were produced within a pre-existing visual economy, which played a determining role in how these images were read. Funding mechanisms validated certain initiatives and gave some groups space to exhibit. Wall mountings, reproduction qualities, and labelling inscribed certain conceptions of photographic value and determined the ways in which the images could be read. Despite the best efforts of activists and volunteers, these community images often had little impact in how the inner city was imagined in the national and international media. However, through composing, making, and displaying affirmative and authentic images, these projects were intended to raise self-esteem and empower individuals and groups. Indeed, community photography's combination of the social and the subjective showed how notions of power and exclusion became entwined with notions of the visible during the latter decades of the twentieth century.

With the exception of the celebrated work of Belfast Exposed, community photography in Ireland has been largely overlooked by both social historians and art historians, sitting awkwardly between social activism and art practice. But despite this, the movement played an important role at a crucial historical juncture. Indeed, through community photography a wide sector of the public in Ireland were taught how to read images and to develop visual literacy. In this context, the movement played a formative role in shaping how the period was visualized, and how these depictions were read during a moment of perceived crisis in Irish cities. This chapter explores this story, first looking at the purpose and practices of the community photography movement in Ireland in the 1970s and 1980s, and then going on to examine three projects in greater detail: the work of Buzz Logan and the Shankill Photographic Workshop, Derry Camerawork, and the work of those associated with the North Centre City Community Action Project in Dublin. Through an assemblage of oral histories, newspaper coverage, and photographs produced as part of these projects, this chapter aims to do two things: first, to explore the cultural politics and affective practices of community photography in Ireland; and second, to use the photographic output of these projects on their own terms, to explore ideas of ordinary life and community during a period of urban crisis.

Leaving community photography undefined

'Community' is a protean word with a lofty rhetorical appeal which is often seen appended to municipal swimming pools and gardens. Writing in 1976, Raymond Williams established the evolution of the word 'community', stretching back through medieval civic formation and Ferdinand Tönnies's distinction between pre-modern *Gemeinschaft* and modern *Gesellschaft*. However, he noted that 'more recently' the word 'community' had developed 'a polemical edge…as in community politics, which is distinct not only from *national politics* but from formal *local politics* and normally involves various kinds of direct action and direct local organization "working directly with people"'.[18] As he indicated, in this period the word community provided a way of thinking about sociability rooted in location, activism, and campaigning, which often functioned as a substitute for class-based politics.[19] This took many forms: Muintir na Tíre was formed in 1937 and initiated Ireland's first community development schemes in order to help rural populations improve their own areas; Michael Young founded the Institute for Community Studies in 1954, exploring the extended kinship networks of the urban working class; and during the 1970s and 1980s, a range of community action projects were initiated in particular focusing on the problems of poverty and drugs.[20] As Williams averred, the 'complexity of community' therefore arose from 'the difficult interaction between the tendencies originally distinguished in the historical development'.[21]

Community photography existed across these multiple definitions of community, taking a range of forms and objectives inspired by these

[18] Raymond Williams, *Keywords: A Vocabulary of Culture and Society* (Oxford, 1985), 75–6.

[19] David Ellis, 'Pavement Politics: Community Action in Leeds, c. 1960–1990', PhD thesis, University of York (2015), http://etheses.whiterose.ac.uk/11727 (accessed9 August 2018).

[20] Lise Butler, 'Michael Young, the Institute of Community Studies, and the Politics of Kinship', *Twentieth Century British History* 26/2 (2015), 203–24; George Thomason, 'Muintir na Tir's role in Irish Community Development', *Studies* 51/203 (1962), 408–18; Ben Jones, 'The Uses of Nostalgia: Autobiography, Community Publishing and Working-Class Neighbourhoods in Post-war England', *Cultural and Social History* 7/3, 355–74 (2010).

[21] Raymond Williams, *Keywords*, 75–6.

differing lineages. As such, the movement was disparate and amorphous; indeed, there was no definitive method for including or excluding groups or projects from the designation; indeed, its inclusive ethos—in contrast to the perceived elitism of the art world—was part of its ethic. The journal *Camerawork*, framed debate on these ideas.[22] A special issue entitled 'Photography in the Community' in March 1979 explained that:

> Community photographers continue both a photographic and communal tradition. Photographers since Lewis Hine and Jacob Riis have shown the things in our society that need to be changed. People have done community work since the great charitable settlements were established in our big cities during the last century. Community photographers, however, want to give more than charity or expose social injustices. They believe that people can use photography to make their own demands and help make them free.[23]

This excerpt provides a sense of the range of work and practices which could come under the label of community photography. It included both the photographic work of local activists and work done by amateurs, and images which depicted localities in both a positive and negative light. Projects varied across a range of topics and themes, including explorations of the identity of the community, photographic evidence to document poor housing conditions, or archives to preserve the history of the neighbourhood. These photographic projects operated with a wide range of intentions including building communal cohesion, campaigning for investment, and exposing injustice.

It was, however, the ambition of community photography to 'help make [people] free', which is both most notable and most enigmatic. Teaching photography to women's groups, Joanne O'Brien recalled that photography was perceived to be part of a broader remedial process: 'it was important that people explored their creative side…that everybody had some talent and they should find an outlet for it, and that it make them happier, and that they could express something about their world, about what they saw around, and learn skills that would give them confidence.'[24] The women in O'Brien's

[22] Matilde Bertrand, 'The Half Moon Photography Workshop and *Camerawork*: Catalysts in the British Photographic Landscape (1972–1985)', *Photography and Culture* (online 18 May 2018); Jessica Starns, 'The Camerawork Archive', *Photography and Culture* 6/3 (2013), 341.

[23] *Camerawork*, March 1979, 1.

[24] Interview with Joanne O'Brien, 12 May 2016.

photography group—and a myriad of others like it—used photography in order to make their view of the world visible, and so gain confidence, a process described by Sam Wetherell as 'therapeutic consciousness-raising'.[25] These activities were based on a notion of the importance of individual creativity which had been in development in social psychology since the 1950s, were further explored by radical theorists including Augusto Boal, Paolo Freire, and Joseph Beuys, and which had their fullest articulation in the women's movement.[26] In this reading, creativity and self-expression led to greater well-being, self-esteem, and self-confidence. This focus on the self, and the mutually constitutive importance of confidence, expression, and creativity as part of a broader process of emancipation within the social and economic order, became a crucial part of the cultural discourse of the era, and a key plank in the ethos of community photography.[27]

But this subjective restitution also had a political purpose. This photographic movement can be understood within notions of 'empowerment' which developed in the new social movements of the 1960s, and which were used by groups considered to be 'marginalized communities' 'to enable the expression of their traditionally silenced points of view'.[28] In this schema, ideas of individual and group psychology coalesced. Communities that had been psychologically damaged by unemployment and the withdrawal of traditional industries, and maligned by negative portrayals in the media, could be given the ability to recuperate through the creation and dissemination of new images which presented an alternative perspective on their places and people. Contesting negative images enabled communities to rehabilitate and raise communal self-esteem, and functioned as part of a broader remedial process aimed at long-term economic and social improvement. However, it was left open as to whether this action was aimed at radical change or reform within the existing system—an interpretation which shifted from activist to activist, and which created an inherent tension within the movement. Nevertheless, like so much of the campaigning of the

[25] Wetherell, 'Painting the Crisis', *History Workshop Journal*, 238.

[26] An example of the influence of notions of visibility in the Irish women's movement is Pat Murphy and Nell McCafferty (eds.), *Women in Focus: Contemporary Irish Women's Lives* (Dublin, 1986). See also Matthew Thomson, *Psychological Subjects: Identity, Culture, and Health in Twentieth-Century Britain* (Oxford, 2006); Joseph LaChapelle, 'Creativity research: Its sociological and educational limitations', *Studies in Art Education* 24/2 (1983), 132.

[27] Emily Robinson, Camilla Schofield, Florence Sutcliffe-Braithwaite, and Natalie Thomlinson, 'Telling Stories about Post-war Britain: Popular Individualism and the "Crisis" of the 1970s', *Twentieth Century British History* 28/2 (2017), 268–304.

[28] Bertrand, '"A Tool for Social Change": Community Photography at Belfast Exposed', *LISA*; Martin Drury, 'Community Arts – Defined but Denied', *Irish Review* 11 (Winter 1991/1992), 100.

1970s, the politics of representation was not so much a corollary of activism, but rather community activists placed representation at the centre of how they operated and how they conceived of political agency.[29] In community photography, the personal and the political were intertwined and representation became a key part of social action.

These notions of self-realization and empowerment were predicated on cultural readings of the camera and the image. This functioned in a variety of ways, combining the subjective, documentary, and mnemonic qualities of the image. The camera's status as conduit of personal viewpoint allowed for the photograph to act as a medium of self-exploration, while the photograph's ability to give a materiality—and hence significance and permanence—to an individual's perspective enabled the camera to function as a device for raising self-esteem for individuals and empowering groups. Furthermore, as *Camerawork* pointed out, a realist conception of photography united much of this work, which drew inspiration from socially motivated photographers such as Lewis Hine and Jacob Riis. At the heart of community photography was the image's documentary status, which underpinned the photograph's ability to generate factual information regarding issues which otherwise might go unrecorded, and its ability to show 'the things in our society that need to be changed'. Moreover, the status, gravity, and authority of documentary provided the appropriate medium for imbuing the participant communities with the status and dignity they might have lacked in other forms of representation. Finally, the photograph's association with memory also played an important role in many projects, allowing groups to capture and record older residents and historic traces. Although nostalgia has been conceived as a determining aspect of many community projects in this period, as Ben Jones has argued, this was not so much a conservative response, but rather can be 'understood as a critique of dominant stigmatizing representations of these neighbourhoods and their inhabitants'.[30] Indeed, the mnemonic qualities of the image were folded into a broader praxis of empowerment throughout many of the projects.

These organizations were largely financed through arts funding and local councils with some additional help from private benefactors, but this ad hoc funding meant that these projects were constantly faced by financial uncertainty. The Arts Council of Northern Ireland gave an interest-free

[29] Stephen Brooke, 'Space, Emotions and the Everyday: The Affective Ecology of 1980s London', *Twentieth Century British History* 28/1 (2017), 110–42.

[30] Ben Jones, 'The Uses of Nostalgia', 356.

loan to finance publication of the *Shankill Bulletin*, and grant-aided the construction and equipment of the dark room and funded running costs and paid towards the subsistence of Buzz Logan.[31] When the money ran out, Logan and the community worker Jackie Redpath attempted to turn the newssheet into a monthly red-top tabloid, intending that the newspaper would report on local issues, while the revenue it generated would be used to fund the darkroom and other community initiatives. However, in this period of prolonged economic crisis in west Belfast, it was impossible to generate the advertising revenue to support the paper, let alone make a profit.[32] Camerawork Darkrooms in Derry was set up with a grant from the Gulbenkian Foundation, while in May 1982, the Community Arts Committee of the Arts Council of Northern Ireland grant aided the group the sum of £2,000 for capital equipment.[33] The Republic of Ireland tended to have fewer funds available for this sort of project, but despite this, the North Centre City Community Action Project received funding from central government's Inner City Group. It was, however, constantly subject to concerns about its funding base.[34] In the early 1980s, the Arts Council attempted to respond to the evolving nature of the arts scene, setting up ACE in conjunction with the Gulbenkian foundation to report on how community arts should best be supported.[35] These funding structures played a crucial role in creating the culture and ethos of the movement. They enabled the state to open up—and shut down—spaces of communal activity and self-expression through the deployment of funding, but meant that the practice of these groups was often dictated by their precarity.

The arts projects shared with local government the language of community as a way of describing working-class culture and urban life. However, while this discourse provided access to funding and a way of rationalizing aims and needs, it was not without its problems. In the view of the philosopher Tom Duddy, writing in *Circa* in 1994, community arts were based 'on a questionable conception of art but also on a questionable conception of community. People who live in regional or inner-city communities are not as isolated, ideologically or structurally, as the community arts policy-makers

[31] PRONI AC10/3/2, Review of Community Arts 1981.

[32] Interview with Jackie Redpath, 2 August 2017.

[33] *Irish Press*, 21 October 1982, 6; PRONI AC10/3/8 Letter from Primrose Finnegan 26 May 1982.

[34] *Irish Independent*, 11 June 1981, 10.

[35] Fitzgerald 'Community Arts', in Carpenter and Murphy (eds.), *Art and Architecture of Ireland*, 421.

seem to think.' However, the use of the term 'community' was problematic, 'sometimes used as if it referred to a kind of semi-autonomous tribal group which has the power to reclaim a lost autonomy or forge a new identity for itself'. But in reality, the sort of communities which lent themselves to community arts projects, were not so much 'marginal' as 'trapped within... a complex social structure in which they happen to occupy structurally subordinate or "subaltern" positions. To say that they have been marginalised is not to say that they are virtually outside society but that they are a long way from the centres of powerful or profitable decision-making.'[36] These tensions of proximity and distance to power, of authority to visualize or be visualized, and the nature and purpose of 'community' ran throughout these projects.

Buzz Logan and landscape photography on the Shankill

Buzz Logan instituted a variety of community photographic initiatives on the Shankill, including classes, exhibitions, and workshops with professional photographers. His own initiation into the world of photography came in his early twenties, when he spent a year documenting the lives of fishermen on arctic trawlers, evoking the tradition of previous documentary makers such as John Grierson and Robert Flaherty, who had also trained their gaze on wild inhospitable seas.[37] From this beginning, he went on to work as a photographer in Dublin during the 1970s, photographing a range of news and feel-good stories for *Nusight*, the *Evening Herald*, and the *Irish Independent*. Alongside this work, he also spent his weekends walking around the north inner city, documenting the physical changes to the area, as local government and private development schemes stripped both population and buildings from much of the inner city, and the tenacity of the communities that remained in these locations.[38] He first started spending time on the Shankill in 1976. A friend who was teaching on the road told him that the conditions in this area were identical to many of the problems facing central Dublin, and indeed on the Shankill he witnessed a process he recognized from the southern capital repeating itself: problems of deindustrialization and poverty, compounded by spatial interventions of road widening and heavy-handed

[36] Duddy, 'Art & Society', *Circa* 67 (1994), 30.
[37] *Nusight*, October 1968, 11–13; *Irish Times*, 22 August 1989, 10.
[38] 'Collapse the Box: Buzz Logan', https://vimeo.com/130849199 (accessed 9 August 2018).

slum clearance.[39] The Shankill was also facing its own particular challenges, due to its location on the interface between unionist and nationalist communities. Logan started coming up to Belfast on his days off, taking photographs and getting to know local activists until, finally, he moved to Belfast permanently.[40]

Responding to these changes he saw around him, in 1979 Logan set up a community photographic studio in partnership with the Shankill Education Workshop, operating from their premises at 95 Shankill Road. It was advertised in the *Shankill Bulletin*: 'It won't be an ordinary camera club nor will it be a commercial photographic shop. It will have two main functions. One will be documentary, the life of the Shankill as it is now and holding exhibitions of pictures. The second function will be teaching photography to anyone even vaguely interested.'[41] From this workshop, Logan taught classes on developing and printing, while he also tutored students one-on-one outside the darkroom on how to select and compose images.[42] He also ran a summer programme in conjunction with the city council of Mac Airt camera clubs around the city at the Markets, Poleglass, Short Strand, the Shankill, Sandy Row, and Lenadoon.[43]

In 1981, Logan emphasized the subjective and ameliorative potential of community arts in a document for the city council. He defined community arts as both 'artistic activities by communities and in communities'. The work involved bringing artistic and cultural events to communities which may have been cut off from or deprived of such activities, and also included activities which heightened 'cultural awareness within communities, stimulate a greater level of artistic activity in the communities, or develop, through exposure to such activity, a greater awareness in the communities of their own identity and potential.'[44] For Logan, the importance of community arts lay in its many forms, and how it could respond to 'the problems of alienation and loss of identity in a mass-produced consumer society and in the desert of the inner city'. This work had a variety of effects, raising consciousness and allowing people to develop a sense of their own agency within broader economic and political structures. Community arts therefore had 'a political

[39] Ron Wiener, *The Rape and Plunder of the Shankill: Community Action – The Belfast Experience* (Belfast, 1980), 74; Sam Sloan, 'A Hard Youth in the Hammer', *Fortnight* 185 (1982), 1–19.

[40] Interview with Jackie Redpath, 2 August 2017.

[41] *Shankill Bulletin* 4, 2.

[42] Interview with Jackie Redpath, 2 August 2017.

[43] Interview with Jackie Redpath 2 August 2017.

[44] PRONI AC10/3/2 Review of Community Arts 1981.

purpose... a radicalizing role which enable a community to comprehend or work out its problems, which stresses the integrity and validity of the cultural experience of the community compared with what it sees as "elitist" art', while it also provided 'a means of helping people resolve or cope with conflict, form relationships as a means of enriching an otherwise drab existence'.[45]

Logan explored his conception of his community, and his role within it, in his photo book *The Shankill*. The book was published in 1979 by the Farset Co-operative Press, 'a community publishing venture, established to help local people get their views and creative ideas into print'.[46] He opened the photo book by stating that this was not a 'book about the "Northern Ireland Troubles"' as the 'public has by now become so used to seeing photographic books of bombings, shootings, rioting and of men with guns, that I must clearly state at the outset that this is not another one'.[47] Instead he focused on the social issues of the documentary tradition, portraying poverty and survival in a way which was both authentic and earnest: in black and white, uncropped, and without the use of a flash. In particular, Logan depicted the problems of urban redevelopment: 'the destruction which you will see reflected here has been caused, in the main, not by the bombs of paramilitaries, but by the bulldozers.'[48] The collection of photographs began with wide-angle shots of empty streets and boarded-up houses. A photo of a range of houses with their doors and windows bricked up was labelled: 'this was the Nick—once it was a community.'[49] This was followed by a great number of photographs of cleared sites and demolished buildings. One image, showing a woman pushing a buggy through an entirely empty landscape, was entitled 'refugees from redevelopment'.[50] The 'proposed site for the new leisure centre' was a derelict site under an ominous grey sky.

After this gloomy beginning, the mood brightened, moving through images of children playing, young people having fun on the street on 12 July, and older people and families socializing together (Figure 4.1). Notions of 'close knit community' and 'ordinary people' were central to Logan's introduction, and also framed how he composed his photographs. His images show a functional community, where people were united, smiled for the camera, and battled on through adversity. Indeed, the bulldozers and construction sites of urban modernization also played a role in this

[45] PRONI AC10/3/2 Review of Community Arts 1981.
[46] *Fortnight* (Oct-Nov 1980), 23. [47] Buzz Logan, *The Shankill* (Belfast, 1979), 3.
[48] Logan, *The Shankill*, 4. [49] Logan, *The Shankill Photographs*, 7.
[50] Logan, *The Shankill Photographs*, 14.

Figure 4.1 Shankill Photographs. Courtesy of the Trustees of the Buzz Logan Photographic Archive/Linen Hall Library.

construction of a unified community, antithetically defining the state as powerful, unseen, and creating an identifiable other for the community to rally against. It was a lyrical portrait of a neighbourhood that was seemingly disappearing—Logan's photography displayed his desire to document and celebrate these moments before they slipped finally out of view. Moreover, it was a community whose moments of cohesion, conflict, and formation took place on the street. Indeed, the streets which formed the backdrop to most of the images—the Shankill Road and the Victorian residential terraces around it—were contemporaneously under threat from the car and bulldozer.[51] The last photograph in the book worked within these themes; it was a view up the Shankill, just after it had stopped raining, the wet road glistened in the low sunlight, leading the eye to the wall of the Belfast Hills which dominated the vista. The section of the Shankill pictured was flanked by Victorian buildings, meaning that the photograph has a timeless quality: the road, the hills, and the light could have looked the same 100 years before. It is a photograph which suggests the continuity of the Shankill through time and that, in turn, the road and its residents would triumph over its present concerns.

Alongside its valedictory qualities, Logan's photography also had a utility in the community workers' interactions with the city council. As Jackie Redpath described, his photographs were 'both non-confrontational and massively confrontational'. Indeed, the veracity of the scenes they showed was crucial: 'you can't argue.'[52] The photographs 'told stories' which were simultaneously 'fantastic and ordinary'. A series of Logan's photographs portrayed a woman who was very ill, living in a solitary Victorian terrace in the middle of waste ground when all the other terrace houses around had been knocked down (Figure 4.2). 'You went to a meeting about housing and threw that down in front of the housing authorities…it was a powerful mechanism. And you were able to tell her story, because they weren't coming out to see her. So we took her to them.'[53] Here the perspective of community photography could push against the blind spots within the social surveys and censuses which local government used to make communities like the Shankill comprehensible. While Logan's images could be used to make a powerful statement to those in authority in this context, this campaigning use of photography could also be controversial with residents of

[51] Stephen Brooke, 'Revisiting Southam Street: Class, Generation, Gender, and Race in the Photography of Roger Mayne', *Journal of British Studies* 53/2 (2014), 472.
[52] Interview with Redpath. [53] Interview with Redpath.

Figure 4.2 Shankill Photographs. Courtesy of the Trustees of the Buzz Logan Photographic Archive/Linen Hall Library.

the area, due to community photography's dual purpose as campaigning tool and device for raising communal self-esteem. For example, many were upset by Logan's photograph of a dead dog on a patch of waste ground, considering it a poor reflection of the area.[54]

Unionist culture has often been portrayed in a limited and negative light, reduced to 'the Orange Order and Rangers FC', while Northern Irish Protestants have often perceived themselves as subject to 'cultural disparagement'.[55] In the words of Redpath, not only was Unionism 'badly represented' but also 'it represents itself so badly, that's the double trouble. We don't do the best by ourselves, and we get badly pictured.'[56] Moreover, even as the Shankill struggled to get a fair portrayal of itself in the media throughout the conflict, the community also struggled with questions of definition, aspiration, and identity as the area suffered the effects of conflict alongside the problems of deindustrialization.[57] But Logan's photography gave the residents of the Shankill more traction in shaping how they were represented. Many of the photographs produced by Logan and his students were published in the *Shankill Bulletin*. The magazine also became a forum for the representation and constitution of community life on the Shankill, publishing numerous photographs of social functions around the street, from Christmas at the old people's home to bonfires on Guy Fawkes Day. Moreover, Logan's photographic credentials connected the community activists of the Shankill to a world of journalists in Belfast. In Redpath's assessment, 'That meant we had a lot of access to the media and getting stuff out there, it put a different angle on the Shankill not just from within but through Buzz's media networks and friendships this community got introduced to a lot of people that normally they would be antagonistic to.'[58] They worked with Michael Longley at the Arts Council while Gilles Peress put on an exhibition on the Shankill as a result of his connections with Logan. When the 'A Day in the Life' project came to Ireland in 1985, Charles Traub and Jeremy Nicholl came to the area because of their associations with

[54] Interview with Redpath.

[55] Connal Parr, *Inventing the Myth: Political Passions and the Ulster Protestant Imagination* (Oxford, 2017), 13.

[56] Interview with Redpath.

[57] Colin Coulter, 'The Character of Unionism'; Jennifer Todd, 'Unionist Political Thought, 1920–72', in D. George Boyce, Robert Eccleshall, and Vincent Geoghan (eds.), *Political Thought in Ireland Since the Seventeenth Century* (London, 1993), 190–211; Thomas Hennessy, 'Ulster Unionism and Loyalty to the Crown of the United Kingdom, 1912–74', in *Unionism in Modern Ireland* (Dublin, 1996), 115–29.

[58] Interview with Redpath.

Logan.[59] In this way, Logan's photography gave the Shankill new networks and status from which the community would otherwise have been excluded.

Logan was only one of a myriad of people who sought 'community' on the Shankill. In 1975, Ron Wiener published *The Rape and Plunder of the Shankill*, influenced by the approach and themes of Michael Young and Peter Wilmott. He characterized the Shankill as a community where young people married locally before seeking accommodation close to their mothers, therefore preserving dense networks of mutual support in the area.[60] However, in Wiener's conception, this traditional pattern of working-class community formation was being broken up by urban modernization. Working with similar themes, in 1979, Paul Hamilton compiled and published a book of historic photographs, *Up the Shankill*, which projected an image of the area as a 'tough, hardworking' community which had a golden era of stability and neighbourly cohesion in the earlier years of the twentieth century.[61] Like Hamilton's, Logan's community photography was a visual analogue of contemporaneous sociology, epitomized by Wiener, seeking to trace communal formation and disintegration in British and Irish inner cities at this time. This was a community on the cusp of destruction due to forces outside its control, where working-class culture and solidarity lived on in ever more arduous circumstances.

Camerawork Derry and the Meaning of the Darkroom

During the late 1970s, the East London-based *Camerawork* magazine produced a special issue entitled 'Reporting on Northern Ireland', which included photo essays alongside articles on history, conflict, and surveillance in the province. Through the research for this issue, organizers at the Half Moon Photography Workshop made contact with community organizers in the Derry who were also interested in using photography as part of their practice.[62] From these initial exchanges, it became clear that the city of Derry would benefit from its own darkroom on the Half Moon model. From the summer of 1982, Trisha Ziff was stationed in Derry. Ziff, who was from the United States, had taught photography at Camerawork in Brixton,

59 Red Saunders and Syd Shelton, *Ireland: A Week in the Life of a Nation* (London, 1986).

60 Wiener, *The Rape and Plunder of the Shankill*, 74.

61 Paul Hamilton, *Up the Shankill* (Belfast, 1979), 1.

62 PRONI AC10/3/8 Camerawork Darkroom Derry; *Camerawork* 14 (1979); Graham, *Northern Ireland*, 24–5.

where she had already staged photographic exhibitions relating to children's facilities and the problems of the disabled.[63] In September, a group of six young people from Derry began working with her as voluntary workers, learning camera skills, with the aim that after a year of training they would find funding for wages, and at this point she would leave the project running and return to London.[64] The first months were taken up with learning basic photographic and project management skills and setting up the darkroom in a renovated building in London Street.[65] The volunteer group were then trained in black and white photography, uses of different papers, chemicals, and film, processing of colour slides and Kodachrome, the production of tapeslide shows, sound, and synchronization.[66] The group also had weekly 'educationals' which explored a spectrum of photographic genres, including portraiture, American photography of the 1930s, German photomontage, personal photography, and youth and subcultures.[67] They also built links with other groups around Derry city. They produced a publicity pamphlet, worked with a group from the Derry Youth and Community Workshop, and with an unemployed arts group based in Pilots Row Community Centre, helping them buy and furnish their darkroom and training them in basic black and white photography. It was intended that Derry Camerawork would serve as a hub of community photography in the north west, helping community groups to set up darkrooms and providing access to more specialized equipment.[68]

In the first year, the group were involved in a range of individual and collective projects which reflected local concerns, notions of individual self-expression, and desires to moves away from 'stereotypes' of Derry. For example, teenagers from the Derry Youth and Community Workshop completed projects on punks, old buildings, and a documentary record of the Bogside.[69] An all-women group also started working on an exhibition of documentary photography on ante-natal care in Derry, funded by the Workers Educational Association (WEA), while others documented an environmental scheme funded by Manpower on the Waterside and housing conditions in Rossville Flats.[70] The group also photographed scenes of

[63] *Irish Press*, 21 October 1982, 6.
[64] PRONI AC10/3/8 Camerawork Darkroom Derry.
[65] PRONI AC10/3/8 Camerawork Darkroom Derry.
[66] PRONI AC10/3/8 Camerawork Darkroom Derry.
[67] PRONI AC10/3/8 Camerawork Darkroom Derry.
[68] PRONI AC10/3/8 Camerawork Darkroom Derry.
[69] PRONI AC10/3/8 Camerawork Darkroom Derry.
[70] PRONI AC10/3/8 Camerawork Darkroom Derry.

vandalism around Derry, using 'photographs like this to help various tenants' associations in the city to show the housing executive the state of their areas. When presented with a photograph people are more inclined to listen to the tenants' complaints, again, tenants' associations do not have much money so we charge for the materials only.'[71] During 1988 and 1989, Camerawork held a series of workshops in black and white photography, aimed at introducing photography to those with little experience of the medium.[72] The first was specifically for the unemployed with the rest catering for women, young people, and other interested people.[73] This included a session on 'How to Use a Camera', followed by a slideshow on 'representation which is designed to make students look and think about pictures and what they are saying' with 'the slide show...designed to stimulate discussion' and 'introduce some photographic theory'.[74]

The group's first major exhibition was on youth unemployment, entitled 'Cat on a Bru', and held at the Orchard Gallery in August 1983. The exhibition took a day in the life of eight young unemployed people, with images depicting how they coped with their different situations while being unemployed, accompanied by first-person descriptions of their daily lives.[75] The aim of this exhibition was to move away from media depictions of unemployed young people, as statistics, social problems, or in the context of Derry, 'a rioter or a hood'. Rather, the photographs in the exhibition aimed to represent 'a more accurate and less sensational image'.[76] The photographs communicated something very different to the drama that usually accompanied reporting on the youth of Derry, recording instead the unseen images of how 'individuals cope with existence in a sort of limbo'.[77] A second exhibition concerned the mythical origins of Derry and included photographs of places as they were seen at the end of the 1980s, accompanied by captions explaining the folklore associated with these places. For example, they told the story of how the Foyle and Galliagh rivers got their names, and photographed the small pathways and fields which still existed around the new housing estates, and explained the stories connected with them. They also used sketches and drawings to depict scenes

[71] PRONI AC10/3/8 Camerawork portfolio.
[72] PRONI AC10/3/8 Letter from Julie Doherty, 6 June 1988.
[73] PRONI AC10/3/8 Letter from Julie Doherty, 6 June 1988.
[74] PRONI AC10/3/8 Letter from Julie Doherty, 6 June 1988.
[75] PRONI AC10/3/8 Letter from Julie Doherty, 6 June 1988.
[76] 'Cat on the Bru', *Circa* 12 (1983), 25.
[77] 'Cat on the Bru', *Circa* 12 (1983), 25.

which were impossible to photograph.[78] But the show not only aimed to depict authentic experiences of life in Derry for external observers, but also attempted to alleviate the negative impact of these experiences. Ziff reported that the shows were 'not just about taking photos but about interviews, organizing meetings, going out with a camera, all these things were new and took confidence'.[79]

Notions of communal and individual empowerment were central to Derry Camerawork's programme of projects. An article in *Fingerpost* magazine described how Derry City 'had been photographed, filmed, reported on and written about by journalists from all over the world', and Camerawork had been 'established primarily to give Derry people the chance to answer back, to show our city and our lives from our point of view'.[80] Indeed, the aim of much of their work was to 'make photographic and communication skills in this area accessible to communities who are already articulate about their needs and feelings but have no access to make these things heard, or to articulate them in a visual or presentable format'. In this, they 'operated an open door policy' for those who wanted to use their facilities, but gave 'priority to working with young people, the unemployed and especially women, since photography is historically a male dominated skill'.[81] This 'answering back' took several forms, both showing local activities, people, and places that did not make it into these international depictions, such as the boredom of unemployment and the vernacular knowledge of local routes and legends.[82] Indeed, these attempts to present an alternate, more authentic vision of the city were also acts of subjective restitution; the groups worked to 'articulate [the] feelings, fears beliefs and fantasies' of Derry residents in order to validate and celebrate local perspectives and concerns.

In 1985, the Channel 4 documentary *Picturing Derry* explored the tensions of representation and practice which provided much of the driver of Camerawork Derry's concerns. In this documentary, British photojournalists Terry Fincher and Clive Limpkin were portrayed as distant and lacking in empathy, viewing the violence in Derry as a sort of blood sport, with their sense of achievement coming from managing to photograph the day's most shocking image. Those involved in Camerawork Derry had a different perspective. A young woman reported being asked 'Why don't you take

[78] PRONI Letter from Trisha Ziff, 28 March 1986.
[79] PRONI AC10/3/8 Camerawork Darkroom Derry.
[80] PRONI AC10/3/8 Camerawork Darkroom Derry.
[81] *Fingerpost* 2/1 (1987), 48.
[82] PRONI AC10/3/8 Camerawork Darkroom Derry.

photographs of scenery?', a question to which she replied, 'If we take photograph of bushes, we don't know what's hiding behind them... my husband was shot dead in a really scenic setting.'[83] In the same programme, Willie Doherty described his ominous, silent photographs of Derry landscapes as 'my first act of resistance'.[84] These voices communicated the difficult choices photographers made when taking pictures in Derry, combining the need to portray the overlooked ordinariness of lives in the city, while also acknowledging the unique situations which they lived through every day. In Colin Graham's formulation, this made for 'an assertive stance' which was 'at once social and political', and in which the two ways of envisaging the city often came into conflict.[85] Moreover, this communal sense of aggrievement at being mis-portrayed also contributed to a heightened sense of ownership about who had the right, or authority, to represent the city.

Dublin and the recital of an incident that illuminates destinies

In the early 1970s, Mick Rafferty was living on Sherriff Street, near to Dublin's docks. He was working as an electrician while also involved in the British and Irish Communist Organization, spending his evenings and weekends organizing protests against the Vietnam War. However, during this period the focus of his political energies shifted from the global to the local. Through a friend living nearby, he began volunteering at a tenants' group that provided after school groups for local children, and through this became involved in community organizing. When the city council proposed to put an urban motorway through the area in 1975, Rafferty led the opposition, organizing a festival in Sherriff Street to galvanize the community against the scheme. Through this event, Rafferty met Fergus McCabe and Tony Gregory, and together they formed the North Central Community Council to serve as an umbrella group for local campaigning and activity. In 1978 this group was formalized as the North Centre City Community Action Project (NCCCAP), with Rafferty as its first director.[86] From its headquarters in Summerhill Parade, the NCCCAP organized a range of activities and training courses in the inner city, such as drama, sport, and

[83] *Picturing Derry*, dir. David Fox and Sylvia Stevens (1985).
[84] *Picturing Derry* (1985). [85] Graham, *Northern Ireland*, 31.
[86] Interview with Mick Rafferty, August 2017.

catering, funded by the government training bureau AnCO, which was in turn funded by the European Social Fund.[87] This small community organization rose to national prominence in 1982 when Tony Gregory became a TD and held the balance of power in Dáil Éireann, and Charles Haughey secured his support through promising a massive injection of cash into the inner city.

The 1970s and 1980s were a difficult period for the residents of the streets around Gardiner Street and North Strand Road.[88] The removal of the docks to the mouth of the Liffey alongside containerization had decimated the employment base of the area, while street trading was largely curtailed from 1983, leading to long running conflicts between traders, the gardai, and the city council.[89] From 1980, heroin deluged the Irish market and led to an epidemic frequently said to be at a higher rate in areas of inner city Dublin than comparable neighbourhoods in New York.[90] Many young men and women became addicted to the drug, leading to an increase in crime and large numbers of drug-related deaths. With unemployment as high as 75 per cent in some estates in the city centre, the government had few answers for how to address the structural shifts which were causing these problems. In this context, the 'inner city' developed a reputation for crime and danger, while images of ruined industrial buildings, vacant lots, and unemployed young men came to symbolize the failings of Ireland's modernization.[91]

The NCCCAP stepped into the gap left by the failings of state services and industrial policy. As part of its programme, the NCCCAP organized a range of courses and events based around photography. During 1980, they ran a twenty-week course in literacy and photography, put together through government financing, favours from contacts, and a lot of initiative. The course was held in Rutland Street school, which, 'due to the decay of the inner-city area, had classrooms vacant'. Alan Lund, who had been working freelance as a photographer on Ireland's music scene, taught the course.[92]

[87] Interview with Rafferty.

[88] David Limmond, 'Living and Learning in the Docklands of Dublin', *Studies* 97/388 (2008), 403–12.

[89] *Irish Press*, 6 December 1988, 2.

[90] Geoffrey Dean, *Drug Misuse in Ireland 1982–1983: Investigation in a North Central Dublin Area and Galway, Sligo and Cork* (Dublin, 1983).

[91] Erika Hanna, '"There is no Banshee Now: Absence and Loss in Twentieth Century Dublin', in Senia Pašeta (ed.), *Unfinished Futures: Essays about the Irish Past for Roy Foster* (Oxford, 2016), 223–34.

[92] Interview with Alan Lund, July 2017.

He approached Kodak, which provided rolls of film, paper, and chemicals. Rafferty had already made contact with Buzz Logan over their shared fights to block the construction of inner city motorways, and Logan helped them source second-hand cameras and darkroom materials from a shop on the Shankill.[93] More than forty people applied to take part in the scheme; the ten students who were chosen were aged between seventeen and twenty-nine, and had been previously unemployed.[94] They were paid about £18 a week by AnCo. Although some of the students faced the barrier of illiteracy, during the five-month programme they learned all aspects of photography, including composition, developing, framing, and mounting.[95] The final product of this programme was *Inner Word*, a magazine produced by the participants on this course, and a photography exhibition which ran at Rutland Street school during February 1980.[96] This interest in photography also led to other creative activities. In September 1979, the NCCCAP organized the Inner City Festival of Community Arts, a day of music and street theatre in the Gloucester Diamond.[97] They also held the Inner City Looking On Festival in 1982, featuring 'a unique photographic exhibition tracing the history of Dublin's city centre from the earliest days of photography right up to the present day'.[98]

Helena Dillon took one of the NCCCAP's media courses in 1983. Living near the docks, she had left school at the age of fifteen, and began a course on photography and publishing shortly after. The programme, taught in the basement of 29 Mountjoy Square, had developed out of Lund's first course, and combined practical and theoretical aspects of photography and publishing, alongside work experience at *In Dublin*. The journalist Denis Geoghegan taught writing, the author Ronan Sheehan taught history, while Alan Lund taught the mechanics of developing and printing. Through these classes, students learned the history and theory of photography and film and the politics of content and form, a curriculum influenced by the new themes and methods of cultural studies. As part of the course, Dillon went on several excursions across Ireland and further afield. The journalist and photographer Maggie O'Kane arranged for a group of young women from the course to go to Greenham Common with a group of Irish journalists. They spent a weekend at the site, camping with the other

[93] Interview with Rafferty.
[94] *Irish Press*, 7 February 1980, p. 4.
[95] *In Dublin*, 30 May 1980, 12; Interview with Lund.
[96] *Irish Press*, 7 February 1980, p. 4.
[97] *Irish Independent*, 12 September 1979, 8.
[98] *In Dublin*, 30 April 1982, 10.

protestors. They also went to Omagh for the weekend as part of a cross-community cultural initiative.[99] These skills were all used in the publication of *IC: The Inner City Magazine*, which was published by the group to provide 'a clear independent voice that inner-city inhabitants will recognize as their own'.[100] They photographed the neighbourhood and residents, conducted interviews, wrote articles, typeset them, and organized the layout of the page (Figure 4.3). They printed the paper once a month, raising money through advertising local businesses.

These photography courses were suffused with political ambitions. Rafferty and the other community activists of the NCCCAP believed that photography would be an appropriate way in to addressing some of the issues faced by young people in the inner city. At this time, many teenagers were still leaving school 'as if there was a job for them at 14, and they didn't need literacy really'.[101] However, with the collapse of many industries in central Dublin, the jobs their parents had done had largely disappeared from the city. Young men from the neighbourhood around Sherriff Street often ended up unemployed. Photography could provide a route in to complex discussions of identity, agency, and experience for those who might otherwise be locked out of these conversations due to poor literacy skills.[102] As Mick Rafferty explained to Colm Tóibín for an article in *In Dublin*, 'Taking photographs…caused the ten teenagers involved to look around them, to objectify their experience. Each photo makes the subjective process of seeing more valid, more significant. And thus the forces that combine to make such a scheme necessary in the first place can be examined.'[103] Interviewed in 2017, Rafferty quoted the Austrian philosopher Martin Buber to illustrate how he used the arts as part of community work:

> 'An anecdote is a recital of an incident that illuminates destinies.' Isn't that amazing. So when I think about it, amongst what we did to make people aware of where they stood in this city, where they stood in the changes, was instead of that phrase being an anecdote, it could be a photograph. It could be a play, it could be a scene which they developed.[104]

Despite Rafferty's radical ambitions, the aims of the project were in many ways realistic about the needs of the young people in the inner city.

99 Interview with Helena McDonnell.
100 *IC: The Inner City Magazine*, June 1983, 3.
101 Interview with Rafferty.
102 Interview with Rafferty.
103 *In Dublin*, 30 May 1980, 12.
104 Interview with Rafferty.

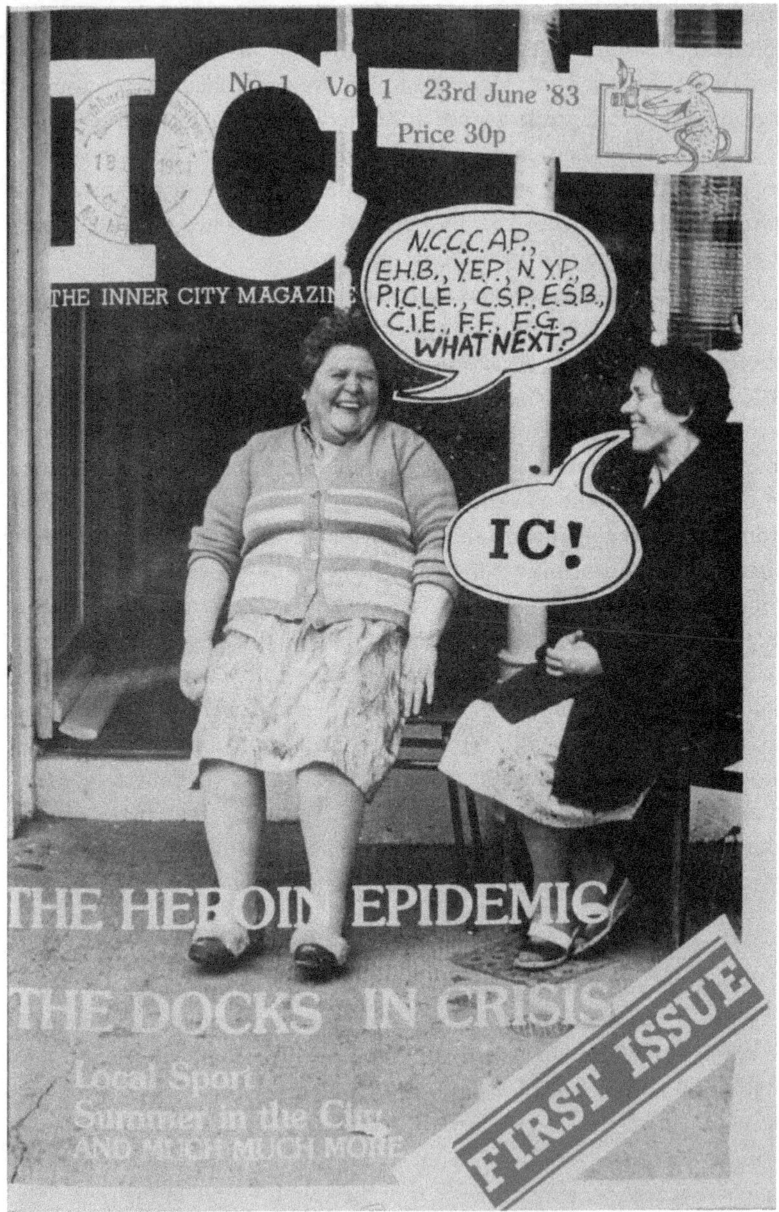

Figure 4.3 IC magazine. Image Courtesy of the National Library of Ireland.

In Dublin reported: 'Three out of the ten are now in full time employment; the other seven have either been employed in a temporary capacity or are being paid by AnCo for a period of four weeks while in employment elsewhere.'[105] Tóibín ended this discussion with a meditation on these tensions, telling the story of one of the students 'who now uses his skills at developing photographs to make a living', but who had difficulty 'reading the handwriting on dockets' who returned to Rutland Street on Wednesday afternoons to improve his reading. This, however, was always a compromised endeavour which, for Tóibín, explored its limitations explicitly: 'Such a course as he has attended cannot afford to indulge in the luxuries of self-discovery and simple creativity but must tackle matters far more basic such as the discovery of talents and potentialities previously hidden by a deprived and alienating environment. A discovery eventually leading to the ultimate aim of self-determination within a social and economic order.'[106]

The courses run by the NCCCAP were not the only initiatives in the city which explored identity and urban change through arts projects. Indeed, they were only part of a broader culture of community photography which led to a variety of projects in the city throughout the 1980s and 1990s. The Urban Folklore Project was organized in conjunction between UCD and FÁS, and provided training and work for ten unemployed young people.[107] It ran for eighteen months from the middle of 1979, depicting the survival of traditional trades, customs, and communities, set against a backdrop of a myriad of disused and unused places (Figure 4.4).[108] In the early 1980s, Fatima Mansions had faced 'two crises', due to Dublin Corporation using the flats as 'transitory' accommodation for 'problem families' from the city centre, and the heroin epidemic.[109] Leading on from this, the Fatima Development Group (FDG) was formed with the objective of engaging in the development of its own community. One of its projects was a community photography workshop run with the aim of documenting the refurbishment of the estate, in order to facilitate communication between the FDG and Dublin Corporation.[110] The Dublin City Community Photographic Archive was begun in 1987 at the Civic Museum, as a base for the photographic history of the contemporary city. The archive combined the work of eight documentary photographers, accompanied by

[105] *In Dublin*, 30 May 1980, 12.
[106] *In Dublin*, 30 May 1980, 12.
[107] Hanna, '"There is No Banshee Now"', 226.
[108] Hanna, '"There is No Banshee Now"', 223–34.
[109] Brian Harvey, *Resource Centres in Ireland* (Dublin, 1990), 25.
[110] Benson, *Art and the Ordinary*, 133.

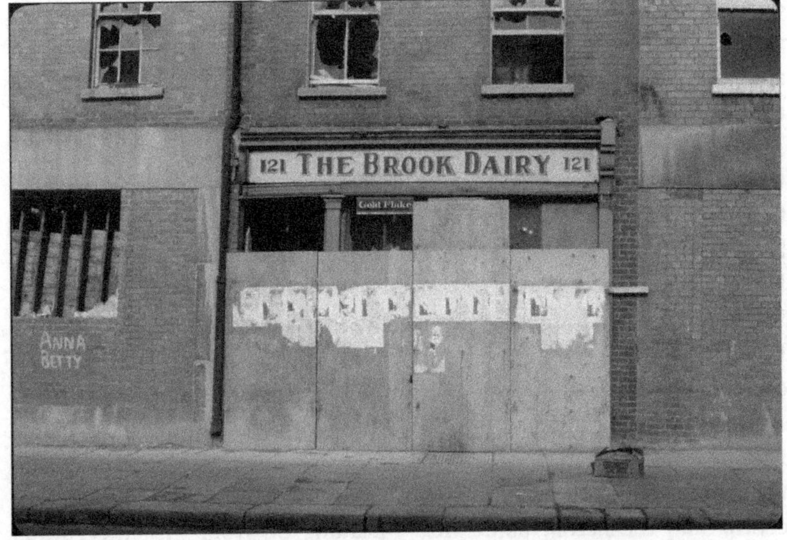

Figure 4.4 The Brook Dairy, Parnell Street, Dublin City (March 1980). Photograph by George McClafferty as part of the Urban Folklore Project. Copyright: National Folklore Collection, UCD.

older 'family snaps'. These collected vernacular photographs were seen to 'provide important details and clues related to past events, styles or activities that might otherwise be lost leaving huge gaps in our knowledge and awareness of the social history of a city and its people'.[111] Beth Rigell, the co-ordinator of the archive, conceived of it as 'a clearing house for photographs made by people who live in the area, their views as opposed to that of the outsider'.[112]

During this period, the economic profile of these urban areas was changing rapidly, as deindustrialization and containerization closed the traditional industries which had sustained them. In Dublin, the government began efforts to create low-taxation zones which would eventually lead to the construction of the International Financial Services Centre (IFSC). While bringing investment into the area, this scheme did little to replace the jobs lost by those who used to work on the docks where it now stood. Similar stories were repeated in Belfast and Derry where the state attempted to mitigate the impact of deindustrialization and violence through the construction of municipal amenities and shopping centres. As this was happening, town planners prospected for roads, commercial precincts, and housing units in these areas, measuring these neighbourhoods in terms of traffic flow and land use, but with little substantive engagement with the needs of the residents or the pre-existing uses and meanings of these spaces. Indeed, when the inner city was scrutinized at all, it tended to be for its problems, with social researchers conducting statistical studies on violence, crime, and drug usage. These reports were validated by a media culture which treated inner city residents with disdain if not outright hostility. The combined impact of these bureaucratic and governmental ways of seeing was a highly partial understanding of the central city which naturalized structural shifts to the economy and—through maps, plans, and graphs—situated the experiences of those impacted by these changes as subsidiary to progressivist narratives around economic growth and modernization. Indeed, they imagined the inner city as a *terra nullis* ready for development.

Representations of the inner city played a determining role in forging the future of these areas, so a great deal rested on whose vision of the area would predominate. In the emerging cultural politics of the radical left, culture was an important concern and creating new representations was a key

[111] National Visual Arts Library archive (NIVAL), 'Dublin Time Capsule: A Travelling Millennial Exhibition of Community Photography'.

[112] Kiang, 'Dublin Time Capsule', *Circa* 41 (1988), 30.

part of social action. Documentary photographs reoriented the gaze to the street, depicting the intimacy of interactions, the texture of skin and clothes, the individuality and cohesion of the community. In short, these photographs were profoundly humanistic in a way that other documents which sought to describe these areas were not. Indeed, similar dynamics were in action in photographic projects which explored the poetics of the ordinary and taxonomized the history of the neighbourhood, which provided ways of valorizing and eulogizing these locations. In the context of these competing portrayals, it is unsurprising that questions emerged over who had the right to visualize these areas; indeed, calls for the depiction of inner-city communities by people who came from within these neighbourhoods was part of a strategy which used the politics of authenticity in order to create space for alternate forms of authority for the future of these places.

But this conflict over the future of urban space was only part of the politics of visuality in the inner city. Political activism bound up with new conceptions of social psychology, which read negative portrayals of a locality or community as emotionally damaging and demoralizing and understood creativity as a conduit for raising self-esteem. Community arts circulated around these issues, teaching people to understand and critique how they were portrayed in the mainstream media, and in turn giving them the skills to generate new representations of themselves and their neighbourhood which more closely reflected their experiences and concerns. In this way, visuality was at the heart of conceptions of individual confidence, communal empowerment, and social justice. Indeed, the discourse of visibility became a key part of campaigns for groups who perceived themselves as marginalized, a discourse which would spread throughout new social movements in the 1980s and has become an accepted plank of campaigns for restorative justice across Ireland since the 1990s.

5

Flesh and Blood

Violence, Truth, and the Troubles, 1965–75

> Constable Robert Simpson: During the period I was there I did not see any civilians throwing stones.
>
> Lord Scarman: But your camera did.
>
> Simpson: Oh yes, I probably did, but as I say I did not see it; my camera was held above my head.[1]

On 12 August 1969, Constable Robert Simpson had been assigned the task of photographing criminal behaviour in Derry for future prosecution. However, as the day progressed and violence between nationalists and the Royal Ulster Constabulary (RUC) intensified, he found it harder and harder to get clear shots of the protagonists. Instead, he resorted to taking general photographs of the unfolding riot for illustrative and contextual purposes. Moving up William Street with a crowd of RUC and civilians, he was unable to see anything at all. Instead he lifted his camera above his head and aimed it in the direction of the noise and movement in front of him. The blurred and crooked photograph that resulted showed a crowd, a building, and some broken windows. During the subsequent tribunal which investigated the violence, the significance of this image was contested: Lord Scarman believed it showed unionist rioters stoning the windows of the nationalist Rossville Flats, an interpretation which Simpson attempted to refute. Instead he asserted that he had not actually *seen* what was in front of him as he took the photograph, and so could not authenticate what the image purported to show (Figure 5.1). The photograph—and the story Simpson told about how he came to take it—was just one of hundreds scrutinized by the tribunal. Indeed, the exchange between Scarman and Simpson is indicative of the complex and contingent processes through which images of violence

[1] *Public Inquiry into the Acts of Violence and Civil Disorder in Northern Ireland* (henceforth *Scarman Inquiry*), Day 17, 17 October 1969 (Constable Robert Simpson), 48, Institute for Advance Legal Studies (IALS).

Snapshot Stories: Visuality, Photography, and the Social History of Ireland, 1922–2000. Erika Hanna, Oxford University Press (2020).
DOI: 10.1093/oso/9780198823032.001.0001

Figure 5.1 Rossville Flats, 12 August 1969 (Robert Simpson). Image courtesy of the Chief Constable of the Police Service of Northern Ireland.

were produced, how they were used to make sense of civil disorder, and the problems and possibilities they contain for historians.

The walled city of Derry, a small city on the north-west border, straddles both sides of the river Foyle where it flows into the Atlantic. During the twentieth century the city suffered long-term problems of unemployment and poor housing, compounded by a Stormont government which directed industry and investment away from the region. These tensions increasingly came to a head in the febrile climate of the late 1960s. In this period, Derry's historic streets were frequently the backdrop to marches, riots, and violence. Catholic demands for housing, jobs, and equal rights were often met with heavy-handed responses both from unionist civilians and security forces; loyalist and republican paramilitary groups increasingly organized and came into conflict, while the government in Stormont oscillated between force and reform.[2] Throughout the summer of 1969, there were fractious exchanges between communities and the police in the city, which reached a crescendo in mid-August when three days of rioting, remembered as the Battle of the Bogside, followed the Protestant Apprentice Boys parade. In subsequent days, street protests spread to cities across Northern Ireland, leading to massive displacement of people, the destruction of property, and the deployment of the British Army.[3] With the introduction of internment during the summer of 1971, attacks on both people and property only increased, with a large part of Derry becoming a no-go area for British security forces. On 30 January 1972, journalists and photographers were back in the city for a banned civil rights march. In the late afternoon, thirteen civilians were shot dead by paratroopers, while another fifteen were wounded; 'Bloody Sunday' became the most famous day of the Troubles, and was an important moment of radicalization for Northern Ireland's Catholic community.[4] Indeed, almost 500 people would die during the course of 1972, the bloodiest year of the Troubles; by the end of that year, violence and divisions were entrenched which would last for a generation.

[2] On the start of the Troubles in Derry, see: Paul Bew, *Ireland: The Politics of Enmity 1789–2006* (Oxford, 2007), 486–555; Richard Bourke, *Peace in Ireland: The War of Ideas* (London, 2012), 81–117; Tim Pat Coogan, *The Troubles* (London, 2002), 71–190; Richard English, *Armed Struggle: The History of the IRA* (Oxford, 2012), 81–147; Thomas Hennessy, *The Origins of the Troubles* (Dublin, 2005), 237–85; Niall Ó Dochartaigh, *From Civil Rights to Armalites: Derry and the Birth of the Irish Troubles* (Cork, 1997), 111–52; Simon Prince, *Belfast and Derry in Revolt: A New History of the Start of the Troubles* (Dublin, 2011), 155–206.

[3] Paul Bew, *Ireland: The Politics of Enmity 1789–2006* (Oxford, 2007), 495.

[4] See, for example, Richard English, *Armed Struggle*, 148–56.

Violence and suffering is often at the centre of how Ireland has been imagined; however, its visual representation has often been characterized by the unease of its absence, with images documenting trace and aftermath rather than the event itself.[5] The Famine, which took place in the decade following the public announcement of the invention of the daguerreotype, is remembered through drawings of emaciated children published in the *Illustrated London News*, but no photographs seem to have been taken in the distressed districts during this time.[6] Photographs of the Easter Rising also tend to be strange and still. Largely taken in the aftermath of conflict, many depict civilians walking in confusion and wonder amongst the rubble of Sackville Street after the events had finished. This focus on the aftermath continued throughout the twentieth century. When a group of IRA activists made their way into Gough Barracks in Armagh in June 1954 and stole 300 rifles and other automatic weapons, Colman Doyle's image showed soldiers standing empty-handed and bemused by an open gate.[7] This sense of heightened emptiness also extended to ominous depictions of absence in the rural landscape, where the remains of poteen stills and cock fights in the provincial press indicated a culture existing just out of view of the authorities. When the Kerry farmer Mossie Moore was murdered over a boundary dispute in 1958, for example, the local press photographer Pádraig Kennelly's images showed the rushes in which his body was found, and a crowd of farmers looking on with a combination of concern and fascination.[8]

With the advent of modern cameras, photography of conflict moved from these traces to the depiction of violence in action. Robert Capa's iconic image of the Spanish Civil War, *Falling Soldier*, was one of the first images that displayed the moment of death for a mass audience. In the post-war era, images of suffering in Biafra and Vietnam, published in high resolution in the photographic press, reinforced photography's ability to depict suffering. A new cohort of photojournalists came to prominence in this period who attempted to use photographs to bear witness, campaign for those without power, and

[5] Themes explored in Justin Carville, 'The Violence of the Image: Conflict and Post-Conflict Photography in Northern Ireland', in Liam Kennedy and Caitlin Patrick (eds.), *The Violence of the Image* (London, 2014), 60–77.

[6] Carville, *Photography and Ireland*, 64; Gail Baylis and Sarah Edge, 'The Great Famine: Absence, Memory, and Photography', *Cultural Studies* 24/6 (2010), 778–800; Emily Mark-FitzGerald, *Commemorating the Irish Famine: Memory and Monument* (Liverpool, 2013); Emily Mark-FitzGerald, 'Photography and the Visual Legacy of Famine', in Oona Frawley (ed.), *Memory Ireland Volume 3: The Famine and the Troubles* (Syracuse, 2014), 121–37.

[7] Colman Doyle, *Ireland: 40 Years of Photographs* (Dublin, 1994), 20.

[8] Padraig Kennelly Archive: http://www.kennellyarchive.com (accessed 10 August 2018).

reveal injustice and wrongdoing. But inevitably these new technologies also brought with them new questions regarding the ethics of seeing. A first wave of photographic theorists, led by Susan Sontag, understood images of conflict to be voyeuristic and clichéd, the instantaneity of the camera divorcing the scene from any causal analysis, and desensitizing the viewer to the suffering in the frame through repeated viewing. Since the 1980s, these polemics have framed debate on taking and looking at photographs of violence, while photojournalists have been condemned for their unethical voyeurism and for using sympathy as spectacle. But more recently a new wave of scholarship has sought to challenge these certainties, and the over-determining conception of the powerlessness of the subject of the image. Susie Linfield has explored the evolution of photojournalism alongside a human rights discourse and has placed the onus on the viewer to develop a more ethnical praxis of looking. Working with similar themes, Ariella Azoulay has explored the 'civil contract' which has allowed people to pursue political agency predicated on notions of photographic citizenship.[9]

Unlike earlier conflicts on Irish soil, during the Troubles photographers were able to catch bombings and shootings at the moment they took place; a visual cacophony of mid-air bricks, hailstorms of glass, and men in running battles on the streets, under an ashen sky. These black and white images appeared repeatedly across the global media throughout the 1970s and 1980s, and played a crucial role in shaping the international visual economy of the conflict.[10] Indeed, during its long course a whole range of photographers turned their gaze on the Troubles, including Gilles Peress, Don McCullin, and Clive Limpkin. These photographs have received extensive treatment by art historians and cultural critics as straddling traditions of social realism and war photography; as part of a genre of 'combat photography that the public had been accustomed to since the Korean and Vietnam wars'.[11] Indeed, in line with broader commentary on images of violence, these

[9] Susie Linfield, *The Cruel Radiance: Photography and Political Violence* (Chicago, 2010); Ariella Azoulay, *The Civil Contract of Photography* (Cambridge, MA, 2012).

[10] Tom Collins, *The Centre Cannot Hold: Britain's Failure in Northern Ireland* (Dublin, 1983); Charles Messenger, *Northern Ireland: The Troubles* (London, 1985).

[11] Justin Carville, 'Renegotiated Territory: The politics of place, space and landscape in Irish Photography', *Afterimage* 29/1 (2001), 6; Carville, *Photography and Ireland*, 125–59; John Taylor, *War Photography: Realism in the British Press* (London, 1991), 116–57; Graham Dawson, 'Trauma, Place and the Politics of Memory: Bloody Sunday, Derry, 1972–2004', *History Workshop Journal* 59/1 (Spring 2005), 221–50; Tom Herron and John Lynch, '"Like 'Ghosts who Walked Abroad": Faces of the Bloody Sunday Dead', *Visual Culture in Britain* 7/1 (2006), 59–77; Trisha Ziff, 'Photographs at War', in Bill Rolston (ed.), *The Media and Northern Ireland: Covering the Troubles*, (London, 1991), 187–206.

photographs were extensively critiqued for the way that they dehumanized both sides, depicted the troubles as an overwhelmingly male affair, and constructed the conflict as a series of 'flashpoints' at street corners divorced from context.[12] But this wasn't the whole story. There were also a large number of—largely local—photographers who, as Colin Graham has noted, 'were committed, either out of a sense of the integrity of documentary truth or the importance of an alternative politics, or both, to telling the story differently'.[13] In Derry, for example, this included the photographers Michael Rodgers, Eamon Melaugh, and Barney McMonagle, who recorded events from a perspective 'inside the community'.[14] However, these photographs only had a limited circulation contemporaneously, which has increased slightly in the aftermath of conflict, but which never rivalled the effect of images by the photo-celebrities of the 1970s. This differential impact indicates that the 'problem' of photography during the Troubles is not just one of cliché, but also one of power and networks.

Debates regarding the ethics of photographing violence often circulate at a theoretical level; it is more difficult to understand why images of violence were taken, or how they were read at the time. However, the Scarman and Widgery tribunals, where the meaning of images was discussed extensively, can provide a range of evidence concerning these issues. On 27 August 1969, Lord Scarman was appointed to lead an inquiry to ascertain the facts of the Battle of the Bogside, the Burning of Bombay Street, and other disturbances across the province during that year. The tribunal sat for more than 300 days; the testimony of its 440 witnesses provided a revealing and detailed picture of a society on the cusp of transformative change. In contrast, the inquiry into Bloody Sunday was much more narrowly focused and reached its conclusions more quickly. Facing outrage across Ireland, on 31 January 1972 the Home Secretary, Reginald Maudling, appointed Lord Chief Justice John Widgery to lead an investigation to determine the circumstances of the civilian deaths on Bloody Sunday. The tribunal soon became another area of grievance for Derry's Catholics; in its scope and conduct the process frequently gave more consideration to the needs of the army than to the victims and relatives of the dead. Moreover, its findings—that soldiers

[12] Belinda Loftus, 'Photography, Art, and Politics: How the English make Pictures of Northern Ireland's Troubles', *Circa* 13 (1983), 10.

[13] Graham, *Northern Ireland*, 10.

[14] Eamon Melaugh, *Derry: The Troubled Years* (Derry, 2005); Niall Ó Dochartaigh and Lisa Rodgers, 'Images from the Inside: Michael Rodgers's Photographs of the Civil Rights Campaign and the Birth of the Troubles in Derry', Field Day Review 9 (2013), 74–99.

were fired upon first, that they shot only at suspected gunmen, and that some of the dead had been handling firebombs or guns—was a second act of violence towards the already traumatized Bogside community. As Dermot Walsh has observed, the inquiry had:

> a devastating effect on nationalist confidence in the rule of law and the integrity of the state. If they could not depend on the judicial arm of the state to deliver justice when they were shot on the streets en masse by British soldiers, why would they withhold support from those within their community who would use force of arms in an attempt to overthrow that state?[15]

An examination of how photographs were used at the Scarman and Widgery inquiries allows us to explore questions surrounding the ethics of seeing in a moment of violence and an era of fast shutter speeds. These tribunals show how photographers negotiated their equivocal role as bystander and participant, and the way that they attempted to use photography in order to campaign for the rights of those in the frame. Reflecting the ambivalence of Seamus Heaney's dictum that 'there is no such thing as innocent bystanding', these photographers attempted to intercede on the behalf of others, with their images inflected by an uneasy combination of sympathy and anger. But the minutes of the tribunals show how the impact of the image was never quite what photographers hoped or expected. Indeed, whether their intervention had any beneficial impact or only resulted in spectacularizing—and aggravating—the situation was both complex and multifaceted.[16] At both tribunals, photographic evidence was accorded a special status due to broadly held perceptions of its truth value in contrast to oral testimony. The effect of the photograph was a product not only of what was caught in the frame but also where the photograph moved and who it was seen by after it was developed. In these tribunals, the existence of certain photographs served to anchor causal narratives of violence around certain places and moments, while each photograph was understood to provide a range of plausible truths which largely mapped on to pre-existing and predetermined concerns. Moreover, the conversations about these photographs focused on the problem of making sense of violence when the image gave

[15] Dermot Walsh, *Bloody Sunday and the Rule of Law in Northern Ireland* (Basingstoke, 2000), 87.

[16] Seamus Heaney, *The Spirit Level* (London, 1996), 36.

no indication of the speed or direction of the action it portrayed; the debates reflected Sontag's critique that photographs are atomizing, punctual, and discrete, and lacking in the narrative coherence necessary for understanding.[17] Despite (or because of) these limitations, these photographs became a crucial technology of state for linking the Bogside and Westminster, and their properties played a constitutive role in constructing and validating state-sponsored narratives of violence in Northern Ireland. The instantaneity of photography became a key part of how narratives were constructed, blame was apportioned, and photographs were re-read to support the arguments of the British state. Indeed, the plausible truths contained in these images relied specifically on the atomized nature of the image and the absence of any sense of long-term causation, qualities which coincided with the predetermined narratives of the British state in Northern Ireland.

Battle of the Bogside and the Scarman Tribunal

On the morning of 12 August 1969, the Protestant Apprentice Boys walked out from St Columb's Cathedral through the city of Derry, retracing their steps, and the steps of their fathers, in marching around the city to commemorate the lifting of the siege of the city in 1689. However, while the suits, sashes, and music echoed what had gone before, in 1969, the city had changed. A combination of housing shortages, unemployment, a civil rights movement at home, and global protest on television had radicalized the Catholic community, and violence was becoming increasingly frequent. The morning had been characterized by low-level disturbances between groups; some Apprentice boys tossed coins from the city walls onto bystanders below, while around 2.30pm Catholic onlookers threw nails at police, followed by stones; 'from this small beginning developed a riot which enveloped the city for two days and nights and which became known as the Battle of the Bogside.'[18] Rippling out from the Bogside, violence spread across Northern Ireland. The impact of these events for both Ireland and Britain cannot be overstated. These riots led to hundreds of injuries, nine deaths, the burning of large areas of residential Belfast, and the displacement of more than 2,000 people from their homes. These disturbances only ended when the British Army was deployed to the streets of Belfast and Derry—heralding the

[17] Judith Butler, 'Photography, War, Outrage', *PMLA* 120/3 (2005), 823.
[18] Hennessy, *The Origins of the Troubles*, 239; Richard Bourke, *Peace in Ireland*, 100.

beginning of Operation Banner, the single longest continuous deployment of the British Army, which continued until 2007.[19]

There were many different types of photographer in Derry during the days of violence in August 1969—for example, Robert Simpson, an RUC photographer, James Gibson O'Boyle, a photographer with an American newspaper, and Bernard McMonagle, a resident of Bogside, all took photographs which appeared before the Scarman Tribunal. Indeed, Scarman estimated that there were approximately 200–300 pressmen in Derry on 12 August, present in the city only to record the anticipated disturbances.[20] These photographers played an important role in creating the atmosphere of tension they sought to record. Many testimonies given at the Scarman Tribunal record the city not only as a site of violence, but also as a site of spectacle—accompanying every crowd throwing stones, there was a second crowd observing and recording events.[21] For example, O'Boyle's 'first hint…of any kind of trouble' was when he was taking pictures of the parade in front of the City Hotel and 'half a dozen or so of the reporters went galloping by with their equipment yelling at me that it had just started down at Waterloo Square'.[22] These photographers also became subject to attack themselves. O'Boyle reported that he was 'was accosted by crowds' in Little James Street, 'stone throwing, threatening to smash the camera, shoving you around, threatening to hit you'.[23] Bernard McMonagle described the cameramen as 'a target for everybody these days…sometimes I would be stopped by the police and sometimes stopped by people in the Bogside.'[24]

The RUC interpretation of the Battle of the Bogside was put forward by Constable Robert Simpson, who presented a book of fifty-seven photographs of the events of 12 August to the tribunal. His role, as a police photographer, was to be present at the scene of violence in order to take photographs of 'persons engaged in crime for identification purposes'.[25] His photographs included images of the crowd watching the Apprentice Boys' parade, a petrol bomb exploding, men throwing stones, and women and TV crews watching events from doorways. Several of the photographs retain the marks of their disciplinary function: many of the images have the faces of stone throwers,

[19] Andrew Sanders and Ian Wood, *Times of Troubles: Britain's War in Northern Ireland* (Edinburgh, 2012), 109.

[20] IALS *Scarman Inquiry*, Day 13, 13 October 1969, 13.

[21] See also Clive Limpkin, 'The Press', in *The Battle of the Bogside* (unpaginated).

[22] IALS *Scarman Inquiry*, Day 21, 30 October 1969 (James O'Boyle), 60.

[23] IALS *Scarman Inquiry*, Day 13, 13 October 1969 (O'Boyle), 15.

[24] IALS *Scarman Inquiry*, Day 25, 13 November 1969 (Bernard McMonagle), 15.

[25] IALS *Scarman Inquiry* Day 16, 16 October 1969 (Robert Simpson), 41.

and even those engaged in minor acts of dissent, such as pushing over crash barriers, ringed and identified.[26] In taking these photographs, Simpson shaped how the disturbances on the streets of Derry were recorded and understood. From the images that he submitted to the tribunal, it is clear that Simpson hid behind police lines, focusing his gaze on the Catholic crowds who confronted him, showing only the backs of RUC officers, and excluding acts of violence towards the Catholic community from the image frame. For example, Simpson's photograph No. 23, taken in Rossville Street, shows a crowd in the distance, while No. 24 shows a group of young men seemingly rioting in isolation—the targets of their stones and any other crowds they were interacting with remain unrecorded (Figure 5.2). Indeed, the effect of Simpson's positioning on how he recorded events can also be seen with regard to his photograph 57 (discussed above). Moving as part of a crowd of RUC and civilians as they entered the Bogside, he was unable to get a clear enough view to record acts of vandalism and assaults against residents of the area.

Many Catholic witnesses called before the tribunal refused to cooperate with the RUC's uses of visual evidence, and in the process suggested the presence of other perspectives on scenes of violence. When Eddie McAteer, the former Nationalist MP for Derry, was shown photographs of stones on the ground, he pointed out that there was nothing to prove whether these had been thrown by Catholic youths, or by Protestant crowds at the Catholic crowd.[27] Eamon Melaugh, a high-profile Catholic activist in Derry in the 1970s and 1980s, who took photographs throughout the Troubles, used his knowledge of photography to attempt to subvert the state's power as personified by the RUC photographer. Asked if Simpson's photograph No. 7 showed a man throwing a stone at the Protestant procession, he replied: 'Well, it could be, yes. You could get that impression. You could also, if you look at the photograph quite closely, get the impression that he was watching a missile coming in his direction and was going to take evasive action.'[28] Pushed again to concede that this man was throwing a stone, he went on: 'I would reluctantly agree although, my Lord, I am somewhat of an expert on photographs, a very keen amateur photographer, and I can assure you that still photographs can give the wrong impression.'[29] He also tried to

[26] IALS Image 2 and Image 8, Disturbances at Relief of Derry Celebration, 12-8-69, Exhibit 32.
[27] IALS *Scarman Inquiry*, Day 7, 26 September 1969 (Edward MacAteer), 50.
[28] IALS *Scarman Inquiry*, Day 24, 12 November 1969 (Eamon Melaugh), 14.
[29] IALS *Scarman Inquiry*, Day 24, 12 November 1969 (Melaugh), 14.

Figure 5.2 Crowd in Little James Street, 12 August (Robert Simpson). Image courtesy of the Chief Constable of the Police Service of Northern Ireland.

push against the logic of these RUC photographs in other ways. On several occasions, when asked to identify people in the photographs, he claimed to 'know them, but I do not know their names', despite the small and close-knit nature of the Catholic community in the Bogside.[30] Seán Keenan, chairman of the Derry Citizens' Defence Association, took a similar tactic when dealing with images presented to him, answering, 'I have seen him around' and 'could be somewhere around there' to questions about several people's names and addresses.[31] Indeed, he failed to recognize a single person from Simpson's fifty-seven photographs.

These RUC images of rioters were also interrogated by photo-journalists who took their photographs from alternate viewpoints, in so doing foregrounding violence *towards* the residents of the Bogside. Two photographs submitted as evidence by Father Mulvey, the Catholic priest for the area, caused considerable controversy and were the subject of intense debate at the tribunal.[32] The first image, labelled Exhibit 6, showed a crowd of men, some in the uniform and helmets of the RUC and some in suits clambering across a barricade. The scene was dominated by a billboard advertising Guinness, declaring jarringly: 'The Most Natural Thing in the World' (Figure 5.3). The second photograph, Exhibit 7, showed another mixed crowded of darkly clothed men, running away from the camera up a street with a high building on the left. For Mulvey, there was a looming sense of determinism about the events of the Apprentice Boys march, which the photographs both contributed to and reinforced. Although he had not been present at the time they were taken, for Mulvey, the photographs he presented showed that what he had 'expected to happen' and 'feared might develop' had occurred: 'these photographs reveal the police in riot equipment moving into the Bogside area accompanied by a certain number of civilians some of whom are throwing missiles';[33] moreover, Protestant civilians and police were acting together in entering the Bogside.[34] Mulvey's comment that 'I would only regard it as a community revolt rather than a street disturbance or a riot' was produced in the final report and has been frequently reproduced by historians; the events 'portrayed in these pictures' were critical to his 'assessment of these riots'.[35]

[30] IALS *Scarman Inquiry*, Day 24, 12 November 1969 (Melaugh), 14.
[31] IALS *Scarman Inquiry*, Day 18, 27 October 1969 (Seán Keenan), 51.
[32] IALS *Scarman Inquiry*, Day 6, 25 September 1969 (Father Mulvey), 63.
[33] IALS *Scarman Inquiry*, Day 7, 26 September 1969 (Father Mulvey), 1.
[34] IALS *Scarman Inquiry*, Day 6, 25 September 1969 (Father Mulvey), 64.
[35] IALS *Scarman Report*, 74; *Scarman Inquiry*, Day 7, 26 September 1969 (Father Mulvey), 1.

Figure 5.3 RUC entry into the Bogside, 12 August 1969 (James Gibson O'Boyle).

These photographs had been taken by James Gibson O'Boyle, a photographer with the *Pottstown Mercury*, a newspaper based in Pennsylvania. O'Boyle had been on his way to Israel in the summer of 1969, but had changed his plans and travelled to Derry when he heard news of the violence in the city. Wholly converted to the cause, a few days after the Battle of the Bogside he abandoned his camera and took an active role in the defence of the Catholic areas of the city. O'Boyle saw himself as a photographer-adventurer; he preluded his discussion of photographs by recounting how he had climbed on to a shed with five or six other photographers on the corner of Rossville Street between 6.30 and 7pm on the day of the Apprentice Boys parade.[36] He described the scene:

> Suddenly there was this breakthrough and as the first people of the crowd started to run I looked round sort of frantically and the one police armoured car drove across and I suddenly saw these civilians there and started taking pictures—these are some of them. I took some pictures and as the police charged by I started to focus again on the civilians. It was almost exclusively civilians who were tearing down the barricade.[37]

When the crowd started to stone O'Boyle and the other photographers on the roof, he had to jump off; but the pictures he took before this played a definitive role in forming the tribunal's line of inquiry regarding the police entry into Rossville Street. He described Exhibit 6 as showing 'the police charging from William Street and Little James Street across the barricades erected at the foot of Rossville Street, and police and civilians charging behind the armoured car in the first photograph'.[38] He told the tribunal that if the photograph could have been extended to the right, 'there would be the crowd from the Bogside running in front of the two armoured cars and there would be also some police and some more civilians—quite a few more civilians'.[39] Exhibit 7 showed 'more of the police charge and civilians throwing stones through the windows of the flats on the right hand side of Rossville Street, facing in'.[40] The events presented by O'Boyle's photographs were corroborated by Bernard McMonagle, a control mechanic and amateur photographer, who ascended to the fourth floor of the high flats on Rossville

[36] IALS *Scarman Inquiry*, Day 13, 13 October 1969 (O'Boyle), 6–7.
[37] IALS *Scarman Inquiry*, Day 13, 13 October 1969 (O'Boyle), 7.
[38] IALS *Scarman Inquiry*, Day 13, 13 October 1969 (O'Boyle), 7.
[39] IALS *Scarman Inquiry*, Day 13, 13 October 1969 (O'Boyle), 7.
[40] IALS *Scarman Inquiry*, Day 13, 13 October 1969 (O'Boyle), 7.

Street in order to record the baton charge by the police towards the Bogside.[41] He told the tribunal: 'No. 1 was the very first photograph I took on the evening of the 12th approximately about a quarter to seven, around that, and in it you will see the first wave of police coming towards the Bogside and in amongst them you will see a lot of civilians and particularly there is one there throwing stones towards the windows of the low maisonettes. There was no attention paid to him at all.'[42]

The RUC officers interviewed resisted the interpretation of events presented in these photographs. They privileged their own memories and experiences above the images captured by O'Boyle, and used their testimonies to shore up the version of events presented by Simpson. County Inspector G. S. McMahon agreed that Exhibit 6 indicated that the police must have been aware of the presence of civilians, but the photograph did not show other important information necessary to assess the scene, including what was 'in the immediate front of the police'.[43] McMahon's reflections on the reality presented by the image provide an echo of Stanley Cavell's observation: 'What happens in a photograph is that *it* comes to an end... When a photograph is cropped, the rest of the world is cut out. The implied presence of the rest of the world, and its explicit rejection, are as essential in the experience of a photograph as what it explicitly presents.'[44] McMahon's acceptance of the image was not typical of RUC officers interviewed. Drawing on a perception that the 'taint of artistry' is 'equated with insincerity or mere contrivance',[45] Head Constable Thomas Fleming used the picture's aesthetic and compositional qualities to throw doubts on its authenticity, stating that 'this gives a very beautiful picture'. But he could not 'relate that photograph to 7pm on 12th October [sic]'.[46] Indeed, many of the RUC officers involved in the operation on the 12 August also used the position and materials of the barricade in order to debate the veracity of the photograph. Sergeant Henry Pendleton stated that 'this barricade was not of this structure at all. At no time did I see what you see in Exhibit 6.'[47] District Inspector Kenneth Cordner said, 'the fact that the barricade does not appear to be the barricade I went over and the Land Rover is not in position, the armoured car is not in

[41] IALS *Scarman Inquiry*, Day 25, 13 November 1969 (Bernard McMonagle), 11.

[42] IALS *Scarman Inquiry*, Day 25, 13 November 1969 (McMonagle), 12.

[43] IALS *Scarman Inquiry*, Day 11, 2 October 1969 (County Inspector G. S. McMahon), 9.

[44] Stanley Cavell, *The World Viewed: Reflections on the Ontology of Film* (Cambridge, MA, 1979), 24.

[45] Susan Sontag, *Regarding the Pain of Others* (London, 2004), 23.

[46] IALS *Scarman Inquiry*, Day 13, 13 October 1969 (Head Constable Thomas Fleming), 81.

[47] IALS *Scarman Inquiry*, Day 14, 14 October 1969 (Sargent Henry Pendleton), 69.

position, there were no police behind it like that, that does not represent what I saw.'[48] Of particular significance, in his recollection 'there were no civilians at Meehans, there was not a soul in that street except police—not a living soul except police'.[49]

Some of the photographs presented before the tribunal showed things that could not be corroborated or remembered by any party. While hearsay or second-hand oral evidence were immediately dismissed by Scarman as having no validity within the court, there was no framework for dealing with similar problems with photographic evidence, which were instead handled uneasily by witnesses and barristers alike. One of the most contentious images debated at the inquiry was a photograph showing a group of policemen in the foreground with their backs to the camera, being stoned by a group of young men located at the back of the photograph (Figure 5.4). On the right-hand side, there was what appeared to be an older man, in a sports coat and felt hat, pointing a gun at the police officers. The existence of the man on the right aiming the firearm was crucial; it was 'one direct piece of evidence of a firearm in the hands of a Bogsider during the August riots'.[50] But this photograph revealed the conflicting and problematic nature of photographs as sources. It was taken by Kenneth Mason, a photographer attached to the *Daily Telegraph* and *Morning Post*, and first appeared in the *Sunday Times* on 17 August. Called to the witness box, Mason attested that the confrontation the image depicted had lasted less than a minute.[51] Indeed, when he took the picture he had not seen 'any figure in the vicinity of that buttress'.[52] He became aware of the figure while he was taking the next shot, and then he moved further to the left to try to get a clearer image of the man with the gun. Mason had some experience of guns; he told the tribunal that the man was handling the weapon 'A little nervously I would say—not used to firearms'.[53] However, he never saw him fire the gun.

None of the policemen who had been present in Columbcille Court remembered the figure by the wall being in possession of a gun. Constable Ian Forbes, who was in the foreground of the image, remembered seeing the man during the incident, but not at the wall, and not with a firearm; rather he remembered the figure amongst the group throwing stones. Constable

[48] IALS *Scarman Inquiry*, Day 16, 16 October 1969 (District Inspector Kenneth Cordner), 22.
[49] IALS *Scarman Inquiry*, Day 16, 16 October 1969 (Cordner), 23.
[50] *Violence and Civil Disturbances in Northern Ireland in 1969*, 79.
[51] IALS *Scarman Inquiry*, Day 15, 15 October 1969 (Kenneth Mason), 3.
[52] IALS *Scarman Inquiry*, Day 15, 15 October 1969 (Mason), 4.
[53] IALS *Scarman Inquiry*, Day 15, 15 October 1969 (Mason), 4.

Figure 5.4 Columbcille Court, 13 August (Kenneth Mason).

Thomas McLaughlin, the policeman on the extreme right of the photograph, also observed the man in the middle of the crowd throwing stones.[54] District Inspector F. I. Armstrong, the officer in charge of the police in this area on 13 August, had received no reports from any of his men of the presence of a gunman or of the existence or use of firearms in Columbcille Court.[55] Despite the dissonance between the photograph and the policemen's memories, this image took on a central importance in the inquiry regarding events in Derry, as the presence of the figure with the gun validated the RUC narrative that they responded legitimately and proportionately to the threat of an IRA rising in the Bogside. Indeed, several RUC officers attempted to reconcile the photograph with their memories. Armstrong stated that 'that man could actually be there with a gun and none of them have seen him', due to the way in which photographs simplified complexities of movement, sound, depth, and time into a single, readable image:

> it is very easy, looking at a photograph, to study it and say why could not, or why would not, they have seen them, but if that were a moving picture it is an entirely different set up, particularly when you have got to watch the stones and we were watching stone throwers all the time. When watching people in action, anybody standing you would not notice.[56]

Indeed, McLaughlin, Forbes, and Constable Albert Neill all remembered having a gun pointed towards them from a different vantage point while in Columbcille Court; McLaughlin attested to the presence of 'a youth on top of the small flats and he had, to me it was a rifle, and several times he was sighting it down the gap there towards the police from the top of the flats'.[57]

As this discussion suggests, at the Scarman Tribunal, photographs submitted by journalists, residents, and the RUC, were co-opted into the judicial process and became loci of debate regarding the course of events. These images served to focus discussion on a series of moments that had been depicted photographically, while a range of competing readings of events were discussed and assessed. The range of plausible interpretations was bounded by the limitations of photographic technologies, alongside the visual tropes of street fighting and urban protest employed by photographers who were

[54] IALS *Scarman Inquiry*, Day 15, 15 October 1969 (Constable Thomas McLaughlin), 70.
[55] IALS *Scarman Inquiry*, Day 12, 12 October 1969 (District Inspector F. I. Armstrong), 23.
[56] IALS *Scarman Inquiry*, Day 12, 12 October 1969 (Armstrong), 24.
[57] IALS *Scarman Inquiry*, Day 15, 15 October 1969 (McLaughlin), 67.

working within the demands of the market in images. This had particular repercussions with regard to the framing of Catholic violence as the activity of the 'hooligan' and the 'mob'. This language was a key element of the vilification of the Catholic community's responses to the police and the military; as Stuart Hall pointed out in 1973, this way of framing urban disorder was a key part of the de-politicization of violence on the streets of the United Kingdom.[58] For example, Lord Scarman described Exhibit 7 as showing 'what I will loosely call the Bogside mob in the distance',[59] while District Inspector Armstrong described the photographs taken in Columbcille Court as taken when they were attempting to 'drive the mob back who were throwing petrol bombs'.[60] The descriptive categories of the 'hooligan' and the 'mob' were reinforced by the Catholic community appearing in the background—as a mass—in many of the photographs taken, placed in this position by photographers who inevitably hid behind police lines, and homogenized by distance and focal depth. Indeed, it is notable how little effort was made to identify participants in many of the photographs shown. This way of seeing a crowd took on a crucial importance during Bloody Sunday where, as Tom Herron and John Lynch have described,

> the British authorities set out to confront, in their terms, a faceless crowd, an indiscriminate mass of Derry Young Hooligans/yobbos/terrorists, organizers of, and participants in, a march that challenged the authority of the state to intern members of the nationalist community without trial and to contain a community within its defined boundary. On that day all of those marching, regardless of their political affiliations, motivations and reservations, were simply a 'crowd'.[61]

Bloody Sunday and the Widgery Tribunal

On 5 February 1972, an RUC officer traced a route around the walls of Derry city, taking photographs of the Bogside below. The photographs he took record an almost ordinary suburban day in Northern Ireland in 1972: boys playing football, a man washing his car, and women in headscarves carrying

[58] Stuart Hall, 'A world at one with itself', in Stanley Cohen and Jock Young (eds.), *The Manufacture of News: Social Problems, Deviance and the Mass Media* (London, 1973), 87.

[59] IALS *Scarman Inquiry*, Day 14, 14 October 1969 (Head Constable Desmond O'Brien), 19.

[60] IALS *Scarman Inquiry*, Day 12, 12 October 1969 (Armstrong), 22.

[61] Herron and Lynch, *After Bloody Sunday*, 36.

bags of shopping home from town (Figure 5.5). The mixture of maisonettes, newly built houses, Victorian terraces, and derelict cleared sites also located the photographs within the specific urban geographies of the post-war settlement. But even a cursory inspection shows that violence was only just beneath the surface of this urban scene. Gun placements, sandbags, and burnt-out cars formed part of the street furniture alongside streetlights, postboxes, and benches. There were few people present on the streets; indeed, the photographs reveal a tense calm on the streets of Derry.

Six days before these photographs were taken, thirteen men had been shot dead and another fifteen wounded by members of the 1st BattalionParachute Regiment, during a Civil Rights march on these residential streets. Contrasting and conflicting versions of events started circulating immediately; spokesmen from the Bogside described how the paratroopers had shot indiscriminately, while the army claimed that the soldiers had opened fire only when fired upon.[62] In the subsequent days, these rival versions were challenged and reinforced by images of Derry which were disseminated around the world. The photographs taken by Gilles Peress, a French photographer with Magnum, appeared in *Life* magazine. Stephen Donnelly's photographs appeared in the *Irish Times*. Robert White's image of men at the barricade appeared in the *Sunday Independent* and in the Derry publication *Republican News*.[63] The subsequent tribunal, led by Lord Chief Justice John Widgery, conducted seventeen public sessions between 21 February and 14 March 1972 which heard 117 witnesses, including priests, press and television reporters, photographers, cameramen and sound recordists, soldiers, police officers, doctors, forensic experts, pathologists, and 'other people from Derry'.[64] Twenty-one pressmen were interviewed by Widgery. Journalists and photographers played a crucial role in putting forward the perspective of those critical of the army because many participants in the march and residents of the Bogside were either not called or had refused to participate in the inquiry. The Scarman and Widgery reports were both published in April 1972; despite the proximity of these two inquiries, it is notable how differently photographic evidence was used at the Bloody Sunday inquiry, due to a range of factors including the differing personalities of those adjudicating, the upsurge in violence in the province, and the different genre of photographs scrutinized.

[62] Thomas Hennessey, *A History of Northern Ireland, 1920–1996* (London, 1997), 206.

[63] See Taylor, *War Photography*, 10 for a discussion of this issue of *Republican News*.

[64] Walsh, *Bloody Sunday and the Rule of Law in Northern Ireland*, 54–5.

Figure 5.5 RUC photographs 5 February 1972 (photographer unknown). Image supplied under the Open Government Licence.

Derrick Tucker was the only Bogside resident to have his photographs examined as part of the tribunal. From his bedroom and living room in the high flats, he had been able to see down Chamberlain Street to William Street, and had observed the crowd approaching the open ground around the Rossville Street flats. He described how the crowd had moved in 'A very quiet manner; just like a Sunday afternoon stroll'.[65] He also witnessed the atmosphere deteriorate as the Saracen armoured cars drove into Rossville Street and the marchers fled in front of them. Using a camera that he normally employed for holiday snaps, he recorded these scenes as the previously peaceful crowd ran away from the approaching military vehicles. Indeed, his were also the only colour photographs submitted to the tribunal; uniquely his photographs record the colours of the cold winter sunset as the army arrived. Tucker continued to watch as the violence of the afternoon unfolded outside his bedroom window; however, his film ran out and he was unable to record what he witnessed.[66] The photographs he took that afternoon played a central role in the subsequent tribunal: Widgery described it as 'the best indication I have had so far of how many people were running into the courtyard' while they were also shown to several soldiers (including Soldier V, below) as an indication that the crowd ran away—and was not aggressive—when they entered Rossville Street.[67]

As Tucker ran out of film in his Rossville flat, photographers in the street below took out their cameras as the paratroopers opened fire. These photographers had a particular relationship to the violence that surrounded them. Their press passes and relative distance from the scenes which surrounded them gave them an ability to move through the city and observe events which most of those who lived locally or had been on the march lacked. When Cyril Cave, a BBC cameraman, heard shots coming from the direction of the soldiers, he recounted how he 'just automatically ran. They said "They're shooting!" And we ran across towards where we thought the shots came from.'[68] Jeffry Morris, a photographer with the *Daily Mail*, described how he 'looked across [Rossville Street] and saw this youth running and being challenged and I saw the paratrooper coming from behind him and I could virtually see what was going to happen, so I started running towards

[65] The National Archives, UK, (TNA) Home Office (HO) 219/8 *Widgery Inquiry*, Day 7, 29 February 1972 (Derrick Tucker), 13.

[66] TNA HO 219/8 *Widgery Inquiry*, Day 7, 29 February 1972 (Tucker), 18.

[67] TNA HO 219/8 *Widgery Inquiry*, Day 7, 29 February 1972 (Tucker), 19.

[68] TNA HO 219/2 *Public Inquiry into the Events of Sunday 30 January 1972 which Led to Loss of Life on that Day* (henceforth *Widgery Inquiry*), Day 1, 21 February 1972, 62.

it to get a better picture'.[69] However, these photographers were also part of the scene they were recording; they were subjects of violence and their presence played a role in shaping how events unfolded. Peress was shot at as he walked across Chamberlain Street, while Fulvio Grimaldi was shot at through a window while hiding in Rossville high flats.[70] Two paratroopers held Morris against a wall with a rifle across his neck. One kneed him in the groin when he tried to get his press-pass out of his pocket, while the other hit him across the face with a rifle when he tried to take a photograph.[71]

Grimaldi provided a narrative of moving through violence, but not being part of it. He described his journey through the Bogside:

> I photographed Doherty as he was dying and I photographed McGuigan as I had seen him dying. At the point I photographed McGuigan the first time there was no Saracen down in Rossville Street, there was no military presence to be seen...I went further down along the front of the shops and I photographed a young man called, I believe, Gilmour, who was dead. As I stood in this place for a couple of minutes a girl was going hysterical. I photographed her.[72]

Grimaldi's seemingly dispassionate photography of those in pain, injured, or dying without coming to their aid provides an example of how he focused on individuated moments of suffering and heightened emotion in his construction of the events of Bloody Sunday. For example, his photographs of Jack Duddy, the first civilian killed as he ran away from the approaching army vehicles, showed Father Daly waving a handkerchief as three others carried Duddy's body; alongside the BBC footage of the same incident, it became one of the most enduring images of the Troubles.[73] Grimaldi's construction of events was matched by many other photographers who focused their gaze on the dead and dying rather than pictures of crowds or the army. This was a notable difference with images of the Battle of the Bogside, perhaps resulting from the photographers' instinctive visual response to death. Peress recorded Patrick Doherty's final moments in a series of four images

[69] TNA HO 219/3 *Widgery Inquiry*, Day 2, 22 February 1972, 49.

[70] For an interview with Gilles Peress regarding Bloody Sunday, see Gilles Peress and Trisha Ziff, 'The Photographer', Trisha Ziff (ed.), *Hidden Truths: Bloody Sunday 1972* (Los Angeles, 1997), 71–82. See also Carville, *Photography and Ireland*, 129.

[71] TNA HO 219/3 *Widgery Inquiry*, Day 2, 22 February 1972, 47–8; TNA HO 219/60 *Widgery Inquiry* (Jeffry Morris written statement).

[72] TNA HO 219/8 *Widgery Inquiry*, Day 7, 29 February 1972 (Fulvio Grimaldi), 59.

[73] Dash, *Justice Denied*, 30.

as he attempted to crawl to safety under a wall bearing the slogan 'Join your local IRA unit'.[74] Hugh Gilmour was shot as he ran away from soldiers in Rossville Street; the moments after he was wounded were captured by Robert White.[75] Barney McGuigan left a position of cover to attend to Patrick Doherty; despite waving a white handkerchief, he was shot almost instantly. Both Grimaldi and Peress photographed his body in the moments after he died, while men and women sheltered from gunfire in the background.[76] Michael Kelly, John Young, Michael McDaid, and William Nash all died in Rossville Street. Kelly was hit first; his body was photographed by the barricade by Robert White, a freelance photographer from Derry.[77] Michael McDaid was pictured in the background of this image in the moments before he was also fatally wounded. Gerald Donaghy, James Wray, Gerald McKinney, and William McKinney were all shot in the northerly courtyard of the Glenfada Park flats; the tribunal scrutinized no photographs of the moments surrounding their deaths (but did examine photographs of Donaghy's body—see below), nor any images relating to the fifteen people who received non-fatal gun wounds.

While these photographers focused on the emotive power of death and victimhood, Widgery's primary aim in examining them was to find validation for his contention that those who had been shot had handled, or could be legitimately thought to have handled, firearms. The photographers' movement towards, rather than away from, gunfire and scenes of violence, driven by an artistic and commercial imperative for a 'successful' photograph, meant that they saw themselves as well-placed to offer a perspective on the presence or absence of weapons in the Bogside on 30 January. On several occasions, photographers and cameramen stated that if civilians had had guns or nail bombs, they would have photographed these. Cave, for example, was adamant that he heard no automatic gunshots coming from the civilians on the barricade. He told Widgery, 'if I had heard automatic fire I would probably have started the camera running to pick it up on the soundtrack.'[78] During questioning, Peress stated that he, like 'any journalist' was anxious to get a photograph of a 'civilian with a weapon': taking this

[74] TNA HO 219/20 *Widgery Inquiry*, Day 19, 16 March 1972 (Gilles Peress), 48.

[75] TNA HO 219/27/9a (Robert White).

[76] TNA HO 219/29/18 *Widgery Inquiry* (Peress written statement); TNA HO 219/30/23 *Widgery Inquiry* (Grimaldi written statement).

[77] TNA HO 219/36/2 *Widgery Inquiry* (William Mailey written statement).

[78] TNA HO 219/2 *Widgery Inquiry*, Day 1, 21 February 1972 (Cave), 59.

kind of photograph was 'something that you cannot help doing'.[79] He also agreed that he would have been keen to take a photograph of 'a weapon lying beside a dead man, or an injured man' or 'if a weapon had been removed from a dead or injured man', but he had at no point seen this occur.[80] Despite these assurances, the tribunal repeatedly sought weapons in the photographs presented to them by these photographers. When Peress's photograph of Duddy being attended to by Father Daly was examined by Edward Gibbens, counsel for the Ministry of Defence, the central focus of the scene was not the priest and the dying teenager but rather the object in the hand of the man crouched beside them. Gibbens told Peress that 'that can be…a stick or it could be other things'; the 'other things' he had in mind was a gun.[81] Similarly, when the images he took of Patrick Doherty attempting to crawl away from army gunfire were examined by Mr Preston, counsel for the tribunal, he asked Peress why Doherty's right hand was in a different position in photographs Nos. 8 and 9 than Nos. 10 and 11, speculating that this could have been because a weapon had been removed from his body.[82]

Whether or not missiles or firearms were being used by Michael McDaid, John Young, and William Nash formed a central part of the inquiry's investigation of how and why they died. A copy of the *Sunday Independent* from 6 February 1972, with an image of the three men at the Rossville Street barricade, was handed in by Gibbens. The image showed Michael Kelly's body being attended to in the foreground; behind him McDaid had his back to the soldiers, while another man held an object between outstretched fingers (Figure 5.6).[83] When Stephen Donnelly, a photographer with the *Irish Times*, was shown the image, he thought that the object looked 'like it could be a nail bomb'.[84] According to Widgery, the man, had 'clearly got something in his hand, about the size of an orange, and it is black'.[85] Gibbens played on the apparent resonances between the poor reproduction of the photograph in the newspaper and the confusion of violence in order to implicate the group, telling Widgery that 'in suitable circumstances of

79 On Peress, see Linfield, *The Cruel Radiance*, 233–58.

80 TNA HO 219/7 *Widgery Inquiry*, Day 6, 28 February 1972 (Peress), 72.

81 TNA HO 219/7 *Widgery Inquiry*, Day 6, 28 February 1972 (Peress), 72.

82 TNA HO 2109/7 *Widgery Inquiry*, Day 6, 28 February 1972 (Peress), 67.

83 The man, not identified at the original tribunal, is Don Mullan. See Don Mullan, *Eyewitness Bloody Sunday: The Truth* (Dublin, 1997); TNA HO219/4 *Widgery Inquiry*, Day 3, 23 February 1972 (Stephen Donnelly), 5.

84 TNA HO219/4 *Widgery Inquiry*, Day 3, 23 February 1972 (Donnelly), 5.

85 TNA HO 219/5 *Widgery Inquiry*, Day 4, 24 February 1972 (Ronald Wood), 65.

Figure 5.6 Barricade in Rossville Street, 30 January 1972. Courtesy of Robert White.

security your Lordship would like to see a nail bomb'; Widgery agreed.[86] The image had been taken by Robert White, a freelance photographer from Derry, who had been at the barricade with another local photographer, William Mailey. Called before the tribunal, Mailey stated that he had not particularly noticed the man or what he was doing as he was taking photographs. However, Gibbens presented Mailey with a particular interpretation of what it showed: 'he is obviously holding some object in a very ginger fashion, is he not, between his extended fingers…do you know that nail bombs are about the size of what he is holding?'[87] Mailey resisted this reading of the photograph, and replied: 'I had a quick glance over at what was happening and obviously I did not want to get involved. Had there been any guns or nail bombs I would not have stayed on the barricade, I had a look, they were simply throwing stones and I felt reasonably safe as long as I moved right out of their way.'[88] Despite Mailey's testimony, and the absence of a positive identification of the man or the object, in the final report of the tribunal Young and Nash were said to have probably discharged firearms.[89] The line of questioning regarding the men on the barricades, Doherty, and the man with Duddy, shows how Widgery and his team of barristers pushed against the meaning of photographs and sought instead the slightest visual evidence for their own narratives of events. In photographs that had used tropes of war and suffering to foreground the victimhood of the Bogsiders, they instead searched irregular patches of light and shade on the edges and in the background in order to assemble plausible weapons in these images in Coleraine County Hall. Indeed, Widgery exploited the tension between the perceived objectivity of photographic evidence and its implicit ambiguities of meaning in order to imply the guilt of the deceased.

The contents of the pockets of Gerald Donaghy formed a crucial part of debates around his death, and photographic evidence was central to this.[90] Donaghy had been with James Wray, Gerald McKinney, and William McKinney near the barricade in the Glenfada Park area when he was shot.[91] Officer PS.34 described how, in the aftermath of these events, he was

[86] TNA HO 219/5 *Widgery Inquiry*, Day 4, 24 February 1972 (Wood), 65.

[87] TNA HO 219/8 *Widgery Inquiry*, Day 7, 29 February 1972 (Mailey), 42.

[88] TNA HO 219/8 *Widgery Inquiry*, Day 7, 29 February 1972 (Mailey), 42.

[89] *Report of the Tribunal appointed to Inquire into the Events on Sunday 30th January 1972 which Led to Loss of Life in Connection with the Procession in Londonderry on that Day* (London, 1972) (henceforth *Widgery Report*), 29.

[90] Walsh, *Bloody Sunday and the Rule of Law in Northern Ireland*, 147–50; Murray, *Bloody Sunday*, 38.

[91] Dash, *Justice Denied*, 37–8; Civil Rights Movement, *Massacre at Derry* (Derry, 1972), 27.

directed to a car park on Foyle Road, where he photographed the body of a youth, a white Cortina, and four nail bombs. He watched as one nail bomb was removed from his pocket, and saw the others removed from the car by the ammunition technical officer, Soldier 127.[92] This series of images was repeatedly shown to witnesses who had attended to Donaghy as he died, who in turn resisted the seemingly damning evidence of the photographs. Hugh Young had been looking for his brother John Young, on the afternoon of the march. He came across Donaghy lying injured in William Street and dragged him by the legs into the home of Raymond Rogan, the Chairman of the Abbey Park Tenant's Association. He then searched the two top pockets of Donaghy's denim jacket, looking for identification.[93] He affirmed: 'If I had known he had a nail bomb I would not have dragged him across the road.'[94] However, 'the pockets of Mr. Donaghy that I searched were completely empty.'[95] Similarly, Rogan, who helped carry Donaghy from his front door into his living room, and Kevin Swords, a doctor who attended to Donaghy, did not come across any nail bombs.[96] When Young and Rogan attempted to drive Donaghy to hospital, they were forcibly removed from their vehicle at a military checkpoint.[97] The car was then driven by a soldier to the Regimental Aid Post of the First Battalion Royal Anglian Regiment where Donaghy was examined by the Medical Officer (Soldier 138) who pronounced him dead, but who, in the course of his examination, discovered no nail bombs.[98] This focus on what, if anything, was in Gerard Donaghy's pockets contained a deliberate effort to change the terms of the debate. Although Widgery was criticized for setting the parameters of the investigation from 'the period beginning with the moment when the march first became involved in violence and ending with the deaths of the deceased and the conclusion of the affair',[99] with reference to Donaghy the main focus of his investigation was whether he had nail bombs in his pockets, not whether or not he had thrown one at the soldiers, or had been intending to use one when he died. Indeed, the photographs served an important function in this respect, anchoring debate over Donaghy's death in the moments

[92] *Widgery Inquiry*, Day 8, 1 March 1972 (Soldier PS.34), 80, TNA HO 219/9.
[93] *Widgery Inquiry*, Day 6, 28 February 1972 (Hugo Young), 12, TNA HO 219/7.
[94] *Widgery Inquiry*, Day 6, 28 February 1972 (Young), 12, TNA HO 219/7.
[95] *Widgery Inquiry*, Day 6, 28 February 1972 (Young), 19, TNA HO 219/7.
[96] *Widgery Inquiry*, Day 6, 28 February 1972 (Raymond Rogan), 7, TNA HO 219/7; *Widgery Inquiry*, Day 6, 28 February 1972 (Kevin Swords), 27, TNA HO 219/7.
[97] *Widgery Inquiry*, Day 6, 28 February 1972 (Rogan), 13, TNA HO 219/7.
[98] *Widgery Inquiry*, 10 March 1972 (Soldier 138), 19–27, TNA HO 219/16; *Widgery Report*, 32.
[99] *Widgery Report*, 2.

after he died, and adding an extra layer of authority to the soldier's version of events.

Just as at the Battle of the Bogside eighteen months previously, photography was used as a coercive and disciplinary mechanism by the state in their efforts to discipline the seemingly unruly Catholic community of the Bogside. But the army and the RUC were certainly not omniscient presences in the Bogside; indeed, the absence of official images of the events was notable and significant. In questioning, General Robert Ford, the commander of the army in Northern Ireland, stated:

> The directive issued to both the Army and the RUC for dealing with illegal marches was that if practicable the leaders would be arrested at the time, either by the RUC under the Public Order Act or by the Military under the Special Powers Act, but that if this was not practicable they would be identified [by photograph] for possible prosecution later.[100]

However, none of these photographs was produced as evidence. The only soldier interviewed by the tribunal who had taken photographs within the Bogside on 30 January was Soldier 028, a press officer for the 22nd Light Air Defence Regiment of the Royal Artillery. He told the tribunal: 'One of the shots is of the ambulance sitting outside Block 1 of the Rossville Flats after the shooting or during the lull in the shooting and some are of some soldiers. I am not a professional photographer and it is not an automatic camera.' He did not bring them with him when he was called to appear at the tribunal because he did not think they were 'particularly relevant'.[101] Similarly, stills from a film taken from a military helicopter of the march were blurred and unclear, and were infrequently called on to provide evidence or contextual information. This absence did not go unnoticed; in his final address, James McSparran, counsel for the next of kin of the deceased, pointed out that alongside the large numbers of press in the city, RUC personnel were also present on top of the Embassy Building, which had a substantial section of the immediate area under view.[102] Not only did the army's evidence run counter to the narrative constructed through images, but also McSparran suggested that the army deliberately suppressed the photographs which prejudiced their case. He pointed out that, despite there being army

[100] *Widgery Inquiry*, Day 10, 3 March 1972 (Major-General Robert Ford), 7, TNA HO 219/11.
[101] *Widgery Inquiry*, Day 17, 14 March 1972 (Soldier 028), 59, TNA HO 219/18.
[102] *Widgery Inquiry*, Day 18, 16 March 1972, 12, TNA HO 219/19.

photographers present in the Bogside on 30 January, no army photographs taken 'from the ground during the trouble' were produced. Indeed, he posed the rhetorical question: 'Is that another situation where the film just did not come out or something happened to prevent that man's photographs being made available to the tribunal?'[103]

When the soldiers of the 1st Battalion Parachute Regiment were questioned, they had no real sense of how the photographs taken by journalists might slot into—or interrogate—their memories or accounts of events. Soldier V, for example, spoke with a sense of indeterminacy and confusion, and had no understanding of what the implications of photographs he was shown were or how they matched to his own memories. He first described how 100 men were at the end of Chamberlain Street, stoning and throwing bottles at the army. However, he was then shown Derrick Tucker's photograph of the crowd running away from an approaching armoured vehicle, and asked, 'it is quite clear on that picture that nobody is turning in your direction to throw anything. They are running in the other way, are they not?'[104] When prompted to reconcile the photographs with his telling of events, he said that he could not.[105] McSparran told him: 'you must have fired, if you are telling the tribunal the truth, when there were a substantial number of people around the forecourt of those flats. What I am suggesting to you is that that photograph proves that.' However, Soldier V resisted the reading of events presented by the photograph; he denied McSparran's contention, and also denied being any of the soldiers in the photograph.[106]

A close reading of how photographs were handled at the Bloody Sunday tribunal reveals the complex ways in which competing truth claims were navigated. On the day the tribunal opened, Lord Widgery had set out to give the proceedings the appearance of rigorous judicial impartiality. He stated, 'The tribunal is not concerned with making moral judgements; its concern is to try and form an objective view of the precise events and the sequence in which they occurred, so that those who are concerned to form judgments will have a firm basis on which to reach their conclusions.'[107] Photographs were central to this process: more than 500 were collected as official exhibits of the tribunal, and their privileged status as devices of positivism and objectivity accorded them a central status in the processes of the

[103] TNA HO 219/19 *Widgery Inquiry*, Day 18, 16 March 1972, 12.
[104] TNA HO 219/14 *Widgery Inquiry*, Day 13, 8 March 1972 (Soldier V), 15.
[105] TNA HO 219/14 *Widgery Inquiry*, Day 13, 8 March 1972 (Soldier V), 20.
[106] TNA HO 219/14 *Widgery Inquiry*, Day 13, 8 March 1972 (Soldier V), 20.
[107] TNA HO 219/1 *Widgery Inquiry*, Day 1, 14 February 1972, 1.

tribunal. However, Widgery used photographic evidence in a highly selective and subjective fashion, pushing at the boundaries of shapes, flaws of images, and ambivalences regarding timing and directions of movement within photographs to reinforce the inquiry's focus on the guilt of those who died. This dualism whereby a rhetoric of photographic positivism was employed alongside an exploitation of the ambivalences of photography was continued in the final report. Indeed, the report described the 'large number of photographs produced by professional photographers' as 'a particularly valuable feature of the evidence'.[108] Images were referred to under headings including 'Narrative' and 'Responsibility' by long reference numbers, giving the investigation the appearance of a fact-finding mission backed by objective source material; but, preventing the possibility of multiple interpretation, copies of the images discussed were not included.

During the Troubles, photographers went to great lengths to record events and bear witness. They became subject to police and communal violence. They ran, hid, got injured, and climbed walls. They constantly negotiated and blurred the distinction between bystander and participant. But they could also walk away, go back to their hotel room, and fly home. As Liam Kennedy has noted, mid-century photojournalism was bound up in a global affective politics of compassion and empathy: 'This philosophy promoted a complex moral economy that was fuelled by abstract principles of liberal humanitarianism, defined categories of human need and harm, and constituted caring and suffering subjects through conventions of visual representation.'[109] This way of conceptualizing photojournalism turned violence into spectacle and shifted the onus of action, agency, and emotion from those in front of the camera to those behind it. However, a closer examination shows how those taking photographs in the Bogside in this period had a range of backgrounds and ties with the area; moreover, they were faced with limited choices and both action and inaction was always fraught with ambiguity. While the ambitions and impact of photojournalists are easy to critique, it is essential we make sense of this tangled moral terrain in order to understand fully the meaning of sympathy, bystanding, and participation in Northern Ireland in the 1970s. Moreover, a full exploration of the politics of the camera allows us a route in to examine how state-sanctioned causal narratives of conflict were constructed and reinforced during the Troubles.

108 Tagg, *The Burden of Representation*, 61; *Widgery Report*, 3.
109 Liam Kennedy, *The Violence of the Image: Photography and International Conflict* (London, 2014), 2.

This politics of the image took on a different tone at each of the tribunals of the early Troubles. Photographs of the Battle of the Bogside tended to be of rioters, stone-throwers, and barricades. But if the Catholic community were often represented as a 'faceless' crowd, the Protestant community were simply absent. It must be noted how few photographs—taken by the RUC, journalists, or amateurs—feature Protestant crowds or Protestant areas; it is as if the violence of these Catholic crowds had no object, and as if the Protestant community barely retaliated. The exceptions to this were photographs by McMonagle and O'Boyle who turned the gaze back upon the RUC, revealing an overstretched police force, and validating the deployment of the British Army. At the Scarman Tribunal the ambiguities around viewpoints, distances, and directions of movement were interrogated, and the implications of these competing readings were discussed. Photographic evidence provided a route to a democratized forum where a range of versions of the same events could be heard and given equal weighting, albeit bounded by photographers with a gaze trained consistently on the activities and spaces of the Catholic community.

However, the photographs examined before the Widgery tribunal were very different. Following photographic conventions of war, photographs of Bloody Sunday focused on the victims; these were photographs suffused with emotion showing bloodied bodies on the concrete of Rossville Street.[110] The framing was tighter and more consistently focused on individuals than the photographs submitted to Scarman. The tendency of photography to decontextualize, to isolate events from longer histories was exploited by Widgery to focus the inquiry on the short moments of shooting, and to pull the events away from longer histories of state policy in the province. The emotive framing of victimhood by professional photographers unintentionally contributed to a process where the focus of the tribunal turned to the actions of the dead, rather than the army. Moreover, at the Widgery Tribunal the range of readings that an image could provide was narrowed, and so too therefore were the range of interpretations of events curtailed. In contrast to the conduct of the Scarman Tribunal, Widgery exploited culturally specific notions of photographic truth to shut down debate about what the photographs presented. However, even as he did this he exploited the malleability of light and shade in the images placed before the tribunal in order to build

[110] Drawing on arguments in Martin Berger, *Seeing Through Race: A Reinterpretation of Civil Rights Photography* (Berkeley, 2011), 1–8. See also Carville, 'Renegotiated Territory', *Afterimage*, 7.

a case for the guilt of those who died.[111] Indeed, these photographs became one of a range of documents which enabled the final report to only deal with the circumstances around which the victims died under the heading 'Were the deceased carrying firearms or bombs?'.[112]

Photographic sympathy did not necessarily help the people of Derry. The images turned long-running conflicts with complex structural causes into staccato moments, while the truth value of different types of image was mobilized in variable ways. Despite the lofty ambitions of many photographers present in the Bogside during the late 1960s and early 1970s, we see how the perceived evidential properties of photographs were also used to provide readings of civil disorder and violence that were appropriate for Stormont and Westminster's purposes. Photographers who saw themselves and their medium as working to tell stories of injustice instead found that their images were read to reinforce the actions the state and security forces had already taken. But action is easier to critique than inaction, and photographers only had a limited range of choices in a market already saturated with images of violence on the streets of Ireland.

[111] Carville, *Photography and Ireland*, 134. [112] *Widgery Report*, 26.

6

Power and Place

Documentary Photography, Politics, and Perspective, 1970–95

> Then came the film and burst this prison-world asunder by the dynamite of the tenth of a second, so that now, in the midst of its far-flung ruins and debris, we calmly and adventurously go travelling.[1]

In April 1980, *Magill* published an extended article entitled 'Poverty in Ireland', featuring photographs by Fergus Bourke, Derek Speirs, and Bill Doyle. The twenty-two photographs which accompanied the article were a grim indictment of the failure of the state and church to provide for the most vulnerable. In these photographs, the Irish landscape was displayed as a ruined site strewn with rubbish, where couples slept on waste ground, homeless men lived in derelict public toilets, and old people inhabited unfurnished, unheated bedsits (Figure 6.1). Poverty was displayed in the faces, frail bodies, and stained clothes of the people in front of the camera. Further, the spaces around the subjects—the empty rooms, and absence of company or support—depicted poverty as profoundly isolating, showing Ireland as a harsh, uncaring society, and Ireland's cities as on the verge of social and physical collapse.[2] Since the nineteenth century, documentary photography has played a crucial role in shaping how people have understood and visualized poverty and defined social problems. But with multifaceted roots in social science, campaigning, and entertainment, these images present something of a problem to those seeking to use them to make sense of the past. On the one hand, they provide a way in to stories which historians often have no other archival access to: of people living outside power

[1] Walter Benjamin, 'The Work of Art in the Age of Mechanical Reproduction', in Howard Eiland and Michael Jennings (eds.), *Walter Benjamin, Selected Writings Vol. 3, 1935–1938* (Cambridge MA, 2002), 117.

[2] *Magill*, April 1980, p. 25.

Snapshot Stories: Visuality, Photography, and the Social History of Ireland, 1922–2000. Erika Hanna, Oxford University Press (2020).
DOI: 10.1093/oso/9780198823032.001.0001

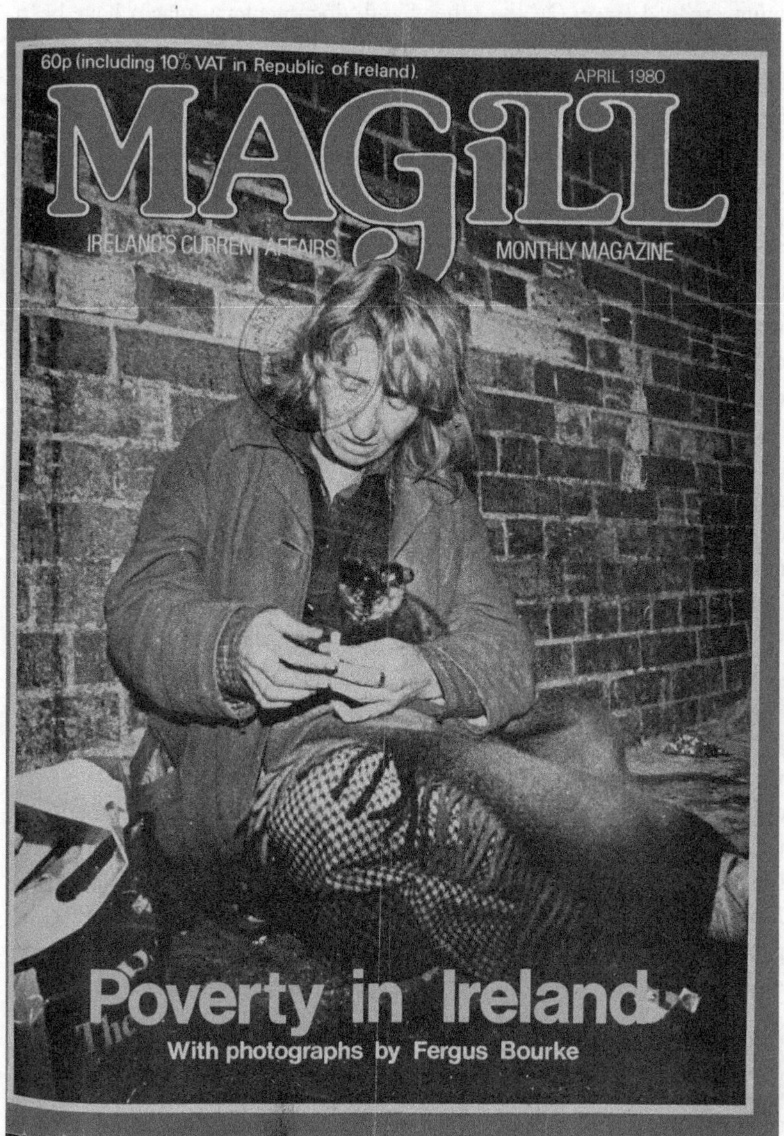

Figure 6.1 'Poverty in Ireland', *Magill* 1980.

and on the edge of society, of individuals and groups who are frequently excluded from the historic record, and of those who frequently left little other archival trace. On the other hand, documentary images have been subject to a deluge of criticism for exploiting their subject, turning people's lives into spectacle, and for the way they reinforce social relations which have caused these problems. It seems self-evident that this body of work should provide an avenue for new insights into Ireland's social history in this period, but what might these sources reveal? And what methods should we use to access this new historical information?

During the 1970s, the country north and south underwent a myriad of bitter confrontations over a range of linked societal and moral questions, while ongoing political instability was punctuated by repeated scandals drawing in those in the upper echelons of power. The north witnessed political collapse, intensified and prolonged violence, and a host of social problems caused by inadequate housing and social infrastructure. The southern state was also affected by this instability. When Patrick Hillery stood on the stage at the Fianna Fáil Ard Fheis in 1971 and shouted at the crowd that 'You can have Boland but you can't have Fianna Fáil', the tension in the room was felt across the country, also straining under the burden of competing political visions. The pressures on both states would only increase during the 1980s. As violence continued, there were also repeated moral panics around linked urban pathologies including heroin, AIDS, and worklessness. At the same time, previously marginalized groups were more vocal in campaigning for change, and new forms of publishing and journalism explicitly worked to expose injustice and puncture hypocrisy in Irish life. Debates over abortion, homosexuality, and contraception verbalized fissures between traditional and modern Ireland, and were increasingly politicized as groups both pro- and anti-liberalization took to the streets with chants and placards. Moreover, repeated revelations around sexual, social, and political abuses of power revealed a more complex relationship between tradition and modernity than many of Ireland's defenders would have allowed, a slow drip of social scandals which would become a deluge in the 1990s and 2000s.

Historians have often neglected the enormous amount of information available in documentary photographs. This is in many ways surprising, as social history and documentary photography emerged from the same intellectual agenda and subsequently mirrored each other in lineage and trajectory. Social history has been concerned with exploring the lives of those outside power—'history from below'—but has often been mired in conflicts about how to access the authentic voice of the marginalized. Indeed, questions of how we can read 'through' an archival document to those who were not involved in its production, and how we can access the *experience* of those outside power have been ongoing throughout various methodological 'turns'. Moreover, if mediators can, or should, communicate for those without access to power has posed fundamental ethical and epistemological challenges to those working within the field. These concerns are equally pressing within debates regarding the historical use of photographs. Documentary images, with their patina of age and the texture of emulsion, have an emotional power for the historian, and they suggest the potential just out of reach to move through the image and understand the past on its own terms. However, documentary photography has been criticized for its (sometimes naïve) attempts to portray authentically the lives of those in difficult circumstances, and the illusory sense it can provide of offering access to an unmediated past. The problem of voyeurism, and of turning suffering into spectacle, has shadowed those who have attempted to use their photography as part of a broader social and political project. In this context, an understandable tentativeness around the complexities of power and agency in the image has made social historians wary of using documentary photography as a source. This has somewhat blinded scholars to the wealth of detail they contain regarding the ephemeral interactions of social relations: gesture, glance, the texture of skin, or the angle of shoulders. Moreover, issues embedded in these images—problems of power, agency, and spectacle—can be worked with, historicized, and used as a starting point for a detailed consideration of these issues within Irish history. Some historians have begun to take on this challenge. New work from Stephen Brooke and Kieran Connell, for example, has taken a more serious approach to the scenes and places shown in the image, using documentary to reorientate the historical gaze to explore 'the street as the key site where social relations were played out' during periods of spatial and societal change, focusing on Roger Mayne's photographs of London in the 1950s and Janet Mendelsohn's work in Birmingham in the 1960s.[3] Using documentary photography can, therefore, not merely provide a new set of sources for filling in the detail of the past, but can also offer access to new possibilities for considering the methodological and epistemological problems of social history—how society and its problems are described, quantified, and made visible.

[3] Kieran Connell, 'Race, Prostitution and the New Left: the Postwar Inner City through Janet Mendelsohn's 'Social Eye', *History Workshop Journal* 83/1 (2017), 301–40; Stephen Brooke, 'Revisiting Southam Street: Class, Generation, Gender, and Race in the Photography of Roger Mayne', *Journal of British Studies* 53/2 (2014), 453–96.

The discipline and lineage of documentary played a formative role in the constitution of political subjectivity for a generation of photographers working in 1980s Ireland. The motivation of serious, earnest emotions, such as sympathy, concern, and responsibility, underlay how they composed images and how they operated as photographers. These were never simple emotions; they contained within them an understanding of power and powerlessness, and complex choices about how to use their limited capacity to act. All photographers working in this period answered these demands in their own way, imperfectly. Nonetheless, in the febrile climate of Ireland in the 1980s, an assessment of documentary practice can allow us to assess how these emotions were understood, and how they shifted as new avenues opened for action. These demands of conscience were evolving rapidly in the distinctive context of Ireland in the 1980s; where the social world was constrained by the boundaries of state and religious institutions, but also receiving a renewed impetus from a newly energetic public sphere forming on the street and in the new media. The seeming gravity of the documentary form and the resonance of the camera's aura of indexicality provided these new photographers with access to an authority and a status that they otherwise would have lacked. Photography allowed them to situate themselves within longer narratives of radicalism stretching back to the foundation of photo-journalism in interwar Europe, and associate with a contemporaneous artistic and political movement in Britain influenced by the writing and practice of Victor Burgin. The camera also provided them with a mobility that otherwise would have been denied to them: to Britain, Europe, across Irish cities and towns, and to the interiors of power. While their photography was informed by their deeply held political convictions, the power of the image was always formed in dialogue with the person in the frame, and by the response of a viewing public. This, however, was never a limitation, but more importantly provided them with a way of understanding photography as a collective endeavour, and their political power as something diffuse.

This chapter examines these issues, using documentary photography to explore three interrelated themes: an attentiveness to the new information present in these images about the Irish 1980s; how photographers strove to use the genre in order to explore their own perspective on Irish life; and finally, attempting to historicize issues of power and the gaze in Ireland in the early 1980s. This chapter focuses on case studies of three photographers who worked in a documentary idiom broadly defined during this period: Derek Speirs, who founded the Irish branch of the photographic agency

Report; Joanne O'Brien, a photographer known for her images of Irish emigrant communities in London; and Frankie Quinn, who has recorded Northern Irish society since the 1980s. The principal source base has been a series of interviews conducted with these photographers, read alongside their images, and in many ways the approach of this chapter has been inspired by the methods and concerns of oral history. Indeed, using interviews and documentary photography in tandem has allowed for a detailed consideration of the intersection of the subjective and the social.[4] These photographers were different from each other in many ways in the tone and emphasis of their work, but taken together their images display the heterogeneity and diversity of work embodied under the label of documentary, and allows for a consideration of how different individuals navigated choices surrounding the ethics of seeing.

Documentary in the 1980s

The documentary movement first came to prominence in the interwar period, as photographers joined with social scientists and writers in their attempts to depict the problems of contemporary society.[5] This genre was pioneered and defined by a diverse group of photographers, including Walker Evans and Dorothea Lange, who both worked for the Farm Security Administration in Depression-era America, and Bert Hardy and Humphrey Spender, who recorded the poverty and mass unemployment of British cities. As is apparent from the subject matter of these photographers, in this era documentary photography was unified by the deep sense of moral responsibility of its practitioners, and their emphasis on using photography to bring the attention of an audience to new and pressing subjects, and therefore to pave the way for social change. It also had close ties with psychoanalysis, through its seeming ability to reveal the unseen; in the words of Walter Benjamin: 'It is through the camera that we first discover the optical unconscious, just as we discover the instinctual unconscious through

[4] Lynne Abrams, *Oral History Theory* (London, 2016); Paul Thompson, *The Voice of the Past: Oral History* (Oxford, 2017); Michael Frisch, *A Shared Authority: Essays on the Craft and Meaning of Oral and Public History* (New York, 1990).

[5] Caroline Knowles and Paul Sweetman 'Introduction', in Caroline Knowles and Paul Sweetman (eds.), *Picturing the Social Landscape: Visual Methods and the Social Imagination* (London, 2004), 1–17.

psychoanalysis.'[6] Due to these associations, documentary photography has been understood to have the power to reveal a societal unconscious, exposing the 'hidden' and the 'invisible' aspects of life through freezing movement, revealing detail, or penetrating dark places and closed doors. The political significance and instrumentality of documentary photographs rested on this purchase on the real, and on the medium's ability to reveal, to expose, and to communicate. Throughout the twentieth century, documentary photographers have attempted to depict their subjects in realistic poses and situations, and to manipulate the image as little as possible in development. For most photographers, this meant uncropped black and white images. But despite these rhetorical appeals to the veracity of the image, the same photographers have also employed a range of compositional devices used in order to stir the responses of the viewer; in John Grierson's famous formulation, documentary was the 'creative treatment of actuality'.[7] Indeed, the diversity of the types of image that fall under the label of 'documentary' is revealing of how the relationship between 'creativity' and 'actuality' has been balanced and interpreted.

Social realist photography in Ireland developed in response to the concerns and problems of life north and south of the border, with photographers working in the idiom from the nineteenth century.[8] In Belfast, Alexander Hogg photographed children and women living in the dirt and decay of the crumbling and overcrowded houses of the central city for Belfast Corporation, prior to these streets' demolition.[9] In the same period, Herbert Cooper photographed the differing sides of life in Strabane, from the prosperous and busy main street to the poor housing conditions of the side alleys.[10] In the 1940s, the *Times Pictorial* followed the format and tone of the popular British title the *Picture Post*, with a photo-essay on a serious theme on the front and back cover of the paper. On 6 December 1941, its first day of publication, it featured a page one story entitled 'Your

[6] Walter Benjamin, 'The Work of Art in the Age of Mechanical Reproduction', 117; Shawn Michelle Smith and Sharon Sliwinski (eds.), *Photography and the Optical Unconscious* (Duke, 2017).

[7] David Phillips, 'Actuality and Affect in Documentary Photography', in Richard Howells and Robert Matson (eds.), *Using Visual Evidence* (Maidenhead, 2009), p. 65.

[8] E. E. Donnell (ed.), *The Genius of Father Browne: Ireland's Photographic Discovery* (London, 1990); Justin Carville, '"The Glad Smile of God's Sunlight': Photography and the Imaginative Geography of Darkest Dublin', in Justin Carville (ed.), *Visualizing Dublin: Visual Culture, Modernity, and the Representation of Urban Space* (Bern, 2014), 181–202; see also the various front covers of the *Times Pictorial* in the 1940s and 1950s.

[9] PRONI Hogg Collection: https://www.flickr.com/photos/proni/sets/72157633602250250.

[10] PRONI Cooper Collection: https://www.flickr.com/photos/proni/sets/72157643792169414.

Daily Bread', which followed wheat production from farm to table as a way of exploring the national drive to meet demands for grain during wartime. Other features from its first years included a profile of men who climbed into the mountains every weekend to cut turf for fuel; a feature on the Marrowbone Lane Fund, which provided meals for poor Dublin children; initiatives to help unemployed youth; and a feature on Travellers.[11] The *Pictorial* attempted to record the view from the street: Ken Gray recorded walking the length of O'Connell Street on the day the Second World War ended—and on many other days—searching for stories.[12]

These images tended to be benignly supportive of the status quo—if critical of some problems—however, the later 1960s were something of a turning point. During this decade, newly shocking photographs of starvation and brutality from Vietnam and Biafra appeared prominently in Irish papers, and photography took on new urgency and radicalism.[13] Also during this period, new publications, such as *Magill*, *In Dublin*, *Fortnight*, and *Circa*, took photography seriously, displaying it prominently and printing it with a new clarity and definition. New spaces such as the Gallery of Photography (opened in 1978), alongside the Ulster Museum, and the plethora of community photography initiatives created new sites for learning about photography and exhibiting photographs. In line with trends across America and Europe, many of these photographs were urban in their focus. In Belfast and Derry, the photography of the slow boredom of everyday life had a heightened political charge in contrast with the bullets, bricks, and bodies in motion which characterized international reporting on the area. Bill Kirk and Brendan Murphy recorded the dignity and sometimes absurdity of lives lived amongst the disruption of the Troubles, while Chris Steele-Perkins attempted to root the Troubles within its socio-economic factors, by focusing more on sociability, commerce, and housing conditions. Eamon Melaugh documented housing conditions in Derry before urban renewal with a combination of anger at government disregard and respect for the inhabitants of the crumbling Victorian streets.[14] Edna O'Brien's 1976 memoir, *Mother Ireland*, featured some of Fergus Bourke's better-known images from the period, including 'Boys Mitching' and 'The Pickaroon', both of

[11] Mountain bog, *Times Pictorial*, 1 August 1942, p. 1; Marrowbone Lane, *Times Pictorial*, 12 December 1942, p. 1.

[12] *Times Pictorial*, 29 March 1958, p. 4.

[13] Kevin O'Sullivan, 'Humanitarian encounters: Biafra, NGOs and imaginings of the Third World in Britain and Ireland, 1967–70', *Journal of Genocide Research* 16/2–3 (2015), 299–315.

[14] Eamon Melaugh, *Derry: The Troubled Years* (Derry, 2005).

which displayed images of children existing in states of poverty on the edge of society.[15] Brendan Walsh depicted the demolition of tenement areas around Dublin's Gloucester Diamond, with family life continuing in a wrecked landscape of ruined housing, vacant sites, and decaying wallpapered interiors. Tony O'Shea's photographs for *In Dublin* showed the city as a place where poverty was endemic, streets were crumbling, and litter and graffiti covered every surface. Most notable, however, are his photographs of people travelling on buses: a quotidian Dublin culture which had been largely unrepresented in Irish culture. In O'Shea's handling, however, buses were grim and silent, and their packed spaces only accentuated the loneliness of urban travellers. The accumulation of these images meant that documentary photographers played a formative role in creating images of crisis within 1980s Ireland, disseminating ideas about Irish society, and campaigning for political and social change.

The late 1970s and early 1980s were also a key moment in the formation of a critical discourse around documentary photography. These critiques took a variety of forms and emphases, but were clustered around issues of power, the gaze, and the subject/object relationship between photographer and photographed. The founding text in this field, and one which has had a lasting dominance on the shape of photographic studies, is Susan Sontag's *On Photography*, first published as a series of essays during the mid-1970s. Although it has often been used as a textbook for understanding the photographic image, the book's intellectual foundations lie in the art world of 1970s New York; its emphasis on the passivity engendered by the saturation of images is only fully comprehensible in the context of the magazines, television, and white-walled exhibition spaces of that time and place.[16] Nonetheless, other scholars have built on her scepticism. For example, Abigail Solomon-Godeau argued that the focus and framing on the emotional suffering of those in need created a comforting narrative of liberal humanism while simultaneously removing any sense of social or economic causality from the scene.[17] In similar terms, Martha Rosler saw documentary photography as being a synecdoche of the condescension and collusion of liberalism. In her reading, 'documentary as we know it carries information about a group of powerless people to another group addressed

[15] Edna O'Brien, *Mother Ireland* (London, 1976).

[16] Sarah Parsons, 'Sontag's Lament: Emotions, Ethics, and Photography', *Photography and Culture* 2/3 (2009), 289–302; Susan Sontag, *On Photography* (Harmondsworth, 1979).

[17] Abigail Solomon-Godeau, *Photography at the Dock: Essays on Photographic History, Institutions, and Practices* (Minnesota, 1994), 171.

as socially powerful.'[18] It 'assuages any stirrings of conscience in its viewers the way scratching relieves an itch and simultaneously reassures them about their superlative wealth and social position, especially the latter, now that even the veneer of social concern has dropped away from the upwardly mobile and comfortable social sectors.'[19] As such, documentary involved a 'double act of subjugation: first in the social world that has produced its victims, and second, in the regime of the image produced within and for the same system that engenders the conditions it then re-presents.'[20]

Critiques based on this reading of gaze, power, and image were also being developed in Ireland in this period. Most pressingly, photography of the Troubles was extensively and vociferously criticized for being exploitative, voyeuristic, and producing clichéd images of the conflict as a series of set-piece 'flashpoints', a discourse which was invigorated by a postcolonial reading of this external gaze.[21] In her now well-known essay, 'How the English Make Pictures of Irish Troubles' published in 1983, Belinda Loftus condemned the leering spectacularization of Irish violence by British photo-journalists. Photography of social problems was subject to the same critique. In 1991, Fintan O'Toole explored the problems of documentary photography and Irish poverty: 'marginalized communities are visited by television or the newspapers, the awfulness of their plight exposed, and the communities end up feeling abused, feeling that all of the negative images which scare off employers and investment have been copper fastened.'[22] This echoed Rosler's pronouncement that documentary photography represented the 'social conscience of liberal sensibility presented through visual imagery.'[23] Indeed, the salience of this international critique of the documentary moment in the Irish context is significant, in a society which was both socially divided and where problems often remained undiscussed in order to maintain an appearance of societal unity. However, this criticism did not lead to a dismissal of documentary as a genre. In O'Toole's conception, turning a blind eye to poverty and inequality did not provide a better answer: 'the answer can hardly be to ignore deprivation and marginalization, to pretend that everything is all right with the world when it is patently

[18] Martha Rosler, 'In, around, and after thoughts (on documentary photography)', in Richard Bolton (ed.), *The Contest of Meaning* (Cambridge, MA, 1992), 306.

[19] Rosler, 'In, around, and after thoughts', 306.

[20] Solomon-Godeau, *Photography at the Dock*, 176.

[21] Belinda Loftus, 'Photography, Art, and Politics: How the English Make Pictures of Irish Troubles', *Circa* 13 (1983), 10–14.

[22] *Irish Times*, 2 March 1991, 5.

[23] Rosler, 'In, around, and after thoughts', 325.

not all right.'[24] The conflicts that O'Toole identified were not easy to navigate. Indeed, as he opined, 'The line between sensitivity and evasiveness or censorship is a thin one, and it is a line that can be walked by those who have a vested interest in silence, in falsehood, in pretty images that belie the reality of people's lives.'[25] O'Toole's fear of 'silence' as an alternative was not unwarranted in a society where social problems were often ignored and which had done little to solve the entrenched causes of poverty or the long-term problems it produced. Moreover, his swipe at 'pretty images' was trenchant; indeed, it was not that images of poverty had ever been invisible in depictions of Ireland, but their political and social power had been nullified through their use within picturesque depictions of nation and homestead.

This moment of critique of documentary was also a period when the genre was increasingly prominent across the arts and media of Britain and Ireland. Working across theory and practice, Rosler and Allan Sekula speculated—without definitive conclusion—about what a revivified documentary practice would look like. Rosler inferred the 'the germ of another documentary—a financially unloved but growing body of documentary works committed to the exposure of specific abuses caused by people's jobs, by the financiers' growing hegemony over the cities, by racism, sexism, and class oppression, works about militancy, about self-organization, or works meant to support them.'[26] In similar terms, Sekula also sought to move beyond 'A naïve faith in both the privileged subjectivity of the artist, at the one extreme and the fundamental "objectivity" of photographic realism at the other', to a 'recognition of cultural work as praxis' and 'an art that documents monopoly capitalism's inability to deliver the conditions of a fully human life.'[27] Irish documentary photographers were therefore working within the intellectual climate which attempted a renewal of the documentary genre 'predicated on a full awareness of the role played by context, relations between photographer and photographed, and the various structuring mechanisms that determine photographic meaning.'[28]

Due to its lineage, documentary tended to be urban in its focus and left-wing in its politics, therefore it took on a particular resonance in Irish life where iconography of both the city and labour has tended to be underdeveloped. These images therefore played an important role in visualizing

[24] *Irish Times*, 2 March 1991, 5. [25] *Irish Times*, 2 March 1991, 5.

[26] Rosler, 'In, around, and after thoughts', 324–5.

[27] Allan Sekula, 'Dismantling modernism reinventing documentary (Notes on the Politics of Representation)', *The Massachusetts Review* 19/4 (1978), 883.

[28] Allan Sekula, 'The Body and the Archive', *October* 39/102 (1986), 1892.

the social world of a newly urban Ireland.[29] Moreover, working in the context of these charged debates about the nature of documentary practice forced each of these photographers to confront the relationship between themselves, the viewer, and the viewed. Exploring these relationships, and the dynamics of power they embodied, can provide a wealth of detail about the constitution of society during an axial time. Documentary is predicated on entwined notions of justice and exposure, and so, throughout its history, has shifted in tone and content in response to the social context in which it is produced. In mid-twentieth-century Ireland, religious and public institutions dominated the social landscape, taking a controlling role in shaping how the public sphere functioned, and how the insiders and excluded of Irish life were understood. From the 1970s, however, the role of these orders and institutions was being increasingly challenged on the street and in new media. During this period in Ireland, the vocabulary of 'hidden' social problems and 'unseen' social groups permeated discourse on poverty, inequality, and social justice. The revival of documentary took place in the context of these tensions, its concerns and aesthetic rooted in the struggles between modernity and tradition in late twentieth-century Ireland. However, this process was never straightforward; narratives of 'revealing' could often be as problematic as stories of concealing, and photographers had to make their own choices about how to navigate these difficulties.

Derek Speirs and activist imagery

Derek Speirs's photographic life began, like so many others, with a childhood gift of a Brownie 127. However, his story of becoming a photographer is not of finding beauty in the everyday through childhood play, rather his entry into the world of photography came later, through work. When he left school, Speirs got a job in a photofinishing laboratory in Tallaght in West Dublin, 'processing pictures for people'.[30] After work one day, he had been taken for a drink by the manager of the laboratory, and felt that he was being sounded out to see if he was management material. However, he couldn't see that situation 'going anywhere'.[31] To get out of Dublin, and

[29] Justin Carville, 'Refracted visions: Street photography, humanism and the loss of innocence', in Eamon Maher and Eugene O'Brien, *Tracing the Cultural Legacy of Irish Catholicism: From Galway to Cloyne and Beyond* (Manchester 2017), 70–88.

[30] Interview with Derek Speirs.

[31] Interview with Speirs.

away from this middle-managerial career track, he attempted to move from processing photographs to a different register of photographic practice. He applied to a range of photography courses in Britain, finally beginning the BA in Photographic Arts at the Polytechnic of Central London (PCL) in 1971. Speirs entered the PCL at a transitional era in the status of photography within British arts and training; a vigorous debate was taking place within both the artistic establishment and the Arts Council relating to the status of photography, and photographic courses were undergoing a related movement from vocational apprenticeships to artistic education.[32] From 1972, the PCL was the first institution in Britain to award a degree in photography, intended by its organizers to 'raise the status of professional photographers'.[33]

Speirs's practice as a photographer was fundamentally shaped by his encounter with the photographer and writer Victor Burgin, who arrived at the PCL mid-way through Speirs's time there. Burgin was giving lectures to the first years at the PCL, but Speirs—in the third year of his degree—went along. He recalled the immediate impression that Burgin made on him as a young man, thinking after the first lecture: 'this guy is really amazing.'[34] Prior to his encounter with Burgin, the class had studied the history of photography as a Whiggish history of great men and great technological innovations, alongside classes in photographic methods and practices, which had emphasized photography as a mode of self-expression.[35] Burgin brought coherence to the degree, providing a way of conceptualizing how the various aspects of studying and practising photography related to each other, and emphasizing photography as a means of communication. In Speirs's perspective, what Burgin was doing was 'infinitely more advanced' than the subjects he had studied up to that point in his degree. He was so taken by Burgin's approach to photography that after this he went to all of Burgin's lectures and went out of his way to get hold of every single thing Burgin wrote, even down to his MA thesis at the Royal College of Art. Lacking the money to pay for it, he stole a copy of the book *Work and Commentary* from a gallery in Sloane Square, indicative of the divisions of class and distinction which ran through the art world and which Speirs's generation of photographers, educated at the polytechnics, navigated.

[32] May McWilliams, 'The Historical Antecedents of Contemporary Photography Education: A British Case Study, 1966–79', *Photographies* 2/2 (2009), 237–54.

[33] McWilliams, 'The Historical Antecedents of Contemporary Photography Education', 244.

[34] Interview with Speirs.

[35] McWilliams, 'The Historical Antecedents of Contemporary Photography Education', 244.

Alongside a photographic education, London provided excitement, exposure to new cultural forms, and political mobilization. During his time studying at the PCL, Speirs was involved in various aspects of left-wing activism. He squatted near Kings Cross, and became actively involved in the movement. At the same time, he was involved as an extra in Kevin Brownlow's film *Winstanley*, which told the story of the attempt to establish a self-sufficient farming community on common land at St George's Hill in Surrey by a group of seventeenth-century radicals known as the Diggers, and which featured many members of the squatting and anarchist movement as actors.[36] After the PCL, Speirs went on to do graduate work at the Royal College of Art; while there, he joined the Socialist Workers' Party and was involved in the occupation of the College for three weeks in 1976, campaigning on the issues of fees and quotas for overseas students. In Speirs's words, the photographic and the political played a formative role in shaping not just his career, but also his identity: 'So now I'm stuck. I don't know whether I'm an academic, whether I'm a practitioner, what I am.'[37]

After he graduated from the RCA, Speirs attempted to resolve these tensions. During his time at the College he had seen photographs in *Time Out* and other left-wing magazines which had the credit 'Report' written up their right-hand edge. Report's output focused on radical political activity, such as demonstrations and marches and avant-garde cultural events, and the organization employed some of the most prominent press photographers working at that time in Britain, including Andrew Wiard, John Sturk, and Angela Phillips.[38] Out of curiosity about the organization behind these pictures, Speirs went to their offices on Oxford Street, where he met the agency's founder and secretary, Simon Guttmann (1891–1990). Guttmann had been a central figure within the history of photojournalism, linking interwar Berlin with 1970s London. He had been at the heart of the intellectual culture and communist activism of interwar Berlin, associating with figures including Walter Benjamin and Georg Heym and travelling to the Soviet Union in 1923. During his time in Berlin, he had set up 'Deutsche Photo Dienst' (Dephot), one of the first photographic news bureaus, supplying individual photographs and 'Bildserien'—photographic news stories—to magazines such as the *Berliner Illustrirte Zeitung*. He left Germany in 1933, living a peripatetic existence across Europe, finally arriving in London in 1938. In

[36] Interview with Speirs. [37] Interview with Speirs.

[38] Nicholas Jacobs and Diethart Kerbs, 'Wilhelm Simon Guttman, 1891–1990: A Documentary Portrait', *German Life and Letters* 62/4 (2009), 413.

the war years, he worked for a variety of journalistic enterprises including *Picture Post*, and British intelligence, before establishing himself as secretary of Report in 1946.[39] After meeting Guttmann, Speirs began working for Report, taking photographs of social activism and left-wing politics on the streets of 1970s London, a mode of employment and genre of photography that seemed for him to resolve the binary between academic and practitioner. Although Guttmann was at this time crippled by illness and almost entirely confined to Report's offices on Oxford Street, he exercised total control over the output of the organization: handing out assignments, marking up contact sheets, and checking prints before they went out. This assiduous approach to the processes of photography was combined with a subtle understanding of the image, and a forensic knowledge of the politics of radical London. This allowed Guttmann to impose absolutely rigorous standards regarding the relationship between the photographer and that which they photographed; in Speirs's phrasing: 'if he sensed that you had a disrespect, or that you weren't engaged, he could see it straight away and he would just dismiss you.'[40]

In the late 1970s, Guttmann decided that Report, as an international organization, should have an office in Ireland, and called on Speirs to set it up. Speirs returned to Ireland in 1977 with a portfolio, fifty pounds, and a second-hand enlarger, subsidizing his early years back in Dublin with a part time job teaching photography in the National College of Art and Design (NCAD).[41] His politics, and his two mentors, Burgin and Guttman, had a formative impact on his engagement with Irish society, and the market in images. When he had left London, he had a conversation with Guttmann:

> he said, go to Ireland, tell people what you do, don't ask anybody for anything. Just tell them what you do. It was really good advice. And I just did what I did, and gradually people came to me for photographs for magazines and stuff but I didn't go looking for work as such, I just had this mission. And Simon was the sort of the organizational side of it, Victor Burgin was the ideological or the theoretical...In a kind of way the theoretical underpinning because I knew, like I was a graduate of the RCA, I could have decided to prance around the place as an art photographer

[39] Jacobs and Kerbs, 'Wilhelm Simon Guttman', 413; Tim Gidal, 'Modern photojournalism: the first years', in David Brittain (ed.), *Creative Camera: Thirty Years of Writing* (Manchester, 2000), 78–9 (first published in Creative Camera July/August 1982).

[40] Interview with Speirs. [41] Interview with Speirs.

> but, do you know what I mean I wasn't interested in that, I was interested in using the photography as a kind of documentary tool, and then to ally that, to try to work with progressive organizations, the Labour movement, left wing political organizations, the women's movement as well, and that was me.[42]

Guttmann's words functioned as a mantra for Speirs not to compromise his politics or his interests in the photographic work he took on. Building on the influence of Guttmann and Report, he was interested in using both news photography and documentary photography as part of a broader project to advance the left in Ireland. Here he saw his photography as part of 'consciousness-raising', a terminology, politics, and a praxis which was rooted in second-wave feminism. Furthermore, the new cultural studies readings of photography—in which Burgin's work played a part—provided a means of explaining the way in which race, class, and gender were portrayed in words and images in the media, and the way in which images could intervene in these processes. These combined influences provided Speirs with a way of understanding himself as both a photographer and an activist.

During the 1980s, he worked photographing left-wing social movements such as trade unions, feminist groups, Travellers' associations, and homeless charities, alongside work for Dublin's radical press, a photography he understood as part of a broader political and social project (Figure 6.2 and Figure 6.3). Speirs's socially conscious approach to image making was clear in his work for *Magill*, for which he undertook numerous projects, amounting to hundreds of photographs during the 1980s. This ranged from photographs of politicians and trade unionists, to longer photo stories on social issues, usually in combination with the journalist Gene Kerrigan. In the politically charged atmosphere of the 1980s, Speirs photographed the many groups—both pro- and anti-divorce, abortion, and contraception—who took to the streets to make their protest visible. For example, in October 1981, *Magill* published Derek Speirs's images of Irish sub-cultures including punks, while another photo-essay, from February 1982, concerned Dublin's streets at night.[43] In January 1984, he produced a series of colour photographs for an article on Travellers, showed both the distinctive landscape of open ground and tightly packed interiors which produced Traveller culture, situating their poverty within broader socio-economic factors.[44] In September 1986, he

[42] Interview with Speirs.

[43] *Magill*, October 1981, 8–14; *Magill*, February 1982.

[44] *Magill*, April 1984, 24–33.

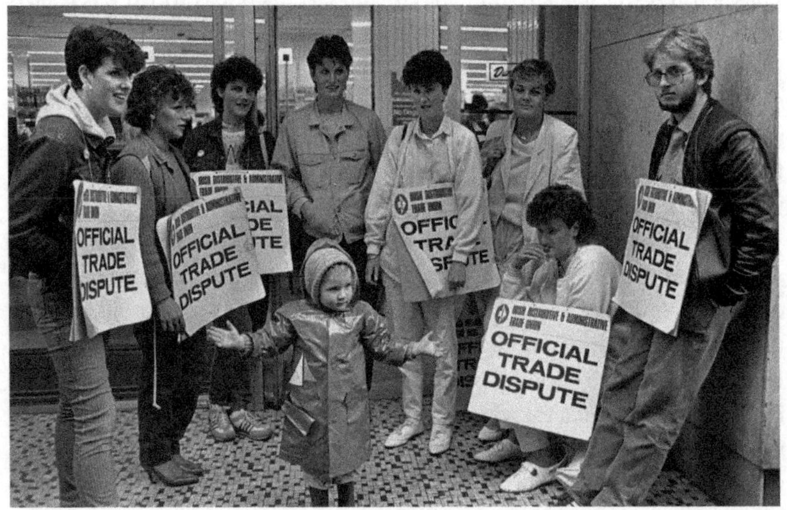

Figure 6.2 Dunnes Store dispute, Dublin (1985) (Derek Speirs).

covered the intimidation of Catholic families in Lisburn, showing ugly inartistic graffiti on the side of a grey council house, barking 'PRODS rule Old Warren', indicating the pettiness of the battles being fought, while a further photograph showed the culmination of this struggle: men loading a mattress and other furniture into a van while another looked on, hands in pockets, bored.[45] This was characteristic of his work in the north of Ireland, which focused largely on street demonstrations, political rallies, and the everyday incidences of the conflict.

The camera was central to Speirs's ability to navigate the volatile climate of politics in the 1980s. Alongside his work with groups associated with the left, his camera also brought him into contact with a burgeoning inner-city arts scene. During the 1980s, he started photographing plays for Passion Machine, a theatre group who performed at the St Francis Xavier Centre, while living on Gardiner Street. John Sutton, the theatre manager, first raised the idea that Speirs should display his work, a suggestion which led to 'Speirs at Large', his first big exhibition, held in the centre in 1990. Like the theatre company, the exhibition emerged from a developing effort to portray the culture of the city; in Speirs's conception, this was part of 'a whole movement of... theatre and publishing relating to a whole new urban class of people a whole, that was quite important'.[46] While photography allowed him to learn more about Dublin's working-class culture, the camera also provided an avenue to the corridors of power. In an attempt to understand and expose the workings of Ireland's 'political mechanism', Speirs spent much of the 1980s following the political career of the on-off Taoiseach Charles Haughey glad-handing through the plush surroundings of government offices and kissing elderly women in draughty school halls across the provinces.[47] But this mechanism encompassed religious institutions alongside political groupings. During the run-up to the 1983 abortion referendum, he attempted to find out more about the Knights of Columbanus, attempting to identify the leadership by photographing people coming in and out of the headquarters in Ely Place. His photography therefore gave him access to spaces and sites of politics, an ability to move across institutional, social, and geographical boundaries, and an intimate understanding of how power in Ireland operated.

[45] *Magill*, September 1986, 26–7. [46] Interview with Speirs.

[47] Derek Speirs and Gene Kerrigan, *Goodbye to All That: A Souvenir of the Haughey Era* (Dublin, 1992), 6.

Figure 6.3 Factory Workers, Connemara (1981) (Derek Speirs).

His images focused on issues of social difference and exclusion on the streets of Ireland. An image of a woman and two boys on a street in central Dublin provides a way of exploring how we can understand Speirs's photographs historically (Figure 6.4). Taken in 1978, it was first published as part of the article 'Poverty in Ireland' in *Magill* in 1980, and then displayed as part of Speirs's first solo show, 'Speirs at Large' in 1990. When it was first published in *Magill*, the caption anchored the image with its description of 'two young boys begging in Dublin's inner city'. Two boys, one in a tracksuit, one in a blazer, stand beside a wall, both looking down. But the focus of the image is not so much on the boys, however, as the relationship between them and the woman looking at them from the left of the image. Well dressed, with set hair, silk scarf, and raincoat, she—unlike them—conformed to the norms through which women presented themselves on the street. Moreover, the distance of class and respectability was presented by the way in which she pulled her upper body away from the boys and—with two fingers—held onto her handbag.[48] In these gazes, glances, gestures, and involuntary movements of the hand and neck we can read a whole set of broader social relations mapped out in miniature in a moment on a street in Dublin. While we gaze at the woman as she gazes at the boys, the photograph seems to suggest a knowing collusion with the children in the light of the woman's distain. Indeed, this image taxonomizes not the boys' poverty, but rather the woman's voyeuristic response. This sensation is compounded by the look of amusement on the boys' faces, an emotion which would normally be out of place within the earnest tone of much documentary practice, but here instead serving to make the woman's response distant and ridiculous. This sense of proximity and distance characterized much of Speirs's work, a theme he returned to a decade later in another photo, taken on Grafton Street at Christmas (Figure 6.5). A woman begs on the side of the street, seemingly without much success. She looks on at the crowd, bored, while her daughter meets Speirs's gaze. A family walk by, averting their gazes. Only the child has not yet learned the rules of comportment that govern the city, and she looks down, in so doing rendering the normalized actions of her mother and grandmother strange. Through both of these images, Speirs refers to a long history of photographing children within the documentary tradition epitomized by Hogg and Cooper, which usually used images of children as a way of asking for pity for poverty from a middle-class viewing public. But that is not the message of these images. Instead, it critiques this very tradition,

[48] *Magill*, April 1980, 25.

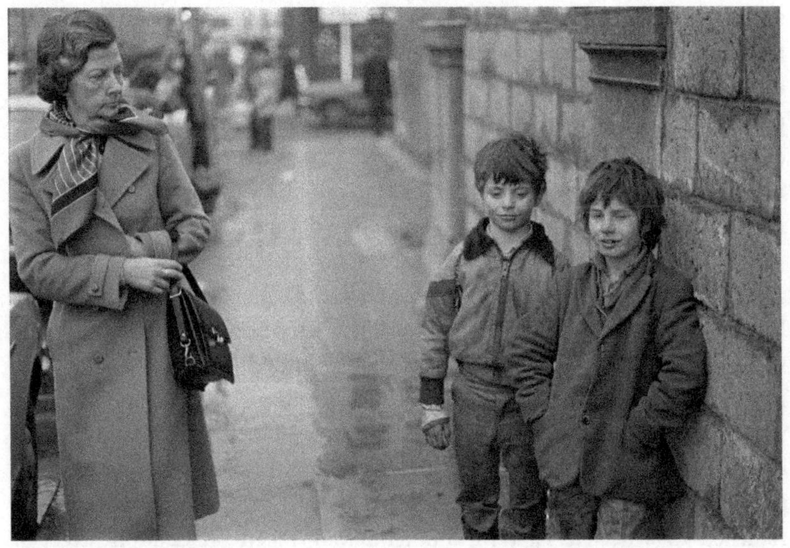

Figure 6.4 Quays, Dublin (1978) (Derek Speirs).

Figure 6.5 Grafton Street, Dublin, 1990 (Derek Speirs).

positioning these children as both wise and active. The focus on the gestures of adults as they looked and looked away showed the fine line which existed in Irish society between pity and contempt, charity and voyeurism.

In common with other documentary photographers working in Ireland in this period, children played a central role in Speirs's photography. These images co-opted an iconography which had run through documentary since the genre's foundation, indicative of the tradition's use of 'rhetorical and aesthetic techniques that combine fact with feeling, information with affect, and factuality with polemic'.[49] However, these images of children had a particular power in the context of 1980s Ireland. The dirty bodies and clothes of these children, playing in a landscape of litter and broken buildings, had a potency for a nation which had a commitment to 'cherish[ing] all her children equally' inscribed in its foundational document. Images of children on inner city streets, playing in derelict sites, or outside Corporation flat blocks indicated state failings to provide adequate facilities for the city's younger population; as morally unblemished victims of state and societal failings, they provided a simple and powerful photographic message untarnished by the complexities of adult agency. But these children did not demand the viewer's pity. They were ambivalent urban actors, who used the city as a playground: playing, exploring, and threatening to destroy or damage, and not conforming to the rules of bodily comportment, gesture, and gaze of the city. They were powerful and active, not supine or pathetic. Indeed, in depicting the child, which has been a locus of middle-class concern, but doing so in a way which challenged these very emotions, Speirs interrogated and revealed the tenor and limits of liberal Ireland's concern for its inner-city neighbours. Thus the portrayal of children posed a set of questions about when society looks—and looks away—and the role that representation plays in social action.

Speirs sought to reconcile the documentary tradition with a broader sense of responsibility as both a photographer and a citizen. However, he was thoughtful about his own responsibility towards those he photographed and the limitations of what could be achieved through photography alone: 'There was the idea that I take these pictures and then I put them in the mainstream media and then people will see them and think that's terrible and then people will change it. I mean, that's reasonable, but if that doesn't happen, I mean what's the purpose?'[50] Rather than conceptualizing

[49] Phillips, 'Actuality and Affect in Documentary Photography', 65.
[50] Interview with Speirs.

documentary photography as a form of middle-class interventionism, he was realistic about the more complex networks of diffuse forms of agency and social change in which his images played a part: 'you would represent a situation, but you would do so in such a way that the people represented can come out feeling positively affirmed even if their circumstances are dire and intolerable because then maybe they have the ability to maybe themselves to engage in some kind of remedial process.'[51] In order to enable this process, he attempted to find, through his photography, 'a way of representing a situation that doesn't reinforce that circumstance as natural to that constituency of people…or inevitable. And people have accepted me working like that.'[52]

Joanne O'Brien and the Migrant Gaze

Throughout her career, Joanne O'Brien has worked across genres including documentary, portraiture, and reportage, and in places from Europe to Asia. When she took up photography in the late 1970s, she was keen to document a wide range of cultural and social issues including health, housing, and education, often working with the trade union movement. During the 1980s, O'Brien established a career photographing subjects including the daily lives of the Irish community in London, demonstrations and political action, and portraits, as well as also freelancing for the *Guardian*, *Independent*, and *Irish Times*. Her photographic subjects have also extended beyond Ireland and Britain. She has documented life in China and Hungary, and in the early 1980s, as the Cold War waned, she accompanied a Europe-wide women's delegation to Washington as part of a campaign to eliminate land-based ballistic missiles. More recently, she has explored the conditions faced by photographers covering the Israeli occupation in Palestine.

Her work on Irish issues has been greatly influenced by her regular travel between Ireland and Britain. The influence of both countries, and the sense of displacement which came from living between them has forged her sense of identity and shaped her photography, themes which were especially important in the early years of her work. Through a series of projects—on Irish women's lives in post-war Britain, on abortion clinics, and on memories of Bloody Sunday—her photography has explored the complexities of Irish-British relations. On one hand, outside their own community, the

[51] Interview with Speirs. [52] Interview with Speirs.

Irish in Britain were invisible and lacking any distinct public identity; they were subsumed into Britishness by a narrative of homogeneity which sought to bolster the political unity of both Britain and Ireland. On the other hand, they were a suspect community, subject to special terrorism laws and a public discourse underpinned by racial and colonial stereotypes. Reciprocally, the projects also interrogated and revealed the way in which Britain has functioned in Irish people's lives, its influence in allowing unpalatable aspects of Irish culture to be concealed and banished: forgotten emigrant groups, hidden abortion trails, and the lasting legacies of trauma after violence has largely ended and newspapers and cameras have departed the scene. Her photography has allowed her to interrogate the boundaries of Irish society, and the role that Britain played in enabling these boundaries to persist. Here, some of these themes in her work on Ireland and the Irish in Britain are explored, examining how she has captured and made sense of these tensions—individual, emotional, and political—between Ireland and Britain in her work.

O'Brien first came to London in 1977, moving into a 'big old house' in Ladbroke Grove.[53] Although she only stayed a year and a half on this occasion, in common with many Irish people who travelled the same route, it was a period of political and personal awakening. She worked as a bus conductor on the route from Golders Green to Wandsworth, a job which gave her a new sense of independence, freedom, and the visual possibilities of the city: 'You got on and... it was your bus.'[54] Her time as a conductor gave her the opportunity to look at the city, and examine her shifting perspective within it. Her daily route gave her a unique visual reading of London, as the view from her bus produced new angles and staccato tableaux: 'You had to be quite philosophical as a bus conductor because... you'd be seeing all these little scenes unfolding... and then you'd be gone... and you couldn't see what happened next. Then, there were beautiful things—the old open backed bus, [with] the light playing on the roof, [and] the reflections from the traffic... [and] it satisfied my desire to be on the move all the time.'[55] These themes also inspired her photography. She had previously been involved in feminist politics in Dublin; from the outset, her approach to photography had a socially aware perspective. But it was while she was

[53] Joanne O'Brien interviewed by Michael-Ann Mullen (British Library Oral History of British Photography).

[54] O'Brien interviewed by Mullen.

[55] O'Brien interviewed by Mullen.

working on this route that her childhood Kodak Instamatic camera 'finally packed up' and she acquired a Zenit, which cost £20. Now, with a newfound ability to control focus and light, and inspired by the scenes and politics of London, O'Brien began to take photography more seriously.[56]

After returning briefly to Dublin to finish a history degree, O'Brien once again travelled to London. She developed her knowledge of the camera during this time, attending evening classes in photography at the Oval House Theatre arts centre and reading photographic theorists such as John Berger.[57] She took an early morning cleaning job, which gave her time to take pictures in the afternoons.[58] Like Speirs, O'Brien taught herself how to compose images and use the camera in the context of a volatile political climate that was manifest on the streets. Her early forays into documentary were through photographing left-wing activism such as demonstrations against the cuts to the welfare state. She also photographed protests against the closure of the South London Hospital for Women and Children, Reclaim the Night marches, anti-apartheid demonstrations, and protests in support of the miners' strike.[59] This was also a period of increased political tension between Ireland and Britain due to the Hunger Strikes, the IRA campaign in Britain, and the intensity of daily conflict in Belfast and Derry (Figure 6.6). O'Brien photographed demonstrations in London associated with the conflict, such as the rallies in support of the hunger strikers, and the annual march in remembrance of Bloody Sunday.[60] The influence of documentary photographers who had gone before her, alongside her training in social history, made her keen to keep a record of this political radicalism. Moreover, in an era of police violence and brutality, she felt protective towards the people whom she photographed. Despite the fact that 'really there wasn't a market for these pictures', she would often cover demonstrations and pickets. She felt that perhaps she could, 'by being there with a camera, act as a kind of restraint on the police or on the authorities, and just let them know that someone was watching what they were doing... What I was doing... was a form of intervention, and creating a record of events.'[61]

In 1983, O'Brien was invited by the photographer Val Wilmer to join a female freelance photographers' discussion group with a view to setting up a new photographic agency. The women-only photography agency Format

[56] O'Brien interviewed by Mullen.
[57] O'Brien interviewed by Mullen.
[58] O'Brien interviewed by Mullen.
[59] Interview with Joanne O'Brien, 12 May 2016.
[60] Interview with O'Brien, May 2016.
[61] Interview with O'Brien, May 2016.

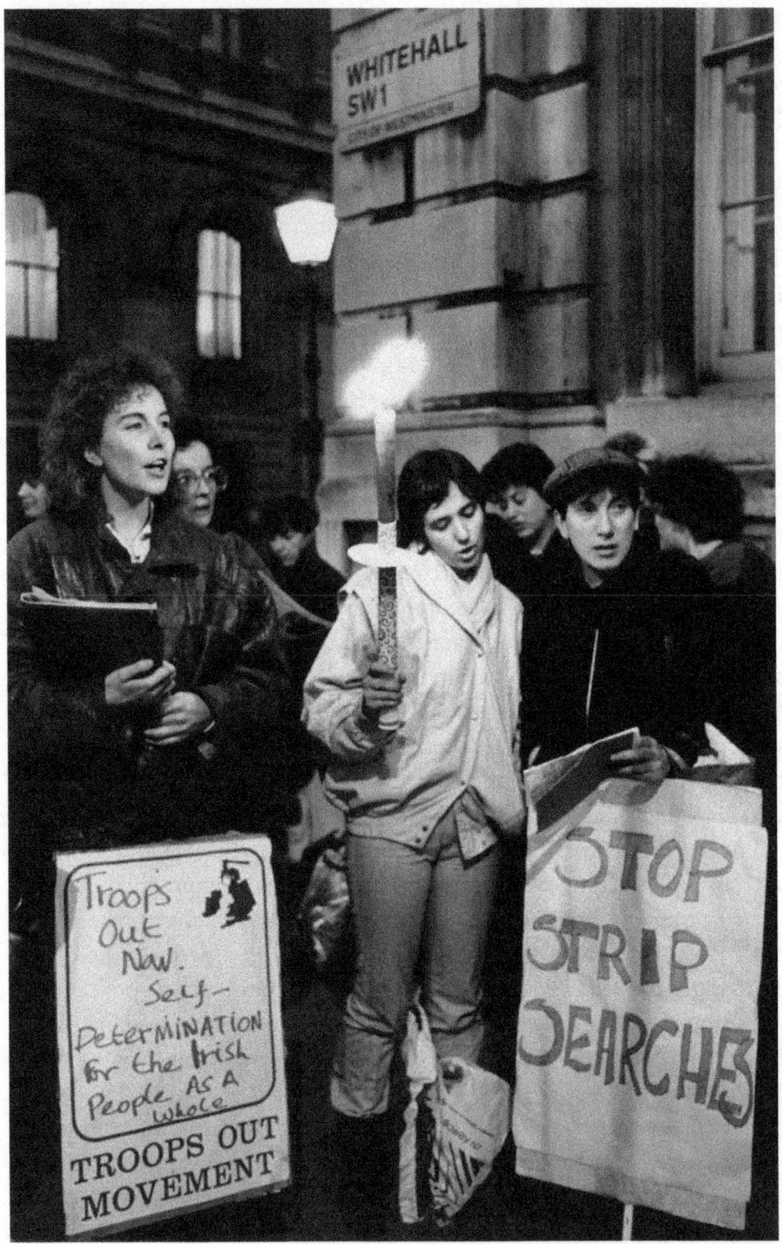

Figure 6.6 London, 8 March 1985. Demonstration outside Downing Street in support of Armagh Gaol women prisoners on International Women's Day (Joanne O'Brien).

was officially set up in May 1984.[62] Working in the context of Thatcher's Britain, they saw their role as visualizing the position of women within stories of deindustrialization, strikes, and political protest, which were often framed as inherently male. In particular, they became known for their coverage of events such as Greenham Common, the miners' strike, lesbian rights campaigns, and social care. In *Feminist Review* in 1984, Format described its mission: 'We... share a concern over the politics of representation—how our photographs are taken, how they are used and where, who sees them.' Although they did not only cover 'women's issues', they saw themselves as approaching and selecting material differently from a male-dominated organization. 'Nobody has to remind us of the "women's angle" on unemployment or the miners' strike. We are women. We feel the necessity to show these things.'[63]

O'Brien was an enthusiastic and busy member of the agency. Yet despite her growing professional recognition, working as an Irish photographer in London in the 1980s during the Troubles left her feeling quite isolated within the photographic world. She frequently felt that her own colleagues in Format and other London freelancers either ignored or misunderstood what was happening in the North of Ireland. Her Irishness gave her a distinct perspective which was out of step with the experiences of her colleagues: 'I think being Irish in that context, I had a different political, social, and cultural outlook.'[64] Moreover, her engagement with Irish politics left her feeling isolated: 'I would come back from Belfast or Derry and I'd be full of the experience, and no one would be interested. I found that incredible.'[65] This sense of disconnection continued when she received an invitation to join an ad hoc editorial group to work on a special issue of *Camerawork* magazine on Northern Ireland. It proved to be a difficult experience. Some of the other members of the group 'didn't realize the subtleties and complexities of the Irish situation. You can't just throw a random selection of Irish people together and expect them all to work together. There were [also] English people in the editorial board [which] I think probably caused a lot of tension too.'[66]

Her experience of migration convinced her that there was a need for a book about Irish women in Britain. Around this time she met Mary Lennon, who also wanted to write on this topic, and together they made contact with

[62] Sheila Gray, Pam Isherwood, Joanne O'Brien, Jenny Matthews, Maggie Murray, Raissa Page, Brenda Prince, and Val Wilmer, 'Format Photographers', *Feminist Review* 18/1 (Winter 1984), 102.

[63] Gray et al., 'Format Photographers', 102.

[64] O'Brien interviewed by Mullen.

[65] Interview with O'Brien May 2016.

[66] O'Brien interviewed by Mullen.

Figure 6.7 Dún Laoghaire, 9 August 1986. Travellers at the ticket office for the Holyhead ferry (Joanne O'Brien).

Marie McAdam. It took the three women five years to finish *Across the Water*. Through a series of oral histories and photographs, they explored the complex and distinctive experiences of Irish women as they took the boat from Dún Laoghaire and built lives in London (Figure 6.7). Whilst many Irish men in Britain lived almost totally within an Irish community through working on a building site, living in lodging houses, and spending their free time in Irish bars, the experience of Irish women was very different.[67] They often worked in occupations such as cleaning or administration, where they might be the only Irish person in the workplace, and they therefore came into contact with racism in different and more intimate ways. Additionally, in their roles as mothers and domestic carers, they sometimes experienced difficult engagements with the welfare state through organizing housing, schooling, and childcare. They also experienced the problems of raising children away from the extended family, and they could be subject to the suspicion of the state, the prejudice of neighbours, and the suffocation of Irish community organizations.[68] These multiple forms of alienation often led to loneliness, and a high incidence of mental health problems.[69] However, whilst migration was often equated with exile, it could also mean escape from stifling social conditions. For Irish women, migration also offered new opportunities and possibilities, and O'Brien and her co-authors wanted to chronicle some of those hitherto unacknowledged achievements.

O'Brien's approach to *Across the Water* was motivated by her own experiences of emigration. She had been living in London for four years when she started working on the project, and had experienced and witnessed racism in a variety of forms: anti-Irish jokes on the bus, police surveillance, and social exclusion. Anti-Irish racism was common, acceptable, and explicit both in everyday occurrences and in the media; it was a feature of British life which was particularly notable for O'Brien, having previously lived in both France and Germany, where anti-Irish racism was not part of the national discourse. For example, she recalls a frightening visit by the Special Branch of the police to the London flat that she shared with other young

[67] Mary Hickman and Bronwen Walter, 'Deconstructing Whiteness: Irish Women in Britain', *Feminist Review* 50/1 (1995), 14.

[68] John Corbally, 'The Othered Irish: Shades of Difference in Post-War Britain, 1948–71', *Contemporary European History* 24/1 (2015), 107; Clair Wills, *The Best are Leaving: Emigration and Postwar Irish Culture* (Cambridge, 2015); Clair Wills, 'Realism and the Irish Immigrant: Documentary, Fiction, and Post War Irish Labor', *Modern Language Quarterly* 73/3 (2012) 373–94.

[69] Mary Lennon, Marie McAdam, and Joanne O'Brien, *Across the Water: Irish Women's Lives in Britain* (London, 1988).

Irish women in the late 1970s, after someone had required an ambulance. The ambulance crew had reported a suspicious object to the police and suggested it was bomb-making equipment. It was in fact a telephone meter used by her flatmates to note their respective telephone usage. 'There was a tremendous amount of anti-Irish attitude. I thought it came from fear...if you treat people badly [it is often because] you are afraid of them.'[70] But O'Brien felt that, while Britain had never come to terms with its colonial role in Ireland, Ireland's relationship with its population resident in Britain was also problematic. Indeed, in her view, Ireland had never come to terms with its own history of emigration. So she and her co-authors saw their book *Across the Water* as having a twofold audience:

> In Ireland, the Irish who go to Britain are somehow never taken notice of...were looked down upon somehow, [but the] people who went to America were up there...It was striking that when you went home to Ireland how no one ever asked you anything about living in London or living in England. The work [I was doing] was directed at the Irish in Britain, and also it was directed at Ireland, to show what was going on, all this stuff that had been [long] ignored.[71]

Throughout the twentieth century, Britain had served as a safety valve, keeping unemployment down, as the historian J. J. Lee remarked, 'Few peoples anywhere have been so prepared to scatter their children around the world in order to preserve their own living standards.'[72] Although Lee was referring to material conditions in his 1989 book on Ireland, emigration to Britain also preserved 'standards' in other ways, disposing of social problems, and providing a home for those who did not fit in. Where there was a certain consciousness in Ireland of migrants in Britain, it was the highly masculine portrayal of the builder or the navvy.[73] Irish women in Britain faced exclusion on multiple fronts—exploited for cheap labour and subject to racism in Britain, but also ignored and forgotten in Ireland.[74]

In this context, *Across the Water* therefore had two aims: firstly to give Irish women in London a sense of their own history and identity, and

[70] O'Brien interviewed by Mullen. [71] Interview with O'Brien.

[72] J. J. Lee, *Ireland 1912–1985: Politics and Society* (Cambridge, 1989), 522.

[73] Louise Ryan, 'Family Matters: (E)migration, Familial Networks and Irish Women in Britain', *The Sociological Review* 52/3 (2004), 351.

[74] Caitríona Clear, *Women's Voices in Ireland: Women's Magazines in the 1950s and* 60s (London, 2015), 124–6.

secondly in order to force people in Ireland to confront both their complacency and hypocrisy regarding the lives and experiences of their relatives in Britain. In their framing of the work and their use of word and image, the authors were profoundly influenced by the work of John Berger, including *Another Way of Telling*, which sought to use new literary and visual forms to explore subjective experiences of European modernization, and *The Seventh Man*, which explored and made visible how the economies of the rich nations of Europe had become dependent during the 1960s on the invisible labour of people from poorer nations.[75] Addressing 'the silence in which are our beginnings', O'Brien and her co-authors sought to use her photography both to empower these female migrants and to make their lives visible.[76] She took portraits of all the women interviewed for the book, asking her subjects to collaborate with her on how they presented themselves to the camera. Through these portraits, she attempted to show the women not as statistics, or as victims, but rather as 'actors in their own lives'.[77] The book also contained photo-essays on topics including culture, work, and the second-generation experience. In taking these photographs, O'Brien attempted to ascribe value to a range of social and cultural activities which had previously been ignored.[78] 

In the early 1990s, O'Brien was commissioned by a Dublin newspaper, the *Sunday Tribune*, to take a series of photographs at an abortion clinic. At the time, there was public controversy surrounding the rape of a fourteen-year-old girl, known only as X, who had been prevented from travelling to the United Kingdom to undergo an abortion. There had been marches and pickets in Ireland and Britain, and a sustained public debate about the realities of contraception and abortion for Irish women. Brian Trench, the picture editor working at the *Sunday Tribune*, 'wanted to try and demystify the experience [of abortion]'.[79] Although taking the plane to London for an abortion had become a relatively common feature of women's lives in 1980s Ireland, the issue tended to remain out of the public sphere. Throughout the latter decades of the twentieth century, the Irish Women's Abortion Support Group (IWASG) and the Irish Abortion Solidarity Campaign (IASC) operated in British cities to help women coming from Ireland get to abortions: meeting them at airports, taking them to clinics, and giving them beds for

75 Berger and Mohr, *Another Way of Telling*, 84.
76 Lennon, O'Brien, and McAdam, *Across the Water*, 9.
77 O'Brien interviewed by Mullen.
78 Interview with O'Brien May 2016.
79 Interview with O'Brien May 2016.

the night. They had, however, generally operated very discreetly, respecting the abortion seekers' right to confidentiality, but also, in so doing, 'pandering to the unspoken wishes of the two Irish states and many Irish community organizations in Britain.'[80] O'Brien looked directly at this area of silence with her camera. The *Sunday Tribune* had negotiated unique access to an abortion clinic in West London. Alongside the journalist Nicola Byrne, she spent a day in the clinic, from 8.30am to 7pm, photographing the waiting room, the doctors and nurses, and the overnight bags of the women who had come on the plane from Ireland. Although initially the staff were adamant that she was not to photograph any of the clients, during the day O'Brien 'struck up a really good rapport with an Italian woman who felt very strongly about the political hypocrisy around the issue, and who wanted to be photographed before, during, and after.'[81] On 1 March 1992, the *Sunday Tribune* led with the story, putting O'Brien's image on the front page.[82] It shows an English operating theatre, moments before an abortion is carried out, reclaiming the experience from the perspective of the woman, a point reinforced by the curtain sweeping around the trolley, making the forms of a vagina (Figure 6.8).

O'Brien's next project was a book on Bloody Sunday, at a moment when personal testimony was being used to 'counter the legitimizing narrative of the British state.'[83] An article in the *Irish Times* on the republication of the 1972 contemporary accounts that had been collected from witnesses to the killings in Derry by the UK's National Council for Civil Liberties (NCCL), in a book edited by Don Mullan, led her to wonder how the survivors and families had coped since the events of that day.[84] However, at first she was tentative about embarking on a project on Bloody Sunday; she was anxious about the emotional pain for the survivors and about asking them to relive traumatic events. What she would do with the material, once she had collected it, was also of concern, as she had no guarantee of publication. But the idea of the project 'wouldn't go away. [It] got me by the scruff of the neck and I was propelled willy-nilly to Derry, for a number of visits during the course of that year.'[85] At this time, the families were still campaigning

[80] Ann Rossiter, *Ireland's Hidden Diaspora: The 'Abortion Trail' and the Making of a London-Irish Underground, 1980–2000* (London, 2009), 26.

[81] O'Brien interviewed by Mullen.

[82] *Sunday Tribune*, 1 March 1992, 1.

[83] Graham Dawson, *Making Peace with the Past? Memory, Trauma, and the Irish Troubles* (Manchester, 2007), 122.

[84] Don Mullan, *Eyewitness Bloody Sunday* (Dublin, 1997).

[85] Interview with O'Brien.

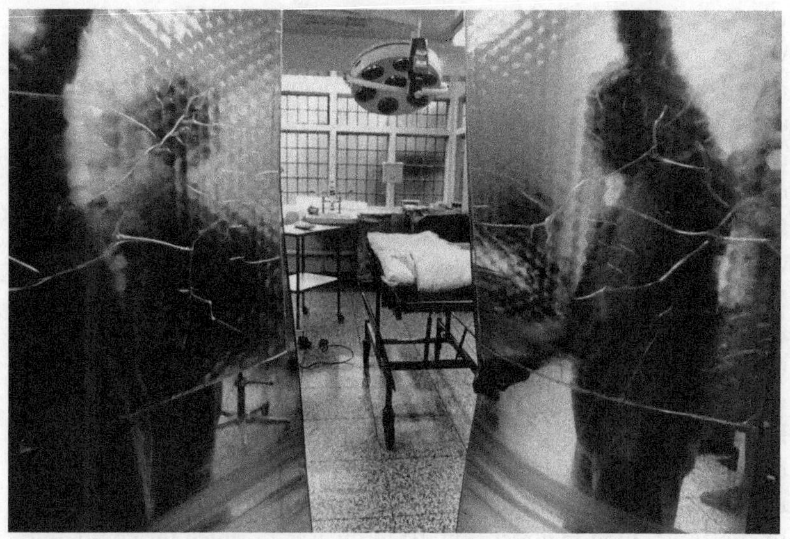

Figure 6.8 West London 1992. Abortion Clinic (Joanne O'Brien).

for a second judicial inquiry into the shootings, and O'Brien initially intended simply to do a series of portraits of relatives and injured survivors at the locations where the shootings had taken place. But 'then people started telling me things. And I started writing them down then taping them. At various times the words took over from the pictures and it became about documenting all these stories.'[86] In January 1998, the *Sunday Business Post* published a special seven-page supplement of her portraits and interviews with the relatives, and then a follow-up the next year focusing on the injured. Her second book, *A Matter of Minutes* (2002), grew out of these publications, and took five years to complete.[87]

O'Brien photographed family members of the deceased on the spot where their relatives had died: 'I asked them to... stand there and to bear witness to what had happened to them, to their family' in order to make 'a record of what had happened... from their point of view'.[88] In framing the aftermath of Bloody Sunday through a series of portraits of the survivors and families of the dead, O'Brien showed the difficulties endured by the community, and using photography's purchase on time to reframe the event not as a 'matter of minutes' but rather as the gruelling decades which had changed the lives of many people.

While O'Brien usually talked to people as she took their photograph, she didn't do that with these photographs, instead staying quiet behind the camera, 'I wanted them at the spot where it had happened and not necessarily relating to me, but relating to the memories and their feelings.'[89] The photographs she took revealed the individual suffering and endurance of those who had lived through Bloody Sunday and dealt with its legacy. By focusing on the individual and subjective experience of loss, the portraits stood in direct contrast to the way in which the community had been treated by the Widgery Tribunal and the security services in the aftermath of the events.[90] In a photograph of Ita and Regina McKinney, for example, the women stand together in front of the remaining low-rise flats on Rossville Street. They clutch each other's hands in support. However, they are lost in their own thoughts, Regina looking down, in a

[86] O'Brien interviewed by Mullen.

[87] Joanne O'Brien, *A Matter of Minutes: The Enduring Legacy of Bloody Sunday* (Dublin, 2002).

[88] Interview with O'Brien. [89] Interview with O'Brien.

[90] Many of the grieving families were subjected to constant harassment by the security services in the wake of Bloody Sunday; see, for example, O'Brien, *A Matter of Minutes*, 72; 94 and 142.

pose of remembrance, Ita gazing out of the image-frame, distraught, caught back in the memory of that day. These images are deeply troubling to look at; through acknowledging the lasting impact of the events of the day on the survivors and families, they serve as a memorial and a marker to the long afterlives of Bloody Sunday.[91] However, the project was also aimed at people in the Republic of Ireland. In O'Brien's view, partition had been a 'blight on the country' which allowed residents of the southern state to 'blank the north' and 'let [the Troubles] go on for so long, [and] that needed to be challenged'.[92]

O'Brien has often felt herself to be an outsider in both Britain and Ireland. Unlike other women in her position, she has used the tropes of the documentary tradition to give herself authority in this system; her photography entwined the subjective and the social, and put a form on her own story and those of millions of women like her who had left Ireland to live in Britain. She worked largely in black and white, which referred back to the men and women who had established the documentary tradition, but also gave her a sense of control, to 'express feeling and shape and line'. The skill of printing was important to her. 'I loved that you could play with perception of the image…by the way you manipulated the negative…that, as Ansel Adams put it, the negative was the score and the print was the performance.'[93] In 1982, John Berger came to the Institute of Contemporary Arts in London to give a lecture. O'Brien went to hear him talk, and afterwards asked him if she could take his portrait, '*Another Way of Telling* had just come out, and I had…read it from cover to cover…I stood him under a tree outside the ICA and he folded his arms…and he said, "I'll be just like Marcel in the book, won't I?" '[94] Berger signed her copy of the book, inscribing it: 'For Joanne and the everyday always ambiguous struggle to wrest some meaning from what we and people live. London September 1982. In solidarity, John.' In his own way John Berger had struck on something fundamental about O'Brien's practice as a photographer—her need to struggle with the unanswerable question of how to be honest as a photographer, and in this process deal with ambiguity, make sense of complexity, and use her images to create a more just society.

[91] See also Carville, 'The Violence of the Image: Conflict and Post-Conflict Photography in Northern Ireland', 73–5.

[92] Interview with O'Brien.

[93] Interview with O'Brien.

[94] Berger and Mohr, *Another Way of Telling*, 36–7. Marcel was a farmer who agreed to have his portrait taken wearing his Sunday best. See chapter 2.

Frankie Quinn's Photographic Eulogies to the Short Strand

Frankie Quinn has spent his entire life living in the Short Strand, an area of red-brick Victorian streets just to the west of the Lagan. As a small Catholic enclave in the largely Protestant East Belfast, it is known for both its close-knit community and the intensity of violence it experienced during the Troubles. Indeed, Gilles Peress described the Short Strand as 'like an island or a prison, depending on what mood you are in.'[95] This experience would be formative in shaping both Quinn's practices and his politics as a photographer.

Quinn's relationship with photography began during the tension and violence of the Hunger Strikes. At this time, he was fifteen years old, and was put under house arrest for nine months, only allowed to leave to go to school. Shortly after his release, his father heard about Buzz Logan's camera club, and bought him a simple Praktica for his sixteenth birthday, which he gave to him with the words, 'There's a camera, stay out of trouble.'[96] The Mac Airt camera club had only the most basic equipment, but from his first visits, Quinn was seduced by the 'alchemy' of photography and the technicalities of image-making. He still remembers 'processing my first film. Getting the negative…And I remember the first time seeing the picture coming up, that was it, that was me hooked.' Moreover, Buzz Logan also taught him a commitment to his subjects, and to the ethics of documentary photography. 'He was a socialist and he cared about people. And you can see the humanity in his photographs. You know that there. He had a training, that's where I got it from, where the picture comes through there, and through here and then to there.' With this statement, Quinn indicated a movement between pressing the button, the eye, and the heart.[97]

From this beginning at Mac Airt camera club, Quinn had a varied career which reflected both the creative tensions and frequent precariousness of photography. In October 1983, he began an apprenticeship at Collins Photographics, a small business doing developing and printing. In the converted garage of Basil Collins, the proprietor, he learned to print colour and to use a range of new equipment.[98] However, the business closed soon after Quinn started working there; while this meant that Quinn lost his job, it also meant that Collins gave him all his photographic equipment. At home

[95] Review of Interface Images by Gilles Peress: http://www.belfastarchiveproject.com/peacelines-review-gilles-peress (accessed 30 July 2019).

[96] Interview with Frankie Quinn, 25 July 2016.

[97] Interview with Quinn.

[98] Interview with Quinn.

in their small house in Short Strand, Quinn's father added a new storey to his pigeon coop, so that Quinn could use the ground floor as a dark room. 'I was like a wee cottage industry, underneath the pigeons.'[99] These new skills and equipment would eventually provide Quinn with further employment. In 1984, the photographer for the Sinn Féin paper, *Republican News*, was paralysed by an RUC plastic bullet, and Quinn took on his job, photographing demonstrations, riots, and political events for the paper. Nine months later, he also started taking pictures for the Irish language newspaper, *Lá*. Soon after he left the paper, going freelance, until in 1989, he got what he described as his 'big break', when he was employed by the *Sunday News*. For this paper he also recorded political events on the streets of Northern Ireland. When that newspaper shut in 1993, pressured out of the market by the new colour Sundays, he again went freelance. Despite his father's orders to 'stay out of trouble', Quinn muses that 'Little did he know it was going to get me into fucking more trouble!'.[100] In the context of 1980s Belfast, Quinn's interest in photography inevitably put him in dangerous situations on several occasions. As a Catholic from the Short Strand, he was immediately under suspicion for photographing the RUC and the British Army, who assumed he was supplying the IRA with photographs, and who frequently harassed him, gave his details to Loyalist paramilitaries, and sent him death threats. Unable to cope with this tension, Quinn left Belfast on two occasions, spending a year working on building sites in London and Australia. In his own words, his early photography 'didn't come easy'.[101]

While Northern Irish photography has been characterized by a turn towards post-modern, non-representational image making practised by photographers such as Victor Sloan and Willie Doherty, Quinn has not followed this approach. Moreover, he has also rejected the exploitative, flash-point photography of violence which has characterized images of Northern Ireland across the world. His distance from both these photographic idioms played an important role in shaping his work. As he described it, people said to him, 'You are not like the fly by photographers who come in, shoot off a few rolls, go back to dinner in the Europa and away the next day.'[102] In contrast, Quinn 'liv[ed] the politics every single day' and 'knew the times he was living through'.[103] He considered his images to come 'from within the community as opposed to people coming in and taking photographs, and

[99] Interview with Quinn.
[100] Interview with Quinn.
[101] Interview with Quinn.
[102] Interview with Quinn.
[103] Interview with Quinn.

that's the difference'. As displayed by his images of back gardens and washing lines in *Interface Images*, this also meant that he had access to scenes other photographers could not get to, which gave him the opportunity to photograph a more diverse set of events and themes.

Growing up in the Short Strand, Quinn's life was shaped by the towering peacelines of corrugated metal, wire, and concrete which surrounded the area on several sides (Figure 6.9).[104] Walls had been built around this small Catholic enclave in east Belfast from the late 1960s, and continued to be erected, extended, and heightened throughout the latter twentieth century.[105] The experience of growing up in the shadow of these walls informed Quinn's first major project, documenting these peacelines, published as *Interface Images* in 1994.[106] In *Circa*, he described the project:

> In September 1992 I began a project to photograph the sixteen so-called 'peacelines' that carve up the working-class areas of Belfast. I thought it necessary to provide a social documentary on the walls, what they represented, and life around them. Since the fall of the Berlin Wall in 1989, no similar structure exists to control and separate any society. The walls represent failure more than anything else. The failure of the Northern Ireland State to create conditions of equality and harmony for all of its citizens for fifty years, ensured that the long-standing psychological barriers that existed for that time were finally given physical expression. For the past 25 years, the peacelines have evolved and spread to most areas where Catholic and Protestant meet, the fact that they are exclusive to working class areas is no coincidence.[107]

An examination of the peacelines provided Quinn with a new way of photographing Belfast during the early 1990s. In the words of Conor McGrady, Quinn's images 'not only capture[d] the architecture of a divided city, but the impact of ideological polarisation and topographical fragmentation on the lives of those who live alongside these structures'.[108] Despite their

[104] Florine Ballif, 'Portraying the Divided city: Photographing the Belfast Peacelines', *Visual Ethnography* 3/1 (2014), 65–91.

[105] Conor McGrady, 'Division and Enclosure: Frankie Quinn's Peaceline Panorama Photographs', in Carolyn Loeb and Andreas Luescher (eds.) *The Design of Frontier Spaces: Control and Ambiguity* (London, 2015), 17.

[106] Nicholas Allen, Review of 'Peacelines: photographs by Frankie Quinn' at the Old Museum Arts Centre, January 1995', *Source* (1995).

[107] 'Vox Pop: Peacelines', *Circa* 71 (Spring 1995), p. 20.

[108] McGrady, 'Division and Enclosure', p. 18.

Figure 6.9 Glenbryn, North Belfast (1980) (Frankie Quinn).

central position in constituting divisions and framing conflict, the photojournalistic emphasis on moments of violence had often pushed the peacelines to the edge or the background of the image-frame. Reorienting the viewer's gaze to these walls provided a new way of looking at Belfast: foregrounding the urban blight caused by these structures, houses with walls claustrophobically placed only feet from bedroom windows, and watch towers looming over quiet residential streets. They also displayed poignant accommodations with these imposing, military walls: washing lines tied to them, children's games played up against them, graffiti scrawled on their large surfaces (Figure 6.10). This depiction of the everyday experiences of the peacelines contained images which explored the sense of the knowing and not knowing that came with living in close proximity and yet entirely divorced from another community, including an image of a boy gazing at the top of a bonfire which could only be partially viewed over the top of the wall, and which cast strange shadows on his street. Quinn's eye for these refigured quotidian moments were simultaneously poignant, beautiful, and revealing of the textures of daily life of during the Troubles. Moreover, these quiet images also contained within them a highly political project. The grim, heavy, still atmosphere of many of the photographs revealed that, as Ronan Bennett stated in response to the collection, 'there is no such thing as a "safe" area in the city', but rather, the 'most dangerous places in Belfast are the areas around the so-called peacelines' where 'people live in a constant state of anxiety; sectarian tension never goes away'.[109] These heavy walls provided visual evidence of a phenomenon so rarely depicted photographically: the state's active efforts to create a sectarian state supported and reinforced in physical objects and infrastructure throughout the province.[110]

More recently, Quinn has turned to a new project on the Orange Order, photographing the organization's marches in Ireland, north and south, England, Scotland, and Canada. He describes his interest in the Orange Order as 'all about geography'.[111] His community in the Short Strand has been 'hemmed in' every 12 July by parades, crowds, and rising sectarian tensions, and the Order's marches. Beginning a project on these parades, his camera gave him a new mobility through his own city: 'It gave me a sense of safety. In fact, you see the old Rolleiflex? People were more interested in the camera than they were in me, and that was great for me. Because there were

109 Ronan Bennett, 'Introduction', in Frankie Quinn, *Interface Images* (Belfast, 1994).
110 Ronan Bennet, 'Introduction', in Quinn, *Interface Images*.
111 Interview with Quinn.

Figure 6.10 Clandeboye Gardens—Cluan Place, East Belfast (2016) (Frankie Quinn).

a couple of safety issues there where it was pretty hairy. I felt a wee bit, intimidated, you know?'[112] Moreover, taking photographs of the Order 'allowed [him] to get really up close', while the studied and focused gaze of the camera gave him a way to attempt to understand a culture which was alien to him, but which was an important tradition for those living close by in Belfast, and a route to explore 'the soul beneath the sash'.[113] Indeed, Quinn noted that the experience of photographing the Orange Order engendered in him 'a wee bit of respect for the whole culture'.[114] This new sense of proximity also allowed him to understand the operation of social capital in the movement. Indeed, the older men associated with the Order used it for networking and social prestige, displayed in their pressed suits and their stiff and formalized bodily composition as they marched (Figure 6.11).[115] However, the organization also attracted a significant group of younger followers, who, in the opinion of Quinn, were exploited as 'cannon fodder', and who, as inevitably as William III defeats James II at Scarva every year, became involved in violence against both the police and the Catholic community.[116]

His photographs of the rituals, regalia, paraphernalia, and gestures associated with the Orange Order show the marches as times of communal camaraderie and celebration. This performance and reinscription of complex spheres of social power and authority took place in front of a backdrop of picnics, deck chairs, ice cream vans, and souvenir stalls. One of his most striking photographs of the Orange marches shows a West Indian family sitting with a picnic waiting to watch the Orange Order go past—a fitting reminder of how Ireland was changing and a significant reversal of the spectacle-spectator dynamic of much colonial photography. It reveals how rituals, which are often taken for granted in Irish life, can be recast as strange, foreign, and anachronistic when composed through a lens. Quinn remembered taking the image: 'See I was waiting for them to come in, I had the camera, and just the right time she turned around. And the whole time I had someone shouting in my ear "Have you been saved?!" and I said, "Let me fucking take this picture then you can do your best." '[117]

Throughout his career, Quinn has put the idea of 'discipline' at the centre of how he has conceived of his work, his technical competency, and how he

[112] Interview with Quinn. [113] Interview with Quinn.

[114] Interview with Quinn.

[115] John O'Farrell, 'Foreword', in Frankie Quinn, *The Orange* (Belfast, 2014), 7; interview with Quinn.

[116] Interview with Quinn. [117] Interview with Quinn.

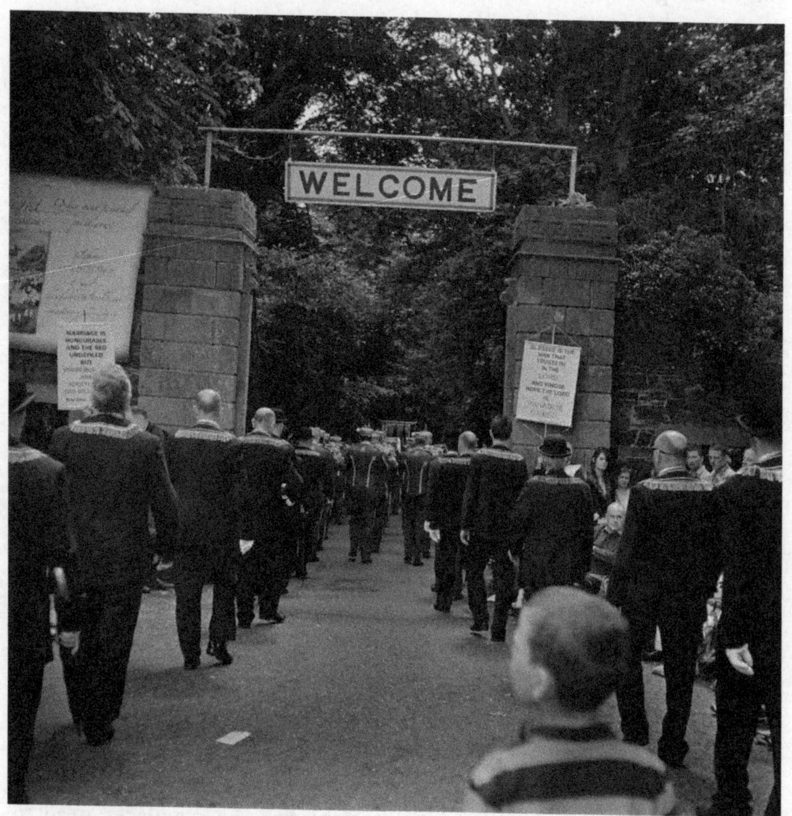

Figure 6.11 Orange Order Parade (2014) (Frankie Quinn).

has behaved as a photographer. Part of this 'discipline' came from economic exigencies: 'I remember you could buy 12 exposure films at the time. 12 exposures. 36 was an absolute luxury. Sometimes it would stay in your camera for weeks. Because the discipline...film was so precious, that everything had to be right before you used that film. And that's discipline I still have.'[118] He has always taken full-frame photographs which are uncropped, 'Because you should get it right when you take it. It's as simple as that, it's a discipline I've learned over the years.'[119] Lacking a traditional art school training, however, Quinn 'hadn't a clue' about photographic traditions when he began taking images.[120] Rather, his early photographic training at the Mac Airt camera club consisted of two simple pieces of advice which would dominate his approach to photography: firstly to 'fill the frame' and secondly to get the relationship between aperture and shutter speed right. However, as he became more experienced he discovered, and was inspired by, the key photographers of the documentary movement: 'I was into it for about five years, maybe more, five or six years, when first somebody gave me a book of Bresson and I hadn't a clue who any of these photographers were.' From this beginning, he also developed an interest in the Magnum photographers, including Ernst Haas, Gilles Peress, Leonard Freed, and Robert Frank.[121] He has also used some of the cameras associated with the history of twentieth-century documentary photography, including a Leica and a Rolleiflex, which produced pristine lines and tones, echoing the work of others who used these cameras such as Bill Brandt and Robert Capa. His photography has also been overwhelmingly in black and white, which echoed the work of these earlier photographers, but also allowed him to create images where lines and forms played a central role. '[The eye] is drawn towards certain colours, and that takes away from the composition. That composition is balanced. It doesn't weigh on either side and that's what I like about black and white. It's the composition.'[122]

In recent years, Quinn's practice has again been reshaped by Northern Ireland's transition to a post-conflict society, and the populace's need to make sense of the events that had shaped their individual and collective pasts. Photography's seeming ability to hold on to the transient makes it uniquely placed to mediate these concerns. In 1994, for example, he discussed his peaceline images:

[118] Interview with Quinn.
[119] Interview with Quinn.
[120] Interview with Quinn.
[121] Interview with Quinn.
[122] Interview with Quinn.

> After two years of photographing the walls, I finally made it to the printers on August 31 of last year, the day of the IRA ceasefire. When the photographs were taken there was war in the streets and now it is seemingly over, history has already overtaken my project…Hopefully sooner rather than later *Interface Images* will become a historical record of Belfast as it once was.[123]

This sense of optimism which characterized the mood in Belfast in the mid-1990s was not wholly substantiated by future events; however, today the photographs retain much of their importance as documents of a period when there was a sense that things were changing and forms of the Troubles were passing into history. For example, the camera's apparent ability to create permanence played an important role in how Quinn conceived of his project on the Orange Order. The Order may have, for him, embodied much that he saw as wrong with Northern Irish culture, but he was also aware of its transience—his photography gave him a sense of how every year the number of marchers was diminishing, the men were getting older, and the sashes were no longer getting passed down through families.

> I'm making this record here because it's a dying thing. It's—if you look at the photographs—they are all old men. There is no doubt about it. When I was in Toronto last year I was told stories of the thirties and forties and fifties when thousands of Orange men marched through Toronto. Last year we counted about a hundred. And they are all grey and all old. There's no young men coming into it. Because the sash doesn't guarantee you anything anymore. It's actually a hindrance. The sash used to be passed down through generations and that guaranteed you a job in one of the heavy industries. And all the industries are gone, all the employment is gone. So you don't need the sash anymore.[124]

Moreover, this sense of the era of the Troubles receding into history has shaped Quinn's business decisions and ability to sell images. During the 2000s, Quinn sold his photographs of the Troubles from a stall in Belfast city centre. 'I said to the guy who owned the stall, fucking hell ten years ago we weren't even allowed into town, let alone set up a stall selling political images.'[125] He used the money he made on the stall to set up the Red Barn, where between 2008 and 2016 he

[123] Frankie Quinn in 'Vox Pop: Peacelines', *Circa* 71 (Spring 1995), 20.
[124] Interview with Quinn.
[125] Interview with Quinn.

exhibited and archived images by photographers working in Northern Ireland during the twentieth century.[126]

Documentary played a formative role in shaping these photographers' life histories: how they have made choices about sympathy, responsibility, and the nature of a social conscience in their own lives. Left-wing politics, ideas of social justice, and notions of authenticity, embedded in the history and ideals of documentary, have played a determining role in how they looked at Irish society and how they understood its problems. Retelling their photographic biographies makes it clear that any simple dynamic between viewer and viewed is simplistic to the point of falsehood—these photographers inhabited the social worlds they photographed and their images were often explorations of the challenges they faced in their own lives. More recently, the cultural resonance of photography has again played a role in shaping their careers; as the photographs they took during the 1980s have been reconceived as mnemonic images they have taken on new and different meanings, as a record—bordering almost on nostalgia—of Ireland when it was poorer and seemingly more authentic, less visibly marked by the signs—and signage—of global consumerism and investment. This reading of their images has come to play an important role in the present day as part of explaining the economic and cultural shifts of recent years and as part of a retroactive renarration of the 1980s as a crucial turning point in the creation of contemporary Ireland.

In the 1980s, the representation of 'authentic' images of Ireland was hard fought within broader battles between the forces of modernity and tradition. Speirs, O'Brien, and Quinn took their documentary images, and magazines published them, because they believed that they pushed at the complacencies of Irish middle-class experience, or—in the linguistic formation of the period—made visible the invisible aspects of Irish culture. Indeed, these photographs sat alongside a whole host of cultural forms, including novels, plays, and memoirs, which sought to recuperate these aspects of Irish society and culture during this period.[127] The very fact that these discourses existed is revealing of the shame and silence which surrounded poverty, emigration, and worklessness in both church and state. But, in this period, these issues became part of the imagination of an increasingly vocal liberal elite, and the way that this largely urban group

126 Bertrand, '"A tool for social change"', *LISA* (online).

127 Examples include Dermot Bolger, *Night Shift* (Dublin, 1985) and Roddy Doyle, *The Commitments* (Dublin, 1987).

made sense of—and critiqued—traditional Ireland. Indeed, the appetite of a new metropolitan press to publish these images is revealing of how the contestation of these issues became the pressure points at which of the identity 'modern' Ireland was being contested and forged.

Despite the serious and thoughtful way in which documentary photographers considered their images, and built relationships with the people they photographed, they had little control over their photographs once they entered public circulation. These photographs were printed thousands of times onto newspaper, loaded into vans, displayed at newsstands, or sold in exchange for a pound coin. As such, each photograph was the product of a set of relations between photographer, photographed, and viewer, and moreover, also embodied a further set of financial and material relations between individuals, the media, and the market. Thus making sense of the processes which brought an image into existence and circulation provides a productive starting point for exploring the constitution of social relations in 1980s Ireland, and the intersection of institutions and capital which brought these perceived 'silences' into formation. The notion of documentary practice in 1980s Ireland was predicated on a wide (social and geographic) gap between rich and poor, a media that profited from it, and an understanding of an elite who would pay to look at these images. These power dynamics were not unique to the documentary image; indeed, they were written through Irish society, and the 'problems' associated with documentary were no different to a similar set of relations embedded in documents such as social surveys, censuses, and reportage. Documentary photography received so much public and strongly worded opprobrium not because it was uniquely voyeuristic but because of the challenging and forthright way it made visible the power dynamics that were embedded in Irish politics and culture.

Conclusion

Digital Analogue Images and the Appearance of Historical Distance

Since I started writing this book, the unknown family album where I began has been digitized. I can now revisit those first moments of archival discovery remotely from my office in Bristol, and re-examine those images of brothers on bicycles, picnics in the garden, and fossil hunting on the coralline shore near Ballyconneely (Figure 7.1).[1] The new viewing function is certainly convenient for researchers working outside Ireland. It also promises to provide more detail and more information, allowing me to blow up the image I seek of the family scrambling together on the beach—in reality no bigger than a business card—to extend across my whole computer monitor. But beyond a limited magnification, the pixelated image breaks down. The photograph becomes a blur of lines and shapes, a meaningless assemblage of browns and greys. I get no closer to finding what I am looking for; despite the possibility suggested by the ability to zoom endlessly, the photograph offers up no more detail. This is a commonplace experience for researchers using photographs. Even photos which are—somewhere—paper documents, we usually see digitally, sitting at a desk in front of a computer. The contours of the archive are flattened as everything is digitized and digitized in the same way, so that photographs which were never looked at when they were first developed now seem obvious and commonplace and the rare and delicate and precious appear everywhere. They are now all the same size, brightly lit, and fill up the screen.

It can feel like some of the magic has gone. There is magic in holding an image by its edges, turning it over, reading the back, smelling the dust.[2] Indeed, there is a very particular set of emotions—of excitement and perhaps relief—we experience in the archive the first time we find a photograph of a person

[1] NLI Family Holidays Ireland Album 2 ALB424b: http://catalogue.nli.ie/Record/vtls000538310#page/1/mode/1up (accessed 23 August 2018).

[2] Carolyn Steedman, *Dust* (Manchester, 2001).

Snapshot Stories: Visuality, Photography, and the Social History of Ireland, 1922–2000. Erika Hanna, Oxford University Press (2020). © Erika Hanna.
DOI: 10.1093/oso/9780198823032.001.0001

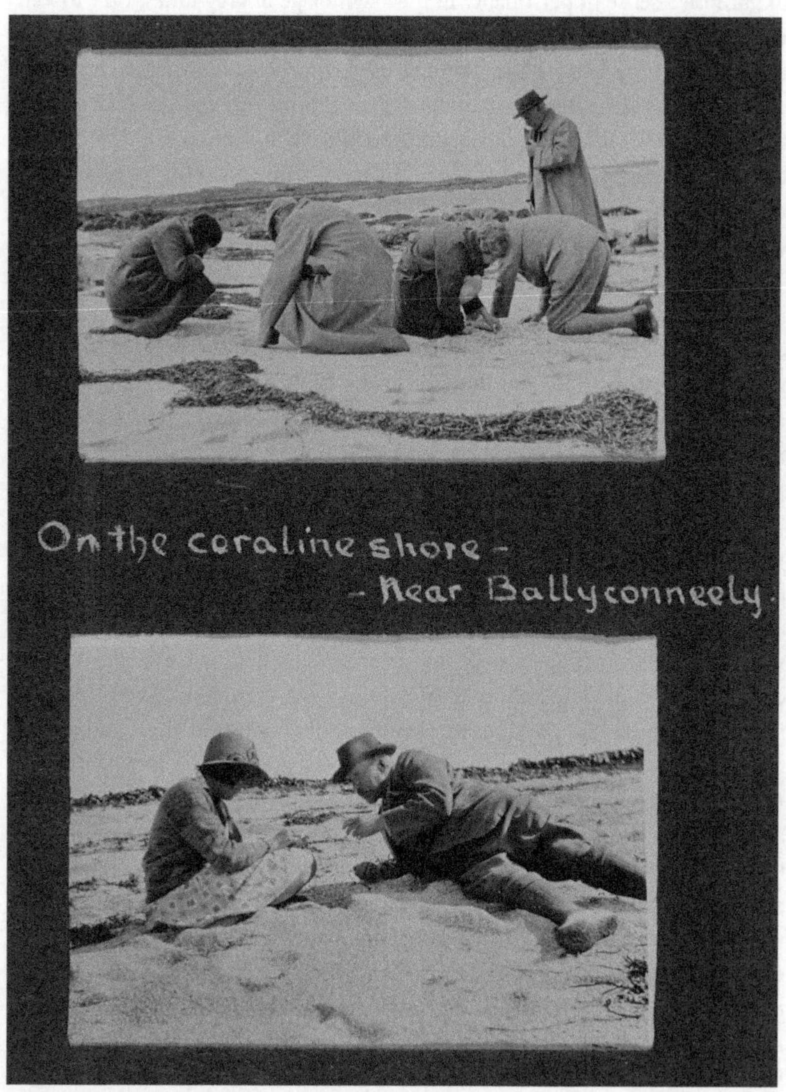

Figure 7.1 On the coraline [sic] shore near Ballyconneely (1929). Image Courtesy of the National Library of Ireland.

we have been looking for. I catch my breath as if the merest whisper of air might disrupt the trace of what remains, and stare hard at the image, to try to glimpse a sense of personality in the assemblage of grey tones. I try to join up wrinkles, clothes, posture in the image with the idea of someone I have assembled in my head. I stare at their eyes, almost attempting to make eye contact across time. But the moment of recognition and connection I seek in the image inevitably does not occur; the blurred image instead epitomizes the gap of historical distance which always animates and frustrates our desire to recover that messy thing we call experience. These photographs stand on the cusp of time, tokens of forgettable moments almost forgotten. The angle of shoulders, the pattern of a tea set, the weather on a day out picnicking are all present and obvious within the frame. Unremarkable details are remembered while information we crave—of structures, systems, processes—escapes us. The images fade, the papers brown, fingerprints corrode and embed themselves in the image, become part of its history. But the images still pull at our heart strings, telling us about our need for the past, even as they resist revealing its details.

The Celtic Tiger changed Ireland. In the twenty-first century, much that we took for granted about who we are, and who we were, is passing into historical time, unknown by the state's younger citizens. Indeed, contemporary Ireland has a difficult relationship with its past; public discourse is often written through with a sense of loss as seemingly distinctive facets of Irish culture slip out of view, held in tension with a self-confidence about the present, and a sense that previous grievances are being faced. The Troubles are over, the abuses of the church are being addressed, the island is considerably more prosperous than it was fifty years ago. However, even as these changes are largely celebrated, a—sometimes joking, sometimes earnest—sentimentality for the authenticity of the past runs through Irish culture, when holidays meant sandblasted days in a clapped-out Opel Kadett at Portrush and celebrity meant a commendation at Young Scientist of the Year. A shape-shifting and sometimes contradictory nostalgia entwined with disavowal of the past permeates Irish cultural life, and even as the meaning of the past is unstable, it is a constant point of reference.[3] These social and cultural transformations have come at a time when the ways in which we record the present and make sense of the historic record are also changing. Digital photographs—stored

[3] For a more detailed exegesis of this topic, see Emilie Pine, *The Politics of Irish Memory: Performing Remembrance in Contemporary Irish Culture* (London, 2011); Oona Frawley (ed.), *Memory Ireland Volume 1: History and Modernity* (Syracuse, 2011), 18–34.

and shared online—seem to provide a new ability to access that past and to reconfigure our relationship with our near and distant history and have played a constitutive role in shaping these tensions. They bring images of the past closer, and circulate more quickly, just at the moment of the past's supposed disavowal.

These changes in our relationship to the past have been underpinned by a revolution in quotidian visual practices. Today images saturate our lives. The figures are staggering: in 2017, 90 per cent of people in the Irish republic had access to a smartphone, while 43 per cent of smartphone users took and shared photographs every day.[4] These statistics are higher than European averages, reflective of Ireland's self-conscious rebranding as a high-tech paradise. The privileges that surrounded taking a photograph dissipated as everyone gained the ability to record and store images—thousands and thousands of images. Moreover, their infinite reproducibility—on Facebook, Instagram, Flickr, and a constantly revolving circus of more fashionable platforms—provides new avenues for dissemination where images are everywhere and yet nowhere, reproducing our images not just in our living rooms, but on everyone else's smartphones too. The sheer number of images makes meaning, significance, and narrative hard to discern. Where one image used to have a treasured significance, this is now replaced by the sensation of clicking through a thousand images; life lived in stutter-framed fast forward. Different tools, which my generation of historians does not possess, are required to make sense of these pixelated photo-histories, and to appreciate how they are reshaping our lives.

Despite their differences of form, many themes which have run through this book persist in today's image world. For example, since emigration recommenced after 2009, ties of family have been preserved by sharing photographs and life stories online, capitalizing on digital media's ability to collapse distinctions of proximity and distance. Irish heritage groups have also protested against the fashion for individuals to post images of themselves performing stunts on ancient Irish heritage sites, including cycling on a ledge along the Cliffs of Moher or posing as characters from *Game of Thrones* at Giants Causeway.[5] In many ways, these controversies merely reflect a

[4] RTÉ, '90% of Irish Population Have Access to a Smartphone, Survey Finds', https://www.rte.ie/news/2017/1205/925007-smartphone (accessed 23 August 2018); Deloitte, 'There's No Place Like Phone', https://www2.deloitte.com/ie/en/pages/about-deloitte/articles/Theres-no-place-like-phone.html (accessed 23 August 2018).

[5] Fintan O'Toole, 'Hunger fails to wrest the narrative from the Hunger Strikers', *Irish Times*, 22 November 2008, https://www.irishtimes.com/news/hunger-fails-to-wrest-the-narrative-from-the-hunger-strikers-1.913725 (accessed 23 August 2018).

longstanding external view of the Irish landscape as a pleasure-ground to be dominated or conquered for the entertainment or self-aggrandizement of the visitor. New moral panics surrounding sharing personal information on the internet have raised new questions about the boundaries of public and private. 'Selfies'—posed, pouting self-portraits, taken in the front seat of the car or in front of a prominent landmark—reimagine the forms through which we constitute the public self.[6] Moreover, they have led to long-running moral panics about the vanity of young women which echo the previous scandals about youth, sexuality, and femininity which accompanied the arrival of short skirts and mass-produced make-up. Indeed, social media has been repeatedly used to shame young women sexually, only aggravating the tendencies of voyeurism and violence which have always come alongside looking at women. Representation and the strategic use of the visual has always been part of Irish protest, and this trend has continued in the digital era. For example, the protests against the introduction of charges for water in 2015 made self-conscious and advantageous use of social media to spread messages declared at demonstrations.[7] More recently, and perhaps more successfully, the visual nature of protests for the repeal of the Eight Amendment capitalized on visually arresting images which were designed to be shared.[8] Images of women with suitcases, and women in *Handmaid's Tale*-style red habits and hoods capitalized on the viral way that images and videos are disseminated on social media in order to raise the profile of the campaign for access to abortion. Indeed, it seems that the pace and reproducibility of digital technologies is reinforcing and exaggerating pre-existing tropes and motifs within Irish photo culture.

But digitization has also created new possibilities for photographic afterlives and new potential for the historical archive. In recent years, archives have ploughed much of their limited resources into digitizing their collections as a way of reducing the burden on staff and preserving original documents, with more and more documents available online every day. The past is not what it used to be. We encounter a tyranny of riches: it is difficult to know where to begin with the Independent

[6] Mary McGill, 'Taking Selfies Seriously' Women Are Boring, https://womenareboring.wordpress.com/2017/11/28/taking-selfies-seriously (accessed 1 August 2018).

[7] 'Water protests first to go viral on Irish social media' *Irish Times*, 2 March 2015, https://www.irishtimes.com/news/politics/water-protests-first-to-go-viral-on-irish-social-media-1.2122292 (accessed 23 August 2018).

[8] Niamh NicGhabhann, 'City walls, bathroom stalls and tweeting the Taoiseach: the aesthetics of protest and the campaign for abortion rights in the Republic of Ireland', *Continuum* (published online 2018).

Newspapers Group's thousands of images which are already online (with millions more in the pipeline), the thousands of images of the Troubles available through the Ulster museum, Ulster University's conflict in Northern Ireland (CAIN) website, or commercial archives such as that of Victor Patterson's Pacemaker collection.[9] The research methods we are used to relying on simply don't stack up in a digital age. Archival 'discoveries' which once might have taken weeks are now only a few clicks away, while instead of bickering over the meaning of fragments, we are instead faced with the problem of sifting through more sources than we can ever process. This can have a strange, distorting impact on archives, as original documents are now often harder to access, and collections which once languished almost forgotten now receiving a dramatic upsurge in attention. The afterlife of the Wiltshire collection is a good example of this. Elinor Wiltshire took street photography in Dublin in the 1960s; however, her images were disseminated to quite a limited sphere at the time, confined to a small Dublin elite, with a few exhibitions at the Green Studio which she co-owned with the husband Reginald, and one touring exhibition to Germany. Since digitization, however, they have appeared on posters across Ireland, been the subject of numerous exhibitions in the National Photographic Gallery, and appeared in a handful of historical publications (including my own). They have come to epitomize a distinctive moment in Dublin's emergent modernity and are far more widespread than they were during the time she was taking them.[10] In this context, whether they tell us more about the 1960s or the twenty-first century is open to debate.

The reformulation of the historical past through digitization has spread far beyond the confines—and the control—of the institutional archive. Websites such as Findmypast and Ancestry also provide new access to impenetrable parish records housed in inaccessible locations. In the words of Alison Light, the internet 'produces its own version of archive fever' as more and more people take up the possibilities offered by the archive to document their own family histories.[11] All of this is overwhelmingly a good thing, democratizing knowledge which was once the preserve of the historian and removing some of the skills required to access historical data.[12] Alongside these commercial websites, which monetize individuals' need to

[9] Victor Patterson, https://www.victorpatterson.com (accessed 1 August 2018).

[10] Elinor Wiltshire collection, https://www.nli.ie/en/udlist/photographs-collections.aspx?page=2&article=19f0ec06-05b7-45ad-8385-1f3ac5dd41d3 (accessed 1 August 2018).

[11] Alison Light, *Common People: The History of an English Family* (London, 2014), 56.

[12] For a sustained discussion of these issues, see Light, *Common People.*

belong in an age of increasing uncertainty, there are an enormous number of private efforts to document and store memories and images of the past on online platforms. On Facebook, examples include the Francis Street photographer, the Belfast History project, and the Historical Tralee page, to name but a few. These online collections of historical images attract millions of clicks every year. The photographs added are not professional images, but rather family photographs or images of street parties and local festivities, reflecting the fact that the era of Kodak photography in Ireland is now rapidly receding into historical time. Shoeboxes are taken out, and photographs are scanned in; forgotten family memories are reanimated as part of a shared public memory. These fora offer the potential for a newly democratized historical space; indeed, those who might not feel comfortable venturing into an archive are given the space and time to scrutinize photographs online, commenting with stories of the people and places in the image, and adding their voice to the construction of the historical past. In places where estates have been demolished, road plans reoriented, and communities scattered, these sites provide a vital opportunity for the reclamation of a sense of lost identity. Indeed, an online community formed through posting images and reminiscences shows the value of nostalgia not as a conservative force, but as a form of cultural capital which enables dispossessed communities to campaign for improved services. Communities have been creating online archives of neighbourhoods and housing estates long before professional historians turned to these topics, and have pioneered the collection of memories and sources.

But this is not a utopian future where the secrets of the past are effortlessly revealed for all. It is notable, during the national convulsions over the secrets of Ireland's recent past, how infrequently photography was used as evidence. A photograph of Magdalene girls in white being led through the street of Dublin, flanked by gardai and crowds, had been used as visual shorthand for a series of historical crises, but less rarely drawn on as a source. Indeed, the government report into the Magdalene Laundries used no photographic evidence at all.[13] The commission of inquiry into the industrial schools, on the other hand, was accompanied by large numbers of contemporary and archival images. However, these images were largely archival images of buildings or carefully composed images of clean and neat

[13] Report of the Inter-Departmental Committee to establish the facts of State involvement with the Magdalen Laundries, http://www.justice.ie/en/JELR/Pages/MagdalenRpt2013 (accessed 1 August 2018).

dormitories or boys busy in workshops.[14] The stories that needed to be told were not in the bound volumes of institutional records, but in the memories and testimonies of those who were victims. The images reveal little; they make these institutions look clean, tidy, and industrious. The moment of recognition we seek does not take place. Indeed, if they can tell us anything it is about how the religious institutions presented themselves to the world and maintained an image of benevolent discipline for so long. These images provide a convincing demonstration of how a society could look but not see anything wrong with a situation, about how ways of seeing have shifted alongside societal standards. In this context, we can see how the image plays an active role in normalizing or concealing practices.

Modern photographic practices have also changed in the light of new technologies and new institutions, and have increasingly responded to these contemporary and historical concerns. Since the 1990s, photography in Ireland has become more experimental and more self-confident, with a range of photographers working at the medium's cutting edge. Anthony Haughey's photography works on themes of home and belonging, migration and distance, exploring these themes through studies on Europe's borders with Africa, Ireland's ghost estates, and disputed territories across the continent.[15] Through these works, he situates Irish themes within a larger European framework, and pushes at the limits of the documentary form through unbalanced centreless composition. Kim Haughton has worked with survivors of child abuse, building on feminist art practices and using a range of media including portrait and landscape photography, oral histories and archival documents both to present a sensitive portrayal of the experiences of survivors and to provide an excoriating critique of the authorities' failure to prosecute anyone for these crimes.[16] Seán Hillen has used photomontage to interrogate myths of Ireland, reworking images of whitewashed cottages and red-haired children alongside spaceships, pyramids, and unlikely meteorological activity in a dizzying interplay of the ludic and the excoriating.[17] These photographers have brought new themes into Irish photography, drawing on ideas of interior worlds, loneliness, and the psychoanalytic potential of the image for depicting the uncanny. Here photographic practice

[14] See, for example, the report on St Joseph's Artane as part of the Commission to Inquire into Child Abuse: http://www.childabusecommission.ie/rpt/pdfs (accessed 1 August 2018); Catriona Crowe, 'The Ferns Report: Vindicating the Abused Child' Eire-Ireland 43/1–2 (2008), 50–73.

[15] Anthony Haughey, http://anthonyhaughey.com (accessed 23 August 2018).

[16] Kim Haughton, 'In Plain Sight' Gallery of Photography, May 2015, http://www.galleryofphotography.ie/in_plain_sight (accessed 23 August 2018).

[17] Seán Hillen website, http://www.seanhillen.com (accessed 23 August 2018).

provides new space for opening up issues of isolation, atomization, and unfulfilled desire in Irish culture.

This burgeoning of artistic culture has been underpinned by shifts in institutional practices. The valorization of Irish arts that accompanied the economic prosperity of the Celtic Tiger and post-conflict Northern Ireland have opened up new possibilities for more people to work in photography in new ways.[18] New spaces have opened for exhibiting photographs while older galleries have also started to exhibit photographic images. Once radical and marginal photographic spaces, such as Belfast Exposed have also changed in ethos and outlook to become part of the city's formal art world. The National College of Art and Design, Dún Laoghaire Institute of Art, Design, and Technology, and Ulster University also began to run courses in photography from the 1990s, moving the teaching of photography in Ireland from a technical apprenticeship to an academic course taught alongside fine arts in the art schools. There is now an active market for Irish photography. Private galleries exhibit photographs, and Irish photo books and prints sell. This shift in institutional practices has brought more money, people, and energy to photography. However, photography's co-option into mainstream art practice—white gallery spaces, high prices for important pieces—poses new questions about the medium's potential for radicalism within the confines of the art market and the routes of dissemination through which photography can have an impact on national debate. Indeed, even as art-photography prospers, it is increasingly difficult for practitioners to make a living from photo-journalism as editors increasingly use freely available online content. Professional and artistic photography is still jarringly masculine, a product of longstanding gendered constructions of both the artist and the public sphere. We await to see if this changes soon.

There are many stories still to be told about the history of photography in Ireland. Each photograph contains a bundle of narratives depending on which methodological thread is pulled. This is a book about seeing and not seeing, power and access to power, agency and resistance. It is about the stories we tell, the things we try to reveal and the things we try to hide. It is a universal story, with a particular Irish inflection, shaped by Irish cultures, habits, and the forms we have in our reach to express and disseminate our views. Within the concentric circles of the home, the town, and the nation,

[18] Colin Graham, 'Luxury, Peace, and Photography in Northern Ireland', *Visual Culture in Britain* 10/2 (2009), 139–54.

people made a range of choices about what to reveal and what to conceal. Studio portraits created an image of respectable prosperity, and hid wrinkles and ailments. Family photograph albums constructed narratives of happy days at the beach and excluded images of work, and life beyond the home. Club photographers depicted images of the Irish landscape but excised images of modernity or poverty. Photographers explored their identity and their place in society, and played with and remodelled tropes of landscape and nation. In these cropped and adapted photographs, we see inferences of emotional histories of shame, vanity, and pride. In recent years, these issues have emerged as crucial historical questions alongside longstanding narratives of state and nation-building.

But photography could also be used to reveal injustice and push at the limits of societal discourse. Throughout the twentieth century, from the photographs of the Church Street collapse to images of housing shortages in the 1960s, there were attempts to render the problems of Irish society visually. During the 1980s, this strand of interrogative photography burgeoned, with a new generation of young people turning to the traditions of documentary to examine their own conceptions of self and state, while new radical publications disseminated this new iconography of a newly urban country to a new viewing constituency. Photographs of inner-city locations, deprived council estates, and Traveller encampments reflected the new realities of Irish society which mirrored new developments in literature and theatre. They developed out of liberal humanism, and also contained within their frames humanism's paradoxes surrounding the ethical politics of interventionism. Photo-journalism of the Troubles provides an example of iterative phases of exposure, which in turn responded to the flaws of a previous generation's image-making. As the Troubles began, a first group of photographers documented injustice in the face of police brutality and English racism, a tendency which soon became voyeurism and clichéd, responded to by a new cohort of Northern Irish photographers who attempted to show a more nuanced depiction of life in the province. Despite this activity, anxieties about the seen and unseen are not quite what we expect them to be. The concerns and moral panics of contemporaneous observers never neatly map on to the historical narratives that we as historians try to construct, and narrative arcs which are visible at a distance are never really apparent up close. Sights that now appear commonplace were once shocking. The archive will always confront us with the agency of the documents it keeps. Attentiveness to these dynamics is revealing; we can make sense of a society through its moral panics about what it deemed to be 'hidden'.

Notions of concealing and revealing run throughout our relationship with the archive. The discourses of 'revealing' 'hidden histories' which often structure social historical work often tell us more about the historian's conceptions of their own historical heroism than about the past or its accreted layers. In similar terms, when historians celebrate the 'discovery' of disappeared stories they often create an image of the past as unproblematic and accidentally forgotten, rather than having a serious and profound engagement with why these stories were actively and conscientiously erased from the historical record, and what the contours of the historical archive can tell us about the past. With a focus on the photograph, its material dimensions, the archival practices which have surrounded it, and moreover, the histories written longitudinally along its life, it can provide us with access to these issues. A more textured sense of the archive as part of our past can emerge through these photographic histories.

Ireland is a visual country. Visuality, as much as orality, has played a crucial role in the formation of social relations and culture. As the photo stories which make up this book suggest, a turn to photographic images provides a new way to do justice to the complexity of Irish lives in the twentieth century, and allows us to tell emotional histories of those who have almost disappeared from the ambit of the historical gaze. Photographs are stashed in shoeboxes and attics all across Ireland, posing interlinked questions about the nature of the archive and the limitations of received historical narratives. Here in these photographs we uncover profound and meaningful stories of how individuals and communities understood Irish society, their place within it, and how through their photographs they created space for themselves and pushed at the certainties which seemingly underpinned Irish life. Through studio portraits, family albums, and camera clubs, people created and disseminated images that expressed something of their own subjectivity and their relationship to place. These images were also constrained in what they could show through the limitations of technology and genre. However, in the interplay between the potentials and limitations of these images, we can make sense of the way in which Irish people made choices about their own agency and identity during the twentieth century. Indeed, unlike other forms such as painting and memoir, the photograph required little technical skill and allowed for a far wider constituency to create photographic images and tokens. Here in these documents we encounter a profound and affective history of what it meant to look—to glance, to stare, to gaze—in modern Ireland.

Bibliography

Primary Sources

1. Manuscript and Archival Sources

Dublin City Archives

Reports and Minutes of Dublin Corporation

Galway County Archive

Minihan Collection

Institute for Advance Legal Studies (IALS)

Minutes of the Public Inquiry into the Acts of Violence and Civil Disorder in Northern Ireland in 1969

Irish Architectural Archive

Hugh Doran Papers

National Archives of Ireland

90/119/2 Emergency Powers (Restrictions on Photography) Order

2011/25/19 Garda Report: George Favilla, 8 Upper Mount Street, Dublin, Emergency Powers (Restriction on Photography) Order 1939

BR Dublin 1182 Business records

IND/22/19 Film Industry: Processing of Colour Film and Cinefilms in Ireland

INDC/IND/22/13 Gevaert Limited, Clarendon Street, Dublin; Kodak Limited; Ilford Limited; Lyall Smith Laboratories, Dublin: proposal to spool roll film in Ireland, processing of colour portrait prints in Ireland

Public Record Office of Northern Ireland (PRONI)

Hogg collection

AC10/3/2 Community Arts

CAB/9/CD/213 Regulations Governing the Control of Photography

D1422 H. F. Cooper papers

D2886 Allison papers

D3479 Paper Relating to the '57 Club, Strabane

D4005 Records of the Belfast Central Presbyterian Association Camera Club

D4194 Maguire and Flanagan Business Papers

The National Archives, Kew, United Kingdom

Home Office HO 219 Widgery Inquiry

National Library of Ireland

Ball photographic collection
Evans collection
Keogh Collection
Stokes Collection
Tully Album
Unidentified albums

National University of Ireland Galway, Special Collections

Pickow Collection

National Visual Arts Library Archive (NIVAL)

Cultural Relations Committee Collection

Waterford County Archive

Brophy Collection

University College Cork, Special Collections

Attic Press/Róisín Conroy Collection

National Photographic Archive

Elinor Wilshire Collection
Alfred Ternan Collection
Poole Collection

Ulster Folk and Transport Museum

Bert Martin Collection

Oral Histories

Joanne O'Brien
Joanne O'Brien interviewed by Michael Ann Mullen (British Library Oral History of British Photography)
Derek Speirs
Frankie Quinn
Jackie Redpath
Mick Rafferty
Alan Lund
Helena McDonnell

2. Printed Primary Sources

a. Journals and Newspapers

Amateur Photographer
The Camera
Camerawork
Capuchin Annual

Circa
Evening Herald
Fingerpost
Fortnight
Hibernia
IC: The Inner City Magazine
In Dublin
Irish Examiner
Irish Independent
Irish Press
Irish Times
The Lens
Life
Magill
Munster Express
Nusight
Republican News
Shankill Bulletin
Strabane Chronicle
Source
Sunday Tribune
Times Pictorial
Tuam Herald
Ulster Herald
Women's Life

b. Printed primary sources

-*A Guide to Photographic Equipment* (Dublin, 1958)
-*Fotofest '93: Dublin Public Libraries Festival of Photography* (Dublin, 1993)
-*Irish Image 1966 Exhibition Catalogue*
Benson, Ciaran, *Art and the Ordinary: Report of the Arts Community Education Committee* (Dublin, 1989)
Civil Rights Movement, *Massacre at Derry* (Derry, 1972)
Dean, Geoffrey, *Drug Misuse in Ireland 1982–1983: Investigation in a North Central Dublin Area and Galway, Sligo and Cork* (Dublin, 1983)
Doyle, Colman, *Ireland: 40 Years of Photographs* (Dublin, 1994)
Government of Northern Ireland, *Violence and Civil Disturbances in Northern Ireland in 1969: Report of Tribunal of Inquiry* (Belfast, 1972)
Gray, Sheila, Isherwood, Pam, O'Brien, Joanne, Matthews, Jenny, Murray, Maggie, Page, Raissa, Prince, Brenda, and Wilmer, Val, 'Format Photographers', *Feminist Review* 18/1 (Winter 1984), 102–8
Hamilton, Paul, *Up the Shankill* (Belfast, 1979)
Harvey, Brian, *Resource Centres in Ireland* (Dublin, 1990)
Irish Tourist Association, *Connacht: Galway, Mayo, Sligo, Leitrim, Roscommon* (Dublin, 1948)

Lennon, Mary, McAdam, Marie, and O'Brien, Joanne, *Across the Water: Irish Women's Lives in Britain* (London, 1988)
Limpkin, Clive, *The Battle of the Bogside* (London, 1972)
Logan, Buzz, *The Shankill Photographs* (Belfast, 1979)
Melaugh, Eamon, *Derry: The Troubled Years* (Derry, 2005)
Murphy, Brendan, *Eyewitness: Four Decades of Northern Irish Life* (Dublin, 2003)
Murphy, Pat and McCafferty, Nell (eds.), *Women in Focus: Contemporary Irish Women's Lives* (Dublin, 1986)
O'Brien, Edna, *Mother Ireland* (London, 1976)
O'Brien, Joanne, *A Matter of Minutes: The Enduring Legacy of Bloody Sunday* (Dublin, 2002)
Quinn, Frankie, *Interface Images* (Belfast, 1994)
Quinn, Frankie, *The Orange* (Belfast, 2014)
Saunders, Red, and Shelton, Syd, *Ireland: A Week in the Life of a Nation* (London, 1986)
Speirs, Derek, and Kerrigan, Gene, *Goodbye to All That: A Souvenir of the Haughey Era* (Dublin, 1992)
Thom's Directory
Town Clerk's Office, *Waterford: A Municipal Directory* (Waterford, 1955), 5
Wiener, Ron, *The Rape and Plunder of the Shankill: Community Action – The Belfast Experience* (Belfast, 1980)
Williams, Herbert, *Portrait Photography* (London, 1937)
Lord Widgery, *Report of the Tribunal appointed to Inquire into the Events on Sunday 30th January 1972 which Led to Loss of Life in Connection with the Procession in Londonderry on that Day* (London, 1972)

Film

Picturing Derry, dir. David Fox and Sylvia Stevens (1985)

c. Websites

100Hours Project: https://ucl100hours.wordpress.com
Anthony Haughey: http://anthonyhaughey.com/
Commission to Inquire into Child Abuse http://www.childabusecommission.ie/rpt/pdfs/
Deloitte: www.deloitte.com
Frankie Quinn: http://www.frankiequinn.com/
Gallery of Photography: http://www.galleryofphotography.ie
Irish Times: www.irishtimes.com
NLI blog: https://blog.nli.ie
Padraig Kennelly Archive: http://www.kennellyarchive.com
Report of the Inter-Departmental Committee to Establish the Facts of State Involvement with the Magdalen
Laundries: http://www.justice.ie/en/JELR/Pages/MagdalenRpt2013
RTÉ: www.rte.ie
Seán Hillen: http://www.seanhillen.com/

TNA Shipping List: https://www.archives.gov/research/immigration/
Women Are Boring: https://womenareboring.wordpress.com
Victor Patterson: https://www.victorpatterson.com/

Secondary Literature

Abrams, Lynne, *Oral History Theory* (London, 2016)

Arensberg, Conrad, and Kimball, Solon, *The Irish Countryman* (Gloucester, Mass., 1937)

Ayoub, Phillip, *When States Come Out: Europe's Sexual Minorities and the Politics of Visibility* (Cambridge, 2016)

Azoulay, Ariella, *The Civil Contract of Photography* (Cambridge, MA, 2012)

Ballif, Florine, 'Portraying the Divided city: Photographing the Belfast Peacelines', *Visual Ethnography* 3/1 (2014), 65–91

Barthes, Roland, *Camera Lucida* (New York, 1981)

Batchen, Geoffrey, *Each Wild Idea: Writing, Photography, History (Cambridge MA, 2001)*

Batchen, Geoffrey, 'Snapshots: Art History and the Ethnographic Turn', *Photographies* 1/2 (2008), 121–42

Batchen, Geoffrey, 'Dreams of Ordinary Life: Cartes-de-Visite and the Bourgeois Imagination', in Long, J. J., Noble, Andrea, and Welch, Edmund (eds.), *Photography: Theoretical Snapshots* (Abingdon, 2008), 80–97

Baxandall, Michael, *Patterns of Intention: On the Historical Explanation of Pictures* (Yale, 1985)

Baylis, Gail, 'Metropolitan Surveillance and Rural Opacity: Secret Photography in Late-Nineteenth-Century Ireland', *History of Photography* 33/1 (2009), 26–38

Baylis, Gail, 'Exchanging Looks: Gap Girls and Colleens in Early Irish Tourist Photography', *Early Popular Visual Culture* 10/4 (2012), 325–43

Baylis, Gail, 'Gender in the Frame: Photography and the Performance of the Nation Narrative in Early Twentieth-Century Ireland', *Irish Studies Review* 22/2 (2014), 184–206

Baylis, Gail, and Edge, Sarah, 'The Great Famine: Absence, Memory, and Photography', *Cultural Studies* 24/6 (2010), 778–800

Beatty, Aidan, *Masculinity and Power in Irish Nationalism* (London, 2016)

Behrend, Heike, 'Love á la Hollywood and Bombay in Kenyan Studio Photography', *Paideuma* 44 (1998), 139–53

Benjamin, Walter, 'The Work of Art in the Age of Mechanical Reproduction', in Eiland, Howard, and Jennings, Michael (eds.), *Walter Benjamin, Selected Writings Vol. 3, 1935–1938* (Cambridge MA, 2002), 101–40

Bennett, Ronan, 'Introduction', in Quinn, Frankie, *Interface Images* (Belfast, 1994)

Berger, John, *Ways of Seeing* (London, 1972)

Berger, John, and Mohr, Jean, *Another Way of Telling* (New York, 1982)

Berger, Lynn, 'Snapshots, or: Visual Culture's Clichés', *Photographies* 4/2 (2011), 175–90

Berger, Martin, *Seeing Through Race: A Reinterpretation of Civil Rights Photography* (Berkeley, 2011)

Bertrand, Mathilde, '"A Tool for Social Change": Community Photography at Belfast Exposed', *Revue LISA/LISA e-journal* (2015)

Bertrand, Matilde, 'The Half Moon Photography Workshop and *Camerawork*: Catalysts in the British Photographic Landscape (1972–1985)', *Photography and Culture* 11/3 (2018), 239–59

Bew, Paul, *Ireland: The Politics of Enmity 1789–2006* (Oxford, 2007)

Bourdieu, Pierre, *Photography: A Middlebrow Art* (Stanford, 1990)

Bourdieu, Pierre, 'The Peasant and his Body', *Ethnography* 5/4 (2004), 579–99

Bourke, Joanna, 'The Best of all Home Rulers: Economic Power of Women in Ireland, 1880–1914', *Irish Economic and Social History* 18/1 (1991), 34–47

Bourke, Richard, *Peace in Ireland: The War of Ideas* (London, 2012)

Breathnach-Lynch, Sighle, *Ireland's Art, Ireland's History: Representing Ireland, 1845 to Present* (Creighton, 2007)

Brody, Hugh, *Inishkillane: Change and Decline in the West of Ireland* (Harmondsworth, 1974)

Brooke, Stephen, 'Revisiting Southam Street: Class, Generation, Gender, and Race in the Photography of Roger Mayne', *Journal of British Studies* 53/2 (2014), 453–96

Brooke, Stephen, 'Space, Emotions and the Everyday: The Affective Ecology of 1980s London', *Twentieth Century British History* 28/1 (2017), 110–42

Buckley, Liam, 'Studio Photography and the Aesthetics of Citizenship in The Gambia, West Africa', in Edwards, Elizabeth, Godsen, Chris, and Phillips, Ruth B. (eds.), *Sensible Objects: Colonialism, Museums, and Material Culture* (New York, 2006), 61–86

Burke, Peter, *Eyewitnessing: The Uses of Images as Historical Evidence* (Cornell, 2002)

Butler, Lise, 'Michael Young, the Institute of Community Studies, and the Politics of Kinship', *Twentieth Century British History* 26/2 (2015), 203–24

Butler, Judith, 'Photography, War, Outrage', *PMLA* 120/3 (2005), 822–7

Byrne, Teresa, 'The Burning of Kilboy House, August 1922', Master's Thesis, National University of Ireland, Maynooth (2006)

Caffrey, Paul, 'Irish Material Culture: The Shape of the Field', *Circa* 103 (2003), 29–32

Cameron, Elizabeth, and Peffer, John (eds.), *Portraiture and Photography in Africa* (Indiana, 2013)

Carville, Justin, 'Renegotiated Territory: The politics of place, space and landscape in Irish Photography', *Afterimage* 29/1 (2001), 5–9

Carville, Justin, '"My Wallet of Photographs": Photography, Ethnography and Visual Culture in J.M. Synge's Aran Islands', *Irish Journal of Anthropology* 10/1 (2007), 5–11

Carville, Justin, 'Mr. Lawrence's Great Photographic Bazaar: Photography, History and the Imperial Streetscape', *Early Popular Visual Culture* 5/3 (2007), 263–83

Carville, Justin, 'Visible Others: Photography and Romantic Ethnography in Ireland', McGarrity, Maria, and Culleton, Clare (eds.), *Irish Modernism and the Global Primitive* (Palgrave, 2009), 93–114

Carville, Justin, 'Visualizing the Rising: Photography, Memory and the Visual Economy of the 1916 Easter Rebellion', in Perreault, Jeanne, Warley, Linda, and Kadar, Marlene (eds.), *Photographs – Histories - Meanings* (New York, 2010), 91–102

Carville, Justin, *Photography and Ireland* (London, 2011)

Carville, Justin, 'The Violence of the Image: Conflict and Post-Conflict Photography in Northern Ireland', in Kennedy, Liam and Patrick, Caitlin (eds.), *The Violence of the Image* (London, 2014), 60–77

Carville, Justin, '"The Glad Smile of God's Sunlight": Photography and the Imaginative Geography of Darkest Dublin', in Carville, Justin (ed.), *Visualizing Dublin: Visual Culture, Modernity, and the Representation of Urban Space* (Bern, 2014), 181–202

Carville, Justin, 'Refracted Visions: Street Photography, Humanism and the Loss of Innocence', in Maher, Eamon, and O'Brien, Eugene, Tracing the Cultural Legacy of Irish Catholicism: From Galway to Cloyne and Beyond (Manchester 2017), 70–88

Casserly, Maeve, and O'Neill, Ciaran, 'Public History, Invisibility, and Women in the Republic of Ireland', *The Public Historian* 39/2 (2017), 10–30

Cavell, Stanley, *The World Viewed: Reflections on the Ontology of Film* (Cambridge, Mass, 1979)

Chalfen, Richard, *Snapshot Versions of Life* (Wisconsin, 1987)

Chambers, Lilian, FitzGibbon, Ger, and Jordan, Eamon (eds.), *Theatre Talk: Voices of Irish Theatre Practitioners* (Dublin, 2008)

Chandler, Edward, *Photography in Ireland: The Nineteenth Century* (Dublin, 2001)

Chandler, Edward, and Walsh, Peter, *Through the Brass Lidded Eye: Photography in Ireland 1839–1900* (Dublin, 1989)

Clarke, Graham, *The Portrait in Photography* (London, 1992)

Clear, Caitríona, *Women of the House: Women's Household Work in Ireland 1921–61: Experiences, Memories, Discourses* (Dublin, 2000)

Clear, Caitríona, *Women's Voices in Ireland: Women's Magazines in the 1950s and 60s* (London, 2015)

Cole, Robert, *Propaganda, Neutrality, and Irish Censorship in the Second World War* (Edinburgh, 2006)

Collins, Tom, *The Centre Cannot Hold: Britain's Failure in Northern Ireland* (Dublin, 1983)

Connell, Kieran, 'Race, Prostitution and the New Left: the Postwar Inner City through Janet Mendelsohn's 'Social Eye', *History Workshop Journal* 83/1 (2017), 301–40

Conor, Liz, *The Spectacular Modern Woman: Feminine Visibility in the 1920s* (Bloomington, IA, 2004)

Coogan, Tim Pat, *Disillusioned Decades: Ireland 1966–1987* (Dublin, 1987)

Coogan, Tim Pat, *The Troubles* (London, 2002)

Corbally, John, 'The Othered Irish: Shades of Difference in Post-War Britain, 1948–71', *Contemporary European History* 24/1 (2015), 105–25

Corbin, Alain, *The Life of an Unknown: The Rediscovered World of a Clog Maker in Nineteenth-Century France* (Columbia, 2001)

Cordery, Simon, 'Friendly societies and the discourse of respectability in Britain, 1825–75', *Journal of British Studies* 34/1 (1995), 35–58

Corkery, Daniel, *The Hidden Ireland: A Study of Gaelic Munster in the Eighteenth Century* (Dublin, 1924)

Coulter, Colin, 'The Character of Unionism', *Irish Political Studies* 9/1 (1994), 1–24

Cronin, Michael, and O'Connor, Barbara (eds.), *Irish Tourism: Image, Culture, and Identity* (Buffalo, 2003)

Crowe, Catriona, 'The Ferns Report: Vindicating the Abused Child', *Eire-Ireland* 43/1–2 (2008), 50–73

Cullen, Fintan, 'Marketing National Sentiment: Lantern Slides of Eviction in Late Nineteenth-Century Ireland', *History Workshop Journal* 54/1 (2002), 162–79

Cullen, Mary, 'Invisible Women and their Contribution to Historical Studies', *Stair: The Journal of the Irish History Teachers' Association* (1982), reprinted in Cullen, Mary (ed.), *Telling it Our Way: Essays in Gender History* (Dublin, 2013), 49–64

Cullen Owens, Rosemary, *A Social History of Women in Ireland, 1870–1970* (Dublin, 2005)

Curtis, Perry, *Apes and Angels: The Irishman in Victorian Caricature* (Smithsonian, 1997)

Curtis, Perry, *The Depiction of Eviction in Ireland, 1845–1910* (Dublin, 2011)

Daly, Mary, *Sixties Ireland: Reshaping Economy, State and Society 1957–73* (Cambridge, 2016)

Daniels, Stephen, *Fields of Vision: Landscape Imagery & National Identity in England and the United States* (Cambridge, 1993)

Dash, Samuel, *Justice Denied: Challenge to Lord Widgery's Report on 'Bloody Sunday'* (New York, 1972)

Dawson, Graham, 'Trauma, Place and the Politics of Memory: Bloody Sunday, Derry, 1972–2004', *History Workshop Journal* 59/1 (Spring 2005), 221–50

Dawson, Graham, *Making Peace with the Past? Memory, Trauma, and the Irish Troubles* (Manchester, 2007)

Deane, Seamus, *Reading in the Dark* (London, 1996)

Doane, Mary Ann, 'Indexicality and the concept of medium specificity', in Kelsey, Robin and Stimson, Blake (eds.), *The Meaning of Photography* (Williamstown, MA, 2008), 4

Donnell, E. E. (ed.), *The Genius of Father Browne: Ireland's Photographic Discovery* (London, 1990)

Downey, Karen, and Hadaway, Pauline, *Portraits from a 50's Archive* (Belfast, 2005)

Drury, Martin, 'Community Arts – Defined but Denied', *Irish Review* 11 (Winter 1991/1992), 99–103

Dube, Leela, Leacock, Eleanor, and Ardener, Shirley (eds.), *Visibility and Power: Essays on Women in Society and Development* (Oxford, 1986)

Duddy, Tom, 'Art & Society: Tom Duddy Analyses the Community Arts Idea and the Politics of Creativity', *Circa* 67 (1994), 28–31

Duffy, Patrick, 'Writing Ireland: Literature and Art in the Representation of Irish Place', in Graham, Brian (ed.), *In Search of Ireland: A Cultural Geography* (London, 1997), 64–83

Dunalley, Lord, *Khaki and Rifle Green* (London, 1940)

Edwards, Elizabeth, 'Photography and the Material Performance of the Past', *History and Theory* 48/4 (2009), 130–50

Edwards, Elizabeth, *The Camera as Historian: Amateur Photographers and Historical Imagination, 1885–1918* (Durham NC, 2012)

Edwards, Elizabeth, 'Objects of Affect: Photography beyond the Image', *Annual Review of Antropology* (2012), 221–34

Edwards, Elizabeth, 'Anthropology and Photography: A Long History of Knowledge and Affect', *Photographies* 8 (2015), 235–52

Edwards, Elizabeth, and Hart, Janice (eds.), *Photographs, Objects, Histories: On the Materiality of Images* (London, 2004)

Eisenhauer, Jennifer, 'Next Slide Please: The Magical, Scientific, and Corporate Discourses of Visual Projection Technologies', *Studies in Art Education* 47/3 (2006), 198–214

Ellis, David, 'Pavement Politics: Community Action in Leeds, c. 1960–1990', PhD thesis, University of York (2015)

English, Richard, *Armed Struggle: The History of the IRA* (Oxford, 2012)

Evans, Emyr Estyn, *The Personality of Ireland: Habitat, Heritage, History* (Cambridge, 1973)

Evans, Jessica, and Hall, Stuart (ed.), *Visual Culture: A Reader* (London, 1999)

Fahey, Tony, 'Housework, the Household Economy and Economic Development in Ireland Since the 1920s', *Irish Journal of Sociology* 2/1 (1992), 42–69

Ferriter, Diarmaid *The Transformation of Ireland, 1900–2000* (London, 2005)

Ferriter, Diarmaid, *Occasion of Sin: Sex and Society in Modern Ireland* (London, 2009)

Ferriter, Diarmaid, *Ambiguous Republic: Ireland in the 1970s* (London, 2014)

Fitzgerald, Sandy (ed.), *An Outburst of Frankness: Community Arts in Ireland – A Reader* (Dublin, 2004)

Fitzgerald, Sandy, 'Community Arts', in Carpenter, Andrew, and Murphy, Paula (eds.), *Art and Architecture of Ireland* 3 (Dublin, 2015), 420–4

Fitzpatrick, Orla, 'Modernity and Irish Photographic Publications, 1922 to 1949' (Ph.D thesis, University of Ulster, 2016)

Fitzpatrick, Orla, 'Portraits and Propaganda: photographs of the widows and children of the 1916 leaders in the *Catholic Bulletin*', in Godson, Lisa, and Brück, Joanna (eds.), *Making 1916: Material and Visual Culture of the Easter Rising* (Liverpool, 2016), 82–90

Fitzpatrick, Orla, 'Photographic Modernism on the Margins: William Harding, *The Camera* and the Irish Salons of Photography 1927 to 1939', *Irish Studies Review* 26/3 (2018), 361–73

Flanagan, Frances, *Remembering the Revolution: Dissent, Culture, and Nationalism in the Irish Free State* (Oxford, 2015)

Foster, Gavin, *The Irish Civil War and Society: Politics, Class, and Conflict* (London, 2015)

Foster, R. F., 'Paddy and Mr Punch', in *Paddy and Mr Punch* (London, 1993), 171–94

Frawley, Oona (ed.), *Memory Ireland Volume 1: History and Modernity* (Syracuse, 2011)

Frisch, Michael, *A Shared Authority: Essays on the Craft and Meaning of Oral and Public History* (New York, 1990)

Garvin, Tom, *Preventing the Future: Why Was Ireland So Poor for So Long* (Dublin, 2004)

Gibbons, Luke, 'Alien Eye: Ireland and Photography', *Creative Camera* (December 1986), 10–11

Gidal, Tim, 'Modern Photojournalism: The First Years', in Brittain, David (ed.), *Creative Camera: Thirty Years of Writing* (Manchester, 2000), 73–80

Gilman, Sander, '"Stand Up Straight": Notes Towards a History of Posture', *Journal of Medical Humanities* 35/1 (2014), 57–83

Girvin, Brian, 'The Origins of Contemporary Ireland: New Perspectives on the Recent Past', *Irish Historical Studies* 38/151 (May 2013), 385–8

Godson, Lisa, and Brück, Joanna (eds.), *Making 1916: Visual and Material Culture of the Easter Rising* (Liverpool, 2016)

Goodman, Nelson, *Languages of Art: An Approach to a Theory of Symbols* (Indianapolis, 1976)

Gordon, Linda, *Dorothea Lange: A Life Beyond Limits* (London, 2009)

Graham, Colin, '"Blame It on Maureen O'Hara": Ireland and the Trope of Authenticity', *Cultural Studies* 15/1 (2010), 58–75

Graham, Colin, 'Luxury, Peace, and Photography in Northern Ireland', *Visual Culture in Britain* 10/2 (2009), 139–54

Graham, Colin, *Northern Ireland: 30 Years of Photography* (Belfast, 2013)

Gray, Mary, *Out in the Country: Youth, Media, and Queer Visibility in Rural America* (New York, 2009)

Hall, Stuart, 'A World at One with Itself', in Cohen, Stanley, and Young, Jock (eds.), *The Manufacture of News: Social Problems, Deviance and the Mass Media*, ed. (London, 1973), 147–56

Hanna, Erika, *Modern Dublin: Urban Change and the Irish Past, 1957–73* (Oxford, 2013)

Hanna, Erika, 'Life's a Beach: The Photo Album of Ireland', *Source* 80 (Autumn 2014), 54–5

Hanna, Erika, 'There is no Banshee Now: Absence and Loss in Twentieth Century Dublin', in Senia Pašeta (ed.), *Unfinished Futures: Essays about the Irish Past for Roy Foster* (Oxford, 2016), 223–34

Haselbeck Flynn, Patricia, *Franz Haselbeck's Ireland* (Cork, 2013)

Heaney, Seamus, *The Spirit Level* (London, 1996)

Hennessy, Rosemary, 'Queer Visibility in Commodity Culture', *Cultural Critique* 29 (1994–5), 31–76

Hennessy, Thomas, 'Ulster Unionism and Loyalty to the Crown of the United Kingdom, 1912–74', in English, Richard, and Walker, Graham (eds.), *Unionism in Modern Ireland* (Dublin, 1996), 115–29

Hennessy, Thomas, *A History of Northern Ireland, 1920–1996* (London, 1997)

Hennessy, Thomas, *The Origins of the Troubles* (Dublin, 2005)

Herron, Tom, and Lynch, John, '"Like 'Ghosts who Walked Abroad": Faces of the Bloody Sunday Dead', *Visual Culture in Britain* 7/1 (2006), 59–77

Herron, Tom, and Lynch, John, *After Bloody Sunday: Representations, Ethics, Justice* (Cork, 2007), 36

Hickman, Mary, and Walter, Bronwen, 'Deconstructing Whiteness: Irish Women in Britain', *Feminist Review* 50/1 (1995), 5–19

Hickman, Mary, and Walter, Bronwen, *Discrimination and the Irish Community in Britain: A Report of Research Undertaken for the Commission for Racial Equality* (London, 1997), 7

Hinton, James, *Nine Wartime Lives: Mass Observation and the Making of the Modern Self* (Oxford, 2010)

Hirsch, Marianna, *Family Frames: Photography, Narrative, and Postmemory* (Cambridge MA, 1997)

Hirsch, Marianne, *The Familial Gaze* (Dartmouth, 1999)
Holohan, Carole, *In Plain Sight: Responding to the Ferns, Ryan, Murphy and Cloyne Reports* (Dublin, 2011)
Houlbrook, Matt, *Prince of Tricksters: The Incredible True Story of Netley Lucas, Gentleman Crook* (Chicago, 2016)
Jackson, Will, 'White man's country: Kenya colony and the making of a myth', *Journal of Eastern African Studies* 5/2 (2011), 344–68
Jacobs, Nicholas, and Kerbs, Diethart, 'Wilhelm Simon Guttman, 1891–1990: A Documentary Portrait', *German Life and Letters* 62/4 (2009), 401–14
Jay, Martin, 'Scopic Regimes of Modernity', in Foster, Hal (ed.), *Vision and Visuality* (Seattle WA, 1988), 3–28
Jencks, Chris, 'The Centrality of the Eye in Western Culture', in Jencks, Chris (ed.), *Visual Culture* (London, 1995), 1–25
Johnston, Kevin, *In the Shadows of Giants: A Social History of the Belfast Shipyards* (Dublin, 2008), 299
Jones, Ben, 'The Uses of Nostalgia: Autobiography, Community Publishing and Working-Class Neighbourhoods in Post-war England', *Cultural and Social History* 7/3 (2010), 355–74
Jordonova, Ludmilla, *The Look of the Past: Visual and Material Evidence in Historical Practice* (Cambridge, 2012)
Joyce, James, *Ulysses* (Paris, 1922)
Kennedy, Liam, T*he Violence of the Image: Photography and International Conflict* (London, 2014)
Kennedy, Catriona, 'Women and Gender in Modern Ireland', in Bourke, Richard, and McBride, Ian (eds.), *Princeton History of Ireland* (Princeton, 2016), 361–81
Keogh, Dermot, *The Lost Decade: Ireland in the 1950s* (Mercier, 2004)
Kiang, Tanya, 'Dublin Time Capsule, Dublin Civic Museum 17 May – 10 June', *Circa* 41 (1988), 30
Kiang, Tanya, 'Playing the Green Card: Contemporary Photography in Ireland', *Aperture* 134 (1994), 54–73
Kinmonth, Claudia, *Irish Country Furniture 1700–1950* (London and New Haven, 1993)
Kinmonth, Claudia, 'Survival: Irish Material Culture and Material Economy', *Folk Life* 38/1 (2000), 32–41
Knowles, Caroline, and Sweetman, Paul, 'Introduction', in Knowles, Caroline, and Sweetman, Paul (eds.), *Picturing the Social Landscape: Visual Methods and the Social Imagination* (London, 2004), 1–17
Kreilkamp, Vera, 'Visualising History', in McAuliffe, Mary, O'Donnell, Katherine, and Lane, Leeann (eds.), *Palgrave Advances in Irish History* (Basingstoke, 2009), 247–68
Kuhn, Annette, *Family Secrets: Acts of Memory and Imagination* (London, 1995)
LaChapelle, Joseph, 'Creativity research: Its sociological and educational limitations', *Studies in Art Education* 24/2 (1983), 131–9
Langhamer, Claire, *The English in Love: The Intimate Story of an Emotional Revolution* (Oxford, 2013)
Lee, J. J., *Ireland 1912–1985: Politics and Society* (Cambridge, 1989)
Light, Alison, *Common People: The History of an English Family* (London, 2014)

Limmond, David, 'Living and Learning in the Docklands of Dublin', *Studies* 97/388 (2008), 403–12

Linfield, Susie, *The Cruel Radiance: Photography and Political Violence* (Chicago, 2010)

Loftus, Belinda, 'Photography, Art, and Politics: How the English Make Pictures of Irish Troubles', *Circa* 13 (1983), 10–14

Lonsdale, John, 'Kenya: Home County and African Frontier', in Bickers, Robert (ed.), *Settlers and Expatriates: Britons over the Seas* (Oxford, 2010), 74–111

Luddy, Maria, 'Writing the History of Irish Women', *Gender and History* 8/3 (1996), 467–70

Luddy, Maria, 'Sex and the Single Girl in 1920s and 1930s Ireland', *The Irish Review* 35 (2007), 79–91

Maguire, W.A., *A Century in Focus: Photography and Photographers in the North of Ireland 1839–1939* (Belfast, 2000)

Mark-FitzGerald, Emily, *Commemorating the Irish Famine: Memory and Monument* (Liverpool, 2013)

Mark-FitzGerald, Emily, 'Photography and the Visual Legacy of Famine', in Oona Frawley (ed.), *Memory Ireland Volume 3: The Famine and the Troubles* (Syracuse, 2014), 121–37

Martin, Peter, *Censorship in the Two Irelands 1922–1939* (Dublin, 2006)

Matless, David, *Landscape and Englishness* (London, 2001), 12

McCarthy, Pat, *The Irish Revolution 1912–23: Waterford* (Dublin, 2015)

McCaughin, Michael, *Steel Ships and Iron Men: Shipbuilding in Belfast 1894–1912* (Belfast, 1989)

McDowell, R. B., *Crisis and Decline: The Fate of Southern Unionists* (Dublin, 1997)

McGrady, Conor, 'Division and Enclosure: Frankie Quinn's Peaceline Panorama Photographs', in Loeb, Carolyn and Luescher, Andreas (eds.), *The Design of Frontier Spaces: Control and Ambiguity* (London, 2015), 17–30

McLellan, Josie, 'From Private Photography to Mass Circulation: The Queering of East German Visual Culture, 1968–1989', *Contemporary European History* 48 (2015), 405–23

McWilliams, May, 'The Historical Antecedents of Contemporary Photography Education: A British Case Study, 1966–79 *Photographies* 2/2 (2009), 237–54

Messenger, Charles, *Northern Ireland: The Troubles* (London, 1985)

Mitchell, W. J. T., *What do Pictures Want? The Lives and Loves of Images* (Chicago, 2005)

Mullan, Don, *Eyewitness Bloody Sunday: The Truth* (Dublin, 1997)

Mullins, Gerry, and Dixon, Daniel (eds.), *Dorothea Lange's Ireland* (Boulder, 1998)

Nead, Lynda, *The Female Nude: Art, Obscenity, Sexuality* (London, 1992)

Nead, Lynda, *The Haunted Gallery: Painting, Photography, Film c. 1900* (New Haven, 2008)

Nead, Lynda, *The Tiger in the Smoke: Art and Culture in Post-War Britain* (New Haven, 2017)

NicGhabhann, Niamh, 'City walls, Bathroom Stalls and Tweeting the Taoiseach: the Aesthetics of Protest and the Campaign for Abortion Rights in the Republic of Ireland', *Continuum* 32/5 (2018), 553–68

Nickel, Douglas, '"Impressed by Nature's Hand": Photography and Authorship', in Howells, Richard and Matson, Robert (eds.), *Using Visual Evidence* (London, 2008), 43–54

de Nie, Michael, *The Eternal Paddy: Irish Identity and the British Press, 1798–1882* (Madison WN, 2004)

Nudds, John, 'The Life and Work of John Joly (1857–1933)', *Irish Journal of Earth Sciences* 8/1 (1986), 84–5

O'Connell, Sean, *The Car in British Society: Class, Gender, and Motoring 1896–1939* (Manchester, 1998)

Ó Dochartaigh, Niall, *From Civil Rights to Armalites: Derry and the Birth of the Irish Troubles* (Cork, 1997)

Ó Dochartaigh, Niall, and Rodgers, Lisa, 'Images from the Inside: Michael Rodgers's Photographs of the Civil Rights Campaign and the Birth of the Troubles in Derry', *Field Day Review* 9 (2013), 74–99

O Drisceoil, Donal, *Censorship in Ireland 1939–1945: Neutrality, Politics, and Society* (Cork, 1996)

Ó Faoláin, Seán, 'Hymneneal', in *The Collected Short Stories of Seán Ó Faoláin*, Vol. 3 (Edinburgh, 1983)

O'Farrell, John, 'Foreword', in Quinn, Frankie, *The Orange* (Belfast, 2014)

O'Sullivan, Kevin, 'Humanitarian encounters: Biafra, NGOs and imaginings of the Third World in Britain and Ireland, 1967–70' *Journal of Genocide Research* 16/2–3 (2015), 299–315

Otter, Chris, *The Victorian Eye: A Political History of Light and Vision in Britain 1800–1910* (Chicago, 2009)

Parr, Connal, *Inventing the Myth: Political Passions and the Ulster Protestant Imagination* (Oxford, 2017)

Parsons, Sarah, 'Sontag's Lament: Emotions, Ethics, and Photography', *Photography and Culture* 2/3 (2009), 289–302

Pasternak, Gil, 'Taking Snapshots, Living the Picture: The Kodak Company's Making of Photographic Biography', *Lifewriting* 12 (2015) 431–46

Pearce, Sandra Manoogian, 'Edna O'Brien's "Lantern Slides" and Joyce's "The Dead": Shadows of a Bygone Era', *Studies in Short Fiction* 32/3 (1995), 437–46

Peress, Gilles, and Ziff, Trisha, 'The Photographer', in Ziff, Trisha (ed.), *Hidden Truths: Bloody Sunday 1972* (Los Angeles, CA, 1997), 71–82

Phillips, David, 'Actuality and Affect in Documentary Photography', in Howells, Richard, and Matson, Robert (eds.), *Using Visual Evidence* (Maidenhead, 2009), 55–77

Pine, Emilie, *The Politics of Irish Memory: Performing Remembrance in Contemporary Irish Culture* (London, 2011)

Pinney, Christopher, *Camera Indica: The Social Life of Indian Photographs* (Chicago, 1998)

Pinney, Christopher, and Peterson, Nicholas (eds.), *Photography's Other Histories* (Durham NC, 2003)

Pinney, Christopher, *Photography and Anthropology* (London, 2011)

Pollock, Vivienne, and Parkhill, Trevor, *Made in Belfast* (Stroud, 2005)

Poole, Deborah, *Vision, Race and Modernity: A Visual Economy of the Andean Image World* (Princeton, 1997)

Praeger, Robert Lloyd, *The Landscape of Ireland* (Dublin, 1953)

Prince, Simon, *Belfast and Derry in Revolt: A New History of the Start of the Troubles* (Dublin, 2011)

Prittie, Terence, *Through Irish Eyes: A Journalist's Memoirs* (London, 1977)

Quinn, Frankie in 'Vox Pop: Peacelines', *Circa* 71 (Spring 1995), 20

Quinn, John, and Doyle, Colman, *All Changed: Fifty Years of Photographing Ireland* (Dublin, 2004)

Rains, Stephanie, *Commodity Culture and Social Class in Dublin 1950–1916* (Dublin, 2010)

Rieger, Bernhard, *Technology and the Culture of Modernity in Britain and Germany* (Cambridge, 2005)

Roberts, John, *The Art of Interruption: Realism, Photography, and the Everyday* (Manchester, 1998)

Robinson, Emily, 'Touching the Void: Affective History and the Impossible', *Rethinking History* 14 (2010), 503–20

Robinson, Emily, Schofield, Camilla, Sutcliffe-Braithwaite, Florence, and Thomlinson, Natalie, 'Telling Stories about Post-war Britain: Popular Individualism and the "Crisis" of the 1970s', *Twentieth Century British History* 28/2 (2017), 268–304

Roper, Michael, *The Secret Battle: Emotional Survival in the Great War* (Manchester, 2009)

Rose, Gillian, 'Practicing Photography: An Archive, A Study, Some Photographs and a Researcher', *Journal of Historical Geography* 26/4 (2000), 555–71

Rose, Gillian, 'On the Need to Ask How Exactly is Geography Visual', *Antipode* 35/2 (2003), 212–21

Rose, Gillian, *Doing Family Photography: The Domestic, the Public, and the Politics of Sentiment* (London, 2010)

Rose, Gillian, *Visual Methodologies* (London, 2013)

Rosenblum, Naomi, *A World History of Photography* (New York, 2008)

Rosler, Martha, 'In, Around, and After Thoughts (on Documentary Photography)', in Bolton, Richard (ed.), *The Contest of Meaning* (Cambridge, MA, 1992), 303–42

Rossiter, Ann, *Ireland's Hidden Diaspora: The 'Abortion Trail' and the Making of a London-Irish Underground, 1980–2000* (London, 2009)

Rowbotham, Sheila, *Hidden from History: 300 Years of Women's Oppression and the Fight Against it* (London, 1977)

Ryan, Louise, 'Negotiating Modernity and Tradition: newspaper Debates on the "modern girl" in the Irish Free State', *Journal of Gender Studies* 7/2 (1998), 181–97

Ryan, Louise, 'Family Matters: (e)migration, familial networks and Irish women in Britain', *The Sociological Review* 52/3 (2004), 351–70

Ryan, James, *Picturing Empire: Photography and the Visualization of the British Empire* (Chicago, 1998)

Sanders, Andrew, and Wood, Ian, *Times of Troubles: Britain's War in Northern Ireland* (Edinburgh, 2012)

Saumarez Smith, Otto, 'The Inner City Crisis and the End of Urban Modernism in 1970s Britain', *Twentieth Century British History* 27/4 (2016), 578–98

Scally, Robert James, *The End of Hidden Ireland: Rebellion, Famine, and Emigration* (Oxford, 1996)

Scott, James, *Seeing Like a State: How Certain Schemes to Improve the Human Condition Have Failed* (New Haven, 1999)

Scott, Joan, 'The Evidence of Experience', *Critical Inquiry* 17/4 (1991), 773–97

Sekula, Allan, 'Dismantling modernism reinventing documentary (Notes on the Politics of Representation)', *The Massachusetts Review* 19/4 (1978), 859–83

Sekula, Allan, 'The Body and the Archive', *October* 39/102 (1986), 3–64

Sheehan, Ronan, 'The Press and the People in Dublin Central: Ronan Sheehan Talks to Tony Gregory, Mick Rafferty and Fergus McCabe', *The Crane Bag* 8 (1984), 44–50

Sichel, Kim, 'Pictorialism: An International Phenomenon', in McCarroll, Stacey, *California Dreamin': Camera Clubs and the Pictorial Photography Tradition* (Boston, 2004), 9–14

Smith, Kate, 'In Her Hands: Materializing Distinction in Georgian Britain', *Cultural and Social History* 11/4 (2014), 489–506

Smith, Shawn Michelle, and Sliwinski, Sharon (eds.), *Photography and the Optical Unconscious* (Duke, 2017)

Solomon-Godeau, Abigail, *Photography at the Dock: Essays on Photographic History, Institutions, and Practices* (Minnesota, 1994)

Sontag, Susan, *On Photography* (Harmondsworth, 1979)

Sontag, Susan, *Regarding the Pain of Others* (London, 2004)

Spence, Jo, and Holland, Patricia (eds.), *Family Snaps: The Meanings of Domestic Photography* (London, 1991)

Starns, Jessica, 'The Camerawork Archive', *Photography and Culture* 6/3 (2013), 341–8

Steedman, Carolyn, *Dust* (Manchester, 2001)

Steele, Karen, 'Gender and the Postcolonial Archive', *CR: The New Centennial Review* 10/1 (2010), 55–61

Sternberger, Paul Spence, *Between Amateur and Aesthete: The Legitimization of Photography as Art in America 1880–1990* (Albuquerque, 2001)

Strassler, Karen, *Refracted Visions: Popular Photography and National Modernity in Java* (Duke, 2010)

Tagg, John, *The Burden of Representation: Essays on Photographies and Histories* (London, 1988)

Taylor, John, *War Photography: Realism in the British Press* (London, 1991)

Thomason, George, 'Muintir na Tir's role in Irish Community Development', *Studies* 51/203 (1962), 408–18

Thompson, John, *Political Scandal: Power and Visibility in the Media Age* (London, 2000)

Thompson, Paul, *The Voice of the Past: Oral History* (Oxford, 2017)

Thompson, Paul, 'Community and Creativity: A Life Stories Perspective', *Oral History* 37/2 (2009), 34–44

Thomson, Matthew, *Psychological Subjects: Identity, Culture, and Health in Twentieth-Century Britain* (Oxford, 2006)

Tinkler, Penny, '"Picture Me As a Young Woman": Researching Girls' Photo Collections from the 1950s and 1960', *Photography and Culture* 3/3 (2010), 261–81

Tinkler, Penny, *Using Photographs in Social and Historical Research* (London, 2013)
Todd, Jennifer, 'Unionist Political Thought, 1920–72', in Boyce, D. George, Eccleshall, Robert, and Geoghan, Vincent (eds.), *Political Thought in Ireland Since the Seventeenth Century* (London, 1993), 190–211
Tóibín, Colm, 'Introduction', in O'Shea, Tony, *Dubliners* (Dublin, 1990), 15–63
Umbach, Maiken, 'Selfhood, Place, and Ideology in German Photo Albums, 1933–45' *Central European History* 48 (2015), 335–65
Valiulis, Maryann, 'Neither Feminist nor Flapper: the Ecclesiastical construction of the Ideal Irish woman', O'Dowd, Mary, and Wichert, Sabine (eds.), *Chattel, Servant or Citizen? Women's Status in Church, State and Society* (Belfast, 1995), 168–78
Walker, Sydney, 'Artmaking in an Age of Visual Culture: Vision and Visuality', Visual Arts Research 30/2 (2004), 23–37
Walsh, Dermot, *Bloody Sunday and the Rule of Law in Northern Ireland* (Basingstoke, 2000)
Walshe, Eibhear, *Cissie's Abattoir* (Cork, 2010)
West, Nancy May, *Kodak and the Lens of Nostalgia* (Virginia, 2000)
Wetherell, Sam, 'Painting the Crisis: Community Arts and the Search for the "Ordinary" in 1970s and '80s London', *History Workshop Journal* 76/1 (2013), 235–49
Williams, Raymond, *The Country and the City* (London, 1973), 149
Williams, Raymond, *Keywords: A Vocabulary of Culture and Society* (Oxford, 1985)
Williams, Val, *Women Photographers: the Other Observers 1900 to the Present* (London, 1986)
Wills, Clair, 'Women, Domesticity and The Family: Recent Feminist Work in Irish Cultural Studies', *Cultural Studies* 15/1 (2001), 33–57
Wills, Clair, 'Realism and the Irish Immigrant: Documentary, Fiction, and Post War Irish Labor', *Modern Language Quarterly* 73/3 (2012), 373–94
Wills, Clair, *The Best are Leaving: Emigration and Postwar Irish Culture* (Cambridge, 2015)
Wolff, Janet, 'The Invisible Flaneuse: Women and the Literature of Modernity', *Theory, Culture, Society* 2/3 (1985), 37–46
Ziff, Trisha, 'Photographs at War', in Rolston, Bill (ed.), *The Media and Northern Ireland: Covering the Troubles* (London, 1991), 187–206
Zuelow, Eric, *Making Ireland Irish: Tourism and National Identity* (Syracuse, 2009)

Index

For the benefit of digital users, indexed terms that span two pages (e.g., 52–53) may, on occasion, appear on only one of those pages.